CREATIVE IDEAS FOR TEACHING EVALUATION

Evaluation in Education and Human Services

Editors:

George F. Madaus, Boston College, Chestnut
  Hill, Massachusetts, U.S.A.
Daniel L. Stufflebeam, Western Michigan
  University, Kalamazoo, Michigan, U.S.A.

Creative Ideas For Teaching Evaluation

Activities, Assignments, and Resources

edited by
Donna M. Mertens
Gallaudet University

Kluwer Academic Publishers
Boston/Dordrecht/London

Distributors for North America:
Kluwer Academic Publishers
101 Philip Drive
Assinippi Park
Norwell, Massachusetts 02061 USA

Distributors for all other countries:
Kluwer Academic Publishers Group
Distribution Centre
Post Office Box 322
3300 AH Dordrecht, THE NETHERLANDS

Library of Congress Cataloging-in-Publication Data

Creative ideas for teaching evaluation : activities, assignments, and
    resources / edited by Donna M.Mertens.
        p.   cm. — (Evaluation in education and human services series)
    Bibliography: p.
    Includes index.
    ISBN 0-7923-9021-0
    1. Educational evaluation.   I. Mertens, Donna M.   II. Series:
Evaluation in education and human services.
LB2855.75.C74   1989
371.1′22—dc20   89-8124
                                                                                  CIP

Copyright © 1989 by Kluwer Academic Publishers

All rights reserved. No part of this publication may be reproduced, stored in a retrieval
system or transmitted in any form or by any means, mechanical, photocopying, recording,
or otherwise, without the prior written permission of the publisher, Kluwer Academic
Publishers, 101 Philip Drive, Assinippi Park, Norwell, Massachusetts 02061.

Printed in the United States of America

Contents

Contributing Authors

James W. Altschuld, Ohio State University
Larry Braskamp, University of Illinois at Urbana-Champaign
Terry R. Berkeley, Gallaudet University
John J. Bowers, The American College Testing Program
Joseph P. Caliguri, University of Missouri at Kansas City
Melinda L. Costello, Syracuse University
Oliver W. Cummings, Arthur Andersen & Co.
Barbara Gross Davis, University of California at Berkeley
Gabriel Della-Piana, University of Utah
K. L. Douglass, Bureau of Research, Evaluation and Analysis,
    Harrisburg, Pennsylvania
David A. Dowell, California State University
D. M. Fye, Bureau of Research, Evaluation and Analysis, Harrisburg, Pennsylvania
Julia Gamon, Iowa State University
J. M. Gibson, Bureau of Research, Evaluation and Analysis,
    Harrisburg, Pennsylvania
Pauline E. Ginsberg, Utica College of Syracuse University
Jennifer C. Greene, Cornell University
Egon G. Guba, Indiana University (1989)
Valerie J. Janesick, Gallaudet University
Karen E. Kirkhart, Syracuse University
James S. Long, Washington State University
George A. Marcoulides, California State University
Geofferey Masters, Australian Council for Educational Research
Jack McKillip, Southern Illinois University at Carbondale
Donna M. Mertens, Gallaudet University
George Morgan, Australian Council for Educational Research
Michael Morris, University of New Haven
Stuart S. Nagel, University of Illinois at Urbana-Champaign
K. L. Nazar, Bureau of Research, Evaluation and Analysis,
    Harrisburg, Pennsylvania
Elizabethann O'Sullivan, North Carolina State University
John C. Ory, University of Illinois at Urbana-Champaign
Hallie Preskill, College of St. Thomas
Frederick K. Richmond, Bureau of Research, Evaluation and Analysis,
    Harrisburg, Pennsylvania
Michael Scriven, University of Western Australia
Helen B. Slaughter, University of Hawaii at Honolulu
Nick L. Smith, Syracuse University
Renata Tesch, Qualitative Research Management
Phyllis M. Thomas, Columbus (Ohio) Public Schools
F. R. Willis, Bureau of Research, Evaluation and Analysis,
    Harrisburg, Pennsylvania
Mark Wilson, University of California at Berkeley

Foreword

In 1976, the first session on the teaching of evaluation was held at an annual meeting of evaluators. A few hardy souls gathered to exchange ideas on improving the teaching of evaluation. At subsequent annual meetings, these informal sessions attracted more and more participants, eager to talk about common teaching interests and to exchange reading lists, syllabuses, assignments, and paper topics. The sessions were irreverent, innovative, lively, and unpredictable. Eventually the group formalized itself with the American Evaluation Association as the Topical Interest Group in the Teaching of Evaluation (TIG: TOE).

As word of TIG: TOE's activities spread, instructors from all over the country clamored for assistance and advice. It became apparent that a handbook was needed, a practical interdisciplinary guide to the teaching of evaluation. Donna M. Mertens, a long-standing member of TIG: TOE and an accomplished teacher of evaluation, volunteered to edit the book, and her skills, sensitivity, and experience in the craft of teaching are apparent throughout.

Both new and experienced faculty will discover here a wide range of creative ideas on topics covered in typical evaluation courses: qualitative methods, needs assessment, proposal writing, personnel evaluation, report writing, professional ethics, policy analysis, and testing and statistics. The contributing authors are leading theorists and practitioners who span the variety of disciplines within which evaluation is taught, including education, psychology, sociology, public administration, and human services. Their recommendations and suggestions are derived from broad professional experience, and at each point they emphasize methods conducive to active learning and problem solving.

For those faced with teaching their first evaluation course or for those looking for new ways to teach such topics as naturalistic interviewing, evaluability assessment, or content analysis, this book provides a useful overview of techniques, methods, and content areas. The classroom activities can be easily implemented in courses at all levels, and sufficient detail is provided so that instructors can readily adapt the activities to their particular teaching circumstance.

We who teach evaluation are deeply indebted to Donna and the contributing authors for their willingness to open the doors of their classrooms and for advancing our understanding of the best ways to pass on the discipline to our students.

Barbara Gross Davis
Director, Office of Educational Development
University of California at Berkeley

CREATIVE IDEAS FOR TEACHING EVALUATION

INTRODUCTION: PRACTICAL AND THEORETICAL FRAMEWORK

Donna M. Mertens

Evaluators are called upon to conduct a number of different kinds
of studies and to use a variety of approaches and tools to
complete these studies. The diversity of demands made on
evaluators and the skills needed by them to perform their tasks
formed the practical basis for this book.

Training of new evaluators should reflect the realities that
they will encounter in their future work. Thus, this book of
creative ideas for teaching evaluation includes innovative and
realistic approaches to teaching program and personnel
evaluation, needs assessment, and policy analysis. Both
quantitative and qualitative approaches to evaluation are
explored as are issues in evaluation utilization and ethics.
Finally, several chapters explain methods for teaching about the
tools that evaluators use, including statistics, measurement, and
computers.

The above-mentioned topics are addressed through a series of
exercises, simulations, assignments, and computer software
applications that are designed to actively engage the student of
evaluation in the learning process. Cognitive learning theory
served as the theoretical framework for the selection of material
for this book. Thus, activities were selected that recognized
learning as a constructive process. Learners try to make sense
out of what the teacher or textbook says and to integrate the
subject matter into some meaningful structure (McKeachie, 1980).
In order to build bridges between the structure of the course
content, the teacher, and the learner, the student must have an
opportunity to participate actively in the learning process.
Talking, writing, doing, interacting, and teaching others are
important ways in which learners restructure their learning. As

teachers, we need to provide opportunities for small group discussion, writing, explaining, or doing something to which the teacher, other students, and the individual learner can respond.

This book reflects the editor's bias that the product of shared input and effort of a group of informed individuals is superior to that of an individual's working alone. Thus, teachers of evaluation from across the world and across the many disciplines that the profession of evaluation encompasses were asked to contribute their ideas for teaching exercises. The contributions do represent the many disciplinary faces of evaluation, including education, psychology, social work, administration, government, extension service, business, special education, public policy, statistics, and computers.

Authors were encouraged to organize their chapters in such a manner as to provide an explanation of a concept, examples, and an opportunity for application. Each chapter begins with an introductory section that explains the concept taught in that activity. Next, materials that are needed for that lesson are listed. Many authors appended exemplary handout materials in their chapters. The heart of each chapter is the Procedures section which explains in step-by-step fashion exactly what a teacher needs to do to use this exercise, simulation, assignment, or software. Authors then discuss any helpful hints that they have about what they have done to ensure the success of the activity. Finally, most authors provide a list of suggested background readings for the teacher and/or students. If the chapter describes use of software, information is also given concerning hardware requirements, cost, and accessibility.

The book is divided into eight sections. The first, Planning and Conceptualizing Evaluation, is the largest section and represents the initial stage of learning about evaluation. In Smith and Costello's "Constructing an Operational Evaluation Design," they present a ten-step planning process based on the work of Brinkerhoff, Brethower, Hluchjy, and Nowakowski (1983). Students select a program with which they are familiar and, through the course of a semester, construct a complete, operational evaluation design. Smith and Costello include an exemplary design of an evaluation for a series of computer training workshops for teachers.

Kirkhart and Scriven, in "Conceptualizing Evaluation: The Key Evaluation Checklist," do **not** present a set of linear steps for planning an evaluation. Rather, they illustrate how to use Scriven's (1983) Key Evaluation Checklist to identify issues, concepts, and dimensions that are relevant to a number of different steps in planning and carrying out an evaluation.

Guba also focuses on the student's conceptualizing of evaluation. However, his exercise, "Journal Writing in

Evaluation," addresses the student's construction of the concept
of evaluation overall, rather than as it applies to the
evaluation of a specific object.

Morris ("Field Experiences in Evaluation Courses") explains
how he has been able to include out-of-class field experiences in
a 13-week course. Students actually plan and conduct small-scale
evaluations in this time period.

Several authors address specific aspects of the evaluation
planning process. Richmond and his colleagues provide a first
step in a logical thought process of selecting, collecting, and
interpreting information to help managers make decisions about
their programs in "Identifying the Evaluation and Its
Usefulness." In "Evaluability Assessment," Ginsberg provides an
exercise in determining if a program is evaluable. Dowell takes
students through several simulation activities to give them
experience in identifying evaluation questions and methods. Long
provides an opportunity to explore alternative evaluation data
collection techniques through a matrix of different settings and
transactions. Ory and Braskamp contribute a scenario based on
the evaluation of a reading program to help the student learn to
establish evaluation boundaries. Altschuld and Thomas provide a
means of integrating several theoretical models with evaluation
planning in their chapter "Alternative Models for Evaluation."
In Caliguri's "Planning a Discrepancy-Based Evaluation," he
explains a planning process based on the discrepancy model of
evaluation.

The second major section of the book includes ideas for
teaching about qualitative approaches to evaluation. Greene
contributed five chapters on this topic that are based on small
group, in-class discussions. In "Naturalistic Interviewing," she
provides students with a framework for exploring key issues that
arise when conducting open-ended, unstructured qualitative
interviews. In "Critical Issues in Participant Observation," she
takes up the issues of methodology, values, ethics, and politics
as they relate to collection of data by participant observation.
The issues of bias, values, and reflexivity are further explored
in her chapter "Naturalistic Data Collection: Case Study
Discussion." Greene then explains a method for teaching about
the issues surrounding trustworthiness in naturalistic inquiry
through the use of audit trails.

Several authors addressed the teaching of qualitative data
analysis and interpretation. Greene based her activity on Miles
and Huberman's (1984) matrix approach to qualitative data
analysis. Slaughter provides an example of writing and
interpreting ethnographic records based on a naturalistic
evaluation of a Chapter 1 writing program. Tesch explains how to
use the computer to assist in the analysis of qualitative data
and provides an example of this based on the evaluation of an

electronic network for faculty and students. Preskill presents a creative approach to teaching content analysis using the comics from the Sunday newspaper. The final chapter in this section presents Caliguri's lessons on "Using Case Records" which focuses on the interpretation and use of information obtained in case records by program administrators.

Alternative approaches to needs assessment are explored in the third major section of the book. Gamon explains methods for teaching the application of the Delphi technique, the Q-sort, and the Charrette technique, and for introducing the concept of focus groups. Cummings takes the reader through a step-by-step process for teaching the nominal group technique and illustrates the application of this technique through an assessment of interdepartmental coordination at a city hospital. Mertens provides ideas for teaching the development of focus group questions within the broader framework of needs assessment.

In the fourth section, two authors address proposal writing in the context of program evaluation. Berkeley combines program development and evaluation in his chapter, "Proposal Writing in Early Childhood Special Education." O'Sullivan explains how to teach proposal writing in response to an informal agency request through a case study of an evaluation of a juvenile offenders program.

Caliguri presents two perspectives on teaching personnel evaluation in the sixth section. In "A Hands-On Experience in Clinical Supervision," he explains how to teach supervisors the technique of evaluating teachers through the use of clinical supervision in an applied setting. He then uses a case study to examine the tensions of a school staff and the accommodation of administrators in validating what happens in the evaluation of staff.

The seventh section of the book addresses several issues that evaluators face, including those related to reporting, utilization, and ethics. Della-Piana provides examples of ways to involve the stakeholders in the reporting process in order to enhance utilization of findings. Janesick's chapter presents a theoretical framework for examining ethical issues as it applies to several evaluation scenarios.

Nagel provided the only chapter in the seventh section on policy analysis. He explains a method of using software to process a set of alternatives to be evaluated, criteria for judging the alternatives, and relations between alternatives and criteria to choose the best course of action in a policy setting.

The final section of the book includes four chapters related to the evaluator's tools: statistics, measurement, and computers. Marcoulides explains the use of software designed to teach users the concept and application of statistical analyses for hypothesis testing. Masters, Morgan, and Wilson describe the use of a software program to teach Item Response theory to construct local variables rather than relying on standardized measures. McKillip presents three techniques for teaching students about regression to the mean: the Clairvoyant Methodology Aptitude Test, Dice Rolling Exercise, and a computer data simulation using SPSSX. In the final chapter, Bowers demonstrates how to teach the use of relational data bases for the purpose of solving evaluation data management problems.

REFERENCES

Brinkerhoff, R.O., Brethower, D.M., Hluchyj, T., & Nowakowski, J.R. (1983). Program evaluation: A practitioner's guide for trainers and educators/Sourcebook and Casebook. Boston, MA: Kluwer-Nijhoff Publishing.

McKeachie, W.J. (1980). Implications of cognitive psychology for college teaching. In W.J. McKeachie (ed.), Learning, cognition, and college teaching. San Francisco, CA: Jossey-Bass.

Miles, M.B., & Huberman, A.M. (1984). Qualitative data analysis: A sourcebook of new methods. Beverly Hills, CA: Sage.

Scriven, M. (1981). Evaluation thesaurus. (Third edition). Inverness, CA: Edgepress.

I CONCEPTUALIZING AND PLANNING AN EVALUATION

1

CONSTRUCTING AN OPERATIONAL EVALUATION DESIGN

Nick L. Smith
Melinda L. Costello

The ten assignments presented here, which are elaborations of material presented by Brinkerhoff, Brethower, Hluchyj, and Nowakowski (1983), are designed to lead students through the construction of a complete, operational evaluation design. The students encounter the assignments sequentially:

1. Program Selection
2. Focus Summary
3. Question Summary
4. Question/Procedure Matrix
5. Procedures Summary
6. Analysis and Interpretation Plan
7. Reporting Summary
8. Management Plan: Personnel
9. Management Plan: Budget
10. Meta-Evaluation Summary.

The students work through the assignments iteratively, revising previous ones as needed, based on work in subsequent assignments. Some assignments are revised four or five times until the student is satisfied with the results. Through interaction with evaluation clients, team discussions, peer reviews, and instructor critiques, each student produces a unique, final evaluation design that is as realistic, pragmatic, and operational as he or she can make it.

MATERIALS

    1. Assignments
    2. Sample Final Report
    3. Assignments Checklist

PROCEDURES

Before reading the rest of this section, review Handout 1: Assignments.

Students select a program with which they are very familiar so that they have an experiential basis for making the many arbitrary tradeoff decisions required in planning an actual study. Selecting their own program to evaluate also increases student interest in the assignments, although the lack of comparability across student work makes the advising and grading task of the instructor more difficult. Students start with the guideline that the evaluation is to take four months and cost a total of $5,000. Designs for larger studies are permitted if students present a convincing argument based on the nature of the program actually being evaluated. (Some students do proceed to implement the designs created in class, but not under the auspices of the course.)

The assignments proceed in a fairly standard design chronology, but become increasingly technical and detailed. The overlap in Assignments 1 and 2 has been found necessary to help students incrementally focus their evaluation designs. The assignments fall into natural cluster of 1-2-3 (which provide the greatest conceptual difficulty for the students), 4-5-6 (which are more difficult for students with no measurement or data analysis background), and 7-8-9 (which are all new for students without project managment experience). The assignments have been used extensively with introductory master's and doctoral students, international and U.S. students, students in their early twenties to late fifties, and students with backgrounds as diverse as art education, social work, engineering, business, and language studies. With sufficient assistance, all types of students have been able to do well on the assignments. The instruction emphasizes the conceptual tasks of designing an evaluation, and de-emphasizes narrative writing by using multiple summary displays to record the evaluation design. These displays help students for whom English is not a dominant language to master the material.

A sample final report is included here as Handout 2. Like most final reports, it underwent numerous revisions and is presented as a complete design rather than as a collection of assignments, although the individual assignments are discernable. This is a strong, representative, student product, included here to illustrate the completion of all ten assignments.

The Assignments Checklist, included here as Handout 3, was developed over several semesters by recording mistakes commonly made by students in working through the assignments. Students are now given the checklist (1) to forewarn them of pitfalls as they work on each assignment, (2) to use in critiquing each other's work, and (3) to retain as an example of the criteria the instructor may employ to grade the completed design.

DISCUSSION

Prior versions of these assignments have been used in six semesters of classes ranging from 3 to 40 students. The variety of supplemental material used to support these assignments is mentioned briefly below, but not described in full due to space limitations.

Student support features have included:

o placing past final reports on reserve for student review (both those with the instructor's critical comments and "cleaned-up" versions),

o offering out-of-class workshops on computer facilities and software (word-processing, spreadsheet, etc.) that are locally available for use in completing the assignments,

o organizing student teams, or assigning classmate consultants, to provide peer support in completing the individual designs.

Feedback and evaluation of student progress has been provided by:

o instructor presentation and discussion of common problems (both of current and past classes),

o weekly peer review of individual assignments,

o instructor critique of individual or clustered (e.g., 4-5-6) assignments,

o formal, written, student critiques of each other's designs (Assignments 1-10) prior to student revisions for final submission,

o a three-hour exam on the basic content of all ten assignments, with feedback and discussion prior to final submission of design.

Supplemental class activities and exercises used to enhance performance on the assignments have included:

o instructor (as evaluator) and a student (as the client) role-playing an initial planning meeting to illustrate the design focusing process,

o small group exercises in identifying and prioritizing key

design aspects,
o extemporaneous development by the instructor in class of
   a preliminary personnel and budget plan to illustrate the
   process of an emerging optimal solution,
o group analysis of a case study of an actual ethical
   problem to provide realistic meta-evaluation practice.

These and other instructional activities can be designed to
support work on the ten assignments, which are typically worked
on over a full semester.

ACKNOWLEDGMENTS

We wish to acknowledge the contributions of many past
students whose thoughtful criticisms and suggestions have
improved the assignments presented here. We are especially
grateful to Joanne Stolp for allowing us to use her final report
as Handout 2. Any additional suggestions, or reports of use of
these assignments, are most welcome and should be forwarded to
the first author.

BACKGROUND READING

Brinkerhoff, R. O., Brethower, D. M., Hluchyj, T., & Nowakowski,
    J. R. (1983). Program evaluation: A practitioner's guide
    for trainers and educators / Sourcebook and casebook,
    Boston, MA: Kluwer-Nijhoff Publishing.

Joint Committee on Standards for Educational Evaluation, (1981).
    Standards for evaluations of educational programs, projects,
    and materials. New York: McGraw-Hill Book Co.

    (Note on notation used in Handout 1: "xix(7)," for example,
    refers to the seventh grouping of standards, Collecting
    Information, on page xix in the Functional Table of Contents
    -- all standards in that group are to be reviewed for this
    particular assignment.)

HANDOUT 1: ASSIGNMENTS

The assignments that follow focus on the development of a design for evaluating a complex service delivery or educational program of your choice.

1. Program Selection

In this course, you will prepare a plan to evaluate some program. Select a program to evaluate. It program should be a complex service delivery, training, or product development effort with which you are very familiar, due to past or current personal contact. Examples include:

- o an employee assistance program for stress management conducted in a small private firm;
- o a national center that trains field workers in family planning assistance;
- o an ad hoc project to revise the entire science curriculum in a large school district;
- o a group assigned to develop new educational exhibits about computers at a regional museum;
- o an adult literacy program conducted by the continuing education department of the nearby community college;
- o an out-patient drug rehabilitation program operated at a community mental health center.

Select this program carefully; it should be a real program that you could conceivably evaluate, given the time, resources, and opportunity.

For Assignment 1, submit a brief description of the program you have selected to evaluate, indicating the program's purpose, clients, basic operation, and the general purpose of the evaluation. Background reading: Brinkerhoff et al. (1983), pp. xiv--xxvii, 35-73; Joint Committee (1981), p. xviii(5).

2. Focus Summary

Begin to focus your evaluation efforts by identifying the major purposes and audiences for your study.

For Assignment 2, submit a description of your study that--

1. describes the object or focus of your study
   -- include major and secondary foci
2. identifies the purposes and audiences of the study
   -- include primary and secondary purposes
   -- include major clients and important stakeholders
3. discusses the major contextual factors affecting the study

> -- include factors likely to influence the study design, implementation, or use of results.

Your summary should be specific, concise, and detailed. (See Brinkerhoff, pp. 49-50, "Product 1: Evaluation Preview," for a condensed example.) Background reading: Brinkerhoff et al. (1983) pp. 5-34; Joint Committee (1981) p. xviii (4,5,6).

3. Question Summary

Now identify the major questions to be answered through your study.

For Assignment 3, submit a statement that--

1. describes the <u>primary questions</u> to be addressed in the study
   -- identify at least five primary questions
   -- provide sufficient examples of subquestions to indicate the coverage and focus of each primary question
2. identifies the <u>audiences</u> interested in each primary question and <u>why</u> it is <u>important</u> that the evaluation answer the question.

Use "Product 2: Outline of the Evaluation Questions" in Brinkerhoff, pp. 50-51, as a model for presenting your question summary. Background reading: Brinkerhoff et al. (1983), pp. 75-116; Joint Committee (1981), p. xix(7).

4. Question/Procedure Matrix

Next, describe the procedures that you will use to collect the information needed to answer the questions identified in Assignment 3.

For Assignment 4, submit a statement that--

1. identifies each of the information <u>collection procedures</u>
   -- your study should employ at least five different data collection procedures
2. summarizes which procedures will be used to address each question.

Use "Product 3: Information Collection: Overall Plan" in Brinkerhoff, pp. 51-52, as a model for presenting your question/procedure summary. Background reading: Brinkerhoff et al. (1983), pp. 75-116, (and 225-236, 278-289, 353-371, as examples); Joint Committee (1981), p. xix(7).

5. Procedures Summary

Summarize each information collection procedure to be used in your study.

For Assignment 5, submit a statement that--

1. indicates the questions each procedure will address
2. lists the data collection schedule
3. names the kinds of respondents
4. indicates how the respondents will be identified (sample).

Use "Product #3: Information Collection: How Each Procedure Works" in Brinkerhoff, p. 53, as a model for presenting your procedures summary (disregard the right-most column on p. 53). Background reading: Brinkerhoff et al. (1983), pp. 75-116 (and 225-236, 278-289, 353-371, as examples); Joint Committee (1981), p.xix(7).

6. Analysis and Interpretation Plan

Prepare a plan for analyzing and interpreting the information you will be collecting.

For Assignment 6, submit a statement that--

1. identifies each evaluation question and subquestion
2. lists the collection procedures used to address it
3. describes how the data will be analyzed
4. identifies the evaluative criteria to be used in interpreting the information
5. describes the procedures that will be used in making judgments.

Use "Product 4: Analysis and Interpretation Plan" in Brinkerhoff, pp. 54-55, as a model for presenting your analysis and interpretation plan. Background reading: Brinkerhoff et al. (1983), pp. 117-147; Joint Committee (1981), p. xvii(2).

7. Reporting Summary

Prepare a reporting summary indicating the formal and informal reporting points you will use to communicate with your various evaluation audiences. Assume that your evaluation study will be conducted over a four month period.

For Assignment 7, submit a statement that--

1. indicates each type of reporting event
2. describes the frequency and format of each event
3. summarizes the scope and content of each report

4. identifies the <u>primary audiences</u> of each report.

Use the "Example of a Report Schedule" in Brinkerhoff, p. 171, as a model for presenting your reporting summary. (Do not forget to include informal reporting points, such as illustrated in the example on p. 56 of Brinkerhoff.) Background reading: Brinkerhoff et al. (1983), pp. 149-174; Joint Committee (1981), p.xx(9).

8. Management Plan: Personnel

Now construct a management plan reflecting what tasks need to be done, when, and by whom, in order to implement your evaluation design.

For Assignment 8, submit a statement that--

1. includes a step by step outline of all <u>major tasks</u> required to accomplish the evaluation
2. identifies which <u>personnel</u> will do each task
3. lists the number of <u>days</u> (and <u>dates</u>) each task requires.

Use "Product 6: Management Plan: Work Plan" in Brinkerhoff, pp. 56-57, as a model for presenting your personnel summary. (Substitute for the X's in Product 6, the number of days (and the dates) required for each task, as illustrated in the example presented below.) Your timeline should cover the full four-month period through which the study will run. Background reading: Brinkerhoff et al. (1983), pp. 175-201; Joint Committee (1981), pp. xvii(1,3), xix(8), xx(10).

9. Management Plan: Budget

Next, prepare a budget for your evaluation. Assume that you are applying for a $5,000 grant to conduct the study and that you are expected to account for the expenditure of all funds.

For Assignment 9, submit a statement that--

1. includes all major budget <u>categories</u>
2. indicates <u>how</u> each item within a budget category was <u>computed</u>.

Use "Product 6: Management Plan: Budget" in Brinkerhoff, pp. 57-58, as a model for presenting your budget, but include more detail as illustrated in the example presented below. (Review the sample budgets on pp. 187-189 of Brinkerhoff for ideas about additional budget categories.) Background reading: Brinkerhoff et al. (1983), pp. 175-201; Joint Committee (1981), pp. xvii(1,3), xix(8), xx(10).

10. Meta-Evaluation Summary
_____

Now conduct a critical review of your evaluation design as
currently reflected in your previous assignments. Review your
past assignments using the standards presented in Joint Committee
(1981). For each standard, consider whether it is not applicable
to your study, is applicable and has been appropriately dealt
with, or is applicable but has not yet been adequately dealt
with. (The summary chart on p. 148 of Joint Committee (1981) may
help you get started.)

For Assignment 10, submit a statement in which you--

   1.   select three standards that are not applicable, or only
        marginally so, to your study, and explain why
   2.   select three standards that are applicable to your
        study and that you feel have been well provided for in
        your current design, and explain why
   3.   select three standards that are applicable to your
        study and that you feel have not yet been well provided
        for in your design, and explain how your design might
        be modified to insure better compliance with these
        standards. Background reading: Brinkerhoff et al.
        (1983), pp. 203-223; Joint Committee (1981), pp. 1-156.

HANDOUT 2: SAMPLE FINAL REPORT

Description of Program Selected for Evaluation:
The Computer Training Program of the Oswego County Teacher Center

Program's Purpose. The object of this evaluation is the Oswego County Teacher Center, one of 91 New York state-funded teacher Resource and Computer Training Centers. It has been in operation since 1984 and has been fully funded by the State Education Department during that time period. Its primary purpose has been to provide educator-requested programs and information and resources. These include--

> *workshops (both one-session and long-term)
> *teacher-to-teacher meetings
> *newsletters and informational mailings
> *professional library resources
> *Material Center
> *mini-grant programs.

The Center is located in a one room office in a relocatable building on the Board of Cooperative Educational Services (BOCES) campus in Mexico, New York. Workshops and meetings are held both at the center and at various schools in the county.

One particular program offered by the Oswego County Teacher Center focuses on the area of computer training. Various computer training workshops have been offered over the last four years to Oswego County teachers. These include introductory, intermediate, and advanced level courses and feature different types of microcomputers. Skills range from word processing/keyboarding to designing and using databases and spreadsheets. These workshops generally run from one to three sessions each and are held in various locations in the county. Some districts offer inservice credit for attendance, but most do not. Most computer training workshops are offered in response to specific teacher requests that are received at OCTC by mail, telephone, or via liaison request forms. Instructors have been area teachers, resource personnel, and professional consultants. The particular purpose of the computer training component of the Oswego County Teacher Center is to provide both reactive and proactive computer training opportunities to county educators.

Clients. The Oswego County Teacher Center is a cooperative staff development effort of nine participating school districts: Altmar-Parish-Williamstown, Central Square, Fulton, Hannibal, Mexico, Oswego, Phoenix, Pulaski, Sandy Creek, their non-public schools, and the Oswego County BOCES. Membership is open to all teachers and administrators who are employed in a probationary or tenured area by participating districts, BOCES, and non-public schools. Other interested parties (such as substitutes, student teachers, interns, nurses, teaching assistants, aides, secretaries, etc.) who are non-members may attend appropriate programs as space allows. Participation in the Center's programs is voluntary. There are approximately 2,035 educators in Oswego County who may use the services provided.

Basic Operation. Staffing consists of five full-time employees: a Coordinator, a Program and Communication Specialist, a Material Center Specialist, and two secretaries. In addition, stipends are paid to 57 elementary and secondary liaisons who disseminate program information and facilitate data collection through needs assessment, surveys, request forms, etc. A Governing Board and Executive Committee consisting of teachers and administrators oversee the Center's policies and procedures.

The Oswego County Teacher Center offers a continuous menu of program workshops, meetings, grants, etc. A newsletter listing and describing these offerings is printed and distributed monthly to all Oswego County educators. Another newsletter disseminating educational information is distributed quarterly. Informational mailings and updates are sent out as needed. Workshops and meetings are generally scheduled after school, Monday through Thursday.

One area of Teacher Center special programming focuses on computer training. The specific computer training objective is, "Teachers will develop skills to utilize in their classrooms for classroom management and student learning in word processing, keyboarding, etc." To meet this objective and others, needs assessment surveys are sent to all 2,035 educators. These surveys may deal with one specific issue, i.e., computer training, or may cover a broad area and include a section on computer training.

After the results of these surveys are compiled, the Coordinator and the Program and Communication Specialist attempt to meet these expressed needs through the avenues of workshops, meetings, literature and research dissemination, and so on. For example, a continuous series of workshops is offered in computer training in areas such as Appleworks and keyboarding. In addition, if the Teacher Center were to receive a request, as it often does, for a specific software course, i.e., IBM PFS:Write, that course would be offered.

Once a need is identified or a request received, a presenter is located who is an expert in that specific area, i.e., IBM Computers PFS:Write. Most consultants come from the ranks of Oswego County teachers. A location is chosen (generally, the school district from which the request was received), and a date and time picked. The course is advertised through newsletters and flyers, and if enrollment reaches ten people, the course is held. Time length of sessions is dependent upon the consultant's determination of need. Post-activity and follow-up activity surveys are given to participants after workshops are completed, and help evaluate presenter, materials, course content, and future interest. Beyond that reactive approach, programs are also designed to integrate recent educational theory into current practice. For example, there has been an increased interest in telecommunications in Oswego County, and a workshop series will be offered in that area in the near future. In this way, programming in computer training is coordinated in a manner similar to programming in other areas.

Evaluation Purpose. The purpose of this evaluation is twofold.

The primary purpose is to evaluate the computer training component of the Oswego County Teacher Center. This will involve an assessment of what the current computer training program is doing, and whether it is needed by educators and useful to them.

Second, the evaluation will serve to determine if and how current computer training services should be modified or expanded. It will seek to discover other areas of upcoming computer usage that are of interest to Oswego County educators and that are not covered by current programming.

FOCUS SUMMARY

Focus of Study

The major focus of the evaluation is the Oswego County Teacher Resource and Computer Training Center, one of 91 New York state-funded Teacher Resource and Computer Training Centers. It offers a wide range of programs designed to meet the expressed needs of Oswego County educators and to satisfy overall proposal objectives approved by the State Education Department. It is currently operating on a three-year proposal that must be updated, amended, and resubmitted yearly. Its primary purpose has been to provide educator-requested programs, information, and resources.

Since, as its name implies, part of its mission is to address the computer training needs of teachers, the Oswego County Teacher Resource and Computer Training Center has as one of its objectives, "Teachers will develop skills to utilize in their classrooms for classroom management and student learning in word processing, keyboarding, etc." OCTC has designed and implemented programs and activities to meet that objective. These include courses and workshops such as Appleworks: Word Processing, Database, and Spreadsheet, Sticky Bear Keyboarding, Logo, etc., offered at numerous locations in Oswego County.

The primary focus of this evaluation, then, is to assess the value of the computer training component of the Oswego County Teacher Center.

The secondary focus is to ascertain other areas of computer needs and services that can be addressed other than those already being included under the above-mentioned objective. What innovations in computer technology are coming to Oswego County? What other types of programming might be of interest to county educators?

Purpose

Specifically, then, the evaluation will focus on whether the computer training courses offered by the Oswego County Teacher Center (OCTC) are needed and useful to the educators in Oswego County. This evaluation will satisfy state requirements and provide needed information to the Coordinator, Program Specialist, and Program Committee to plan the direction or even the need for future computer training. Second, the evaluation will focus on how to improve or modify existing programs for computer training. Hopefully OCTC will be able to increase attendance and impact, and identify currently unknown computer training needs and services.

Audiences

The clients for this evaluation are the Coordinator of the Teacher Center, and the Program and Communication Specialist whose responsibilities include overseeing and directing center operations and planning programming to meet expressed needs. Other audiences include:

1. The New York State Education Department (N.Y.S.E.D) which needs to know how well OCTC is meeting its proposal objectives
2. The Executive Committee and the Governing Board of the Teacher Center
3. The Program Committee of the Teacher Center which is responsible for planning and implementing new instructional programs in all areas
4. The CAI (Computer Assisted Instruction) Committee, a committee branch of the CRC (Curriculum and Resource Center) (BOCES) which, among other things, provides resources and staff development programs through BOCES
5. Teachers who want programs that are a true reflection of their needs.

Interested stakeholders include:

1. Other teacher centers that are developing similar programs
2. Computer trainers and consultants who will need the information to scrap or develop appropriate programs
3. Students who will benefit from having their teachers trained in computer usage.

Major Contextual Factors

1. The evaluation must be completed by May 1988, so that new programs can be developed over the summer months.

2. One of two secretaries is available one afternoon a week to tally results and compile data.

3. Most instruments must be distributed and collected by liaisons who are overworked and often feel as if they are harrassing their colleagues.

4. Instruments need to be agreed upon with the CAI Committee which also surveys teachers so as to avoid duplication and the resultant animosity that arises when teachers are asked to fill out similar surveys for different groups.

5.   Scantron scoresheets are the only means the Teacher Center has available for the processing of thousands of replies to a needs assessment questionnaire if one is necessary.

6.   The Program and Communication Specialist has limited experience as an evaluator and is also relatively new (six months) in her position. The results of the evaluation will produce little reflection or judgment of her past work but will produce future directions for programming ideas.

Question Summary

Evaluation Questions	Subquestions	Audience	Importance
1. Are teachers attending computer training classes and are they aware of what is being offered?	a. How many teachers take computer training courses? b. What kinds of teachers? c. Where are classes held? d. How often? e. How do teachers know about computer training courses? f. Which teachers are not attending training?	1. OCTC Coordinator 2. Program Specialist 3. Governing Board And Executive Committee 4. The N.Y. State Education Dept. (N.Y.S.E.D.) 5. Program Committee 6. Teachers	It is necessary to determine a baseline attendance and gather data that would eliminate variables affecting attendance such as location of classes, timely notification (advertising), etc.
2. What types of computer training are being offered by OCTC?	a. What computer training workshops are being offered? b. What skills are being taught? c. What level of expertise is being addressed by the workshops?	1. OCTC Coordinator 2. Program Specialist 3. Governing Board & Executive Committee 4. CAI Committee 5. N.Y.S.E.D. 6. Program Committee 7. Teachers	This question addresses the primary evaluation question by providing a descriptive model of current computer training programs.
3. Is computer training needed?	a. What courses are being requested? b. How many requests are being received? c. Do teachers use computers in their classrooms? d. Are they required to? e. Are teachers already adequately trained to use computers?	1. OCTC Coordinator 2. Program Specialist 3. Executive Committee & Governing Board 4. CAI Committee 5. Program Committee 6. Teachers	This question also addresses the primary evaluation purpose in helping to determine if the entire OCTC computer training objective is needed.

Evaluation Questions	Subquestions	Audience	Importance
4. Are the computer training workshops useful?	a. What skills do teachers acquire? b. Do they use these skills in their classroom? at home? c. Are courses perceived as useful? d. Are workshops offerings matched with existing hardware and software? e. Are workshops matched to existing levels of skill of teachers? f. Are workshops long enough? thorough enough? g. Are trainers adequate? h. Are teachers satisfied with comp. training workshops?	1. OCTC Coordinator 2. Program Specialist 3. Governing Board & Executive Committee 4. The N.Y. State Education Dept. 5. Program Committee 6. Teachers	This questions deal with the merit of current training programs. Should they be kept or eliminated in their present form? It also attempts to measure audience satisfaction.
5. Should computer-related services be offered?	a. What services exist now? b. Should they? c. Should they be modified? d. What requests does OCTC get? e. What do district curriculum people offer now? f. What do they want OCTC to offer?	1. OCTC Coordinator 2. Program Specialist 3. Governing Board & Executive Committee 4. CAI Committee 5. N.Y.S.E.D. 6. Program Committee 7. Teachers	This provides data for future programing in the area of computer-related services.

Question Procedure Matrix

Information Collection Procedure	1. Teacher Attending/ Knowing? a. How many teachers? b. What kind? c. Where held? d. How often? e. Who is not coming? f. How known?	2. Type of training? a. Kinds of comp. workshops? b. Skills taught? c. What level of expertise?	3. Comp. Training needed? a. Course requests? b. Number requests? c. Teachers use comp. in class? d. Required to? e. Teachers already trained?	4. Comp. workshops useful? a. Acquired Skills? b. Used at school? At home? c. Perceived as useful? d. Matched with hardware & software? e. Matched to level of skill? f. Workshop long enough? g. Trainers adequate? h. Teachers satisfied?	5. Should computer related services be offered? a. What services exist? b. Should they? c. Should they be modified? d. OCTC requests? e. District offerings? f. District requests?
Records analysis (sign-in sheets, database, request forms)	x(a-e)	x	x(a,b)		x(d)
Needs assessment surveys	x(e,f)		x	x	
Post-activity & follow-up surveys		x	x(c,d,e)	x	
Interviews with teachers				x	
Interviews with district curriculum personnel					x(e,f)

Procedure Summary

Procedure	Evaluation Questions Addressed	Schedule for Collection	Respondents	Sample
Records analysis	1a,1b,1c,1d,2,3a,3b,5d	March 21-25 April 25-29	Documents/ "P" (Participants)	All from the past 2 years
Needs assessment surveys	1e,1f,3,5	March 14-25	Oswego County Educators	All
Post-activity survey	2,4	After each workshop (March/April) Review past surveys March 1-4 and April 11-15	All "P's" (Participants)	All in workshops
Interviews with teachers	3c,3d,3e,4,5a,5b,5c	March 7-11 April 18-22 (Planning periods & after school)	Two teachers from each workshop in the last 12 mos.	Approx. 20, chosen randomly from class lists.
Interviews with district curriculum personnel	5e,5f	March 28-31 (during the day)	CAI Committee members & CIC members (at least one per district)	Nine people First interview committee at meeting & informally survey results. Follow-up with individual interviews

Analysis and Interpretation Plan

Evaluation Question	Collection Procedure	Analysis Procedure	Evaluation Criteria	Procedure for Making Judgement
1. Are teachers attending training classes and are they aware of what is being offered?	A. Records analysis (Sign-in sheets, database, request forms)	1. Count teachers attending over past three years. 2. Tally totals by teaching assignment. 3. Count teachers attending from various schools. 4. Tally number of times courses are offered.	These findings will be used as baseline demographic information and blocked against further data that are collected.	Results will be presented to client in the form of a written report with accompanying graphics.
a. How many teachers take computer training courses? b. What kinds of teachers? c. Where are classes held? d. How often?				
1.e. How do teachers find out about workshops? 1.f. Which teachers are not attending?	B. Survey	Block how teachers found out by past participation, by school district, by kind of teacher, by level of experience, etc. Code frequency of awareness methods, list top five.	Top five methods will be listed numerically. There should be no discrepancy between workshop participants and non-participants concerning how they found out about courses.	In general, findings will be summarized. Analysis results will be compared to evaluation criteria and presented in the form of a written report with explanation and recommendations. Client makes judgments based on data.

Evaluation Question	Collection Procedure	Analysis Procedure	Evaluation Criteria	Procedure for Making Judgment
2. What types of computer training are being offered by OCTC? a. What computer training workshops are being offered by OCTC? b. What skills are being taught? c. What level of expertise is being addressed in workshops?	A. Records analysis C. Post-activity survey	1. Frequency count of courses offered. 2. Open-ended questions code into categories of common response (i.e. skills, levels)	All areas of skills from beginner to advanced should be represented. Course frequencies will indicate areas of interest in computer training.	Report results. Discrepancies should be noted.

Evaluation Question	Collection Procedure	Analysis Procedure	Evaluation Criteria	Procedure for Making Judgment
3. Is computer training needed? a. What courses are being requested? b. How many requests?	A. Records analysis B. Surveys	Tally frequency of responses. List needs according to frequency. Compare requests to actual courses offered. Compare number of attendees to number of requests for specific courses. Compare location of courses offered.	There should be high correlation (>.5) between items in all comparisons.	Present discrepancies to client.
3.c. Do teachers use computers in their classrooms? 3.d. Are they required to? 3.e. Are teachers already trained to use computers?	B. Surveys D. Interviews with teachers.	1. Tally frequency of computer usage. 2. Tally required use. 3. Compare percent of teachers using computers to percent of teachers required to percent of teachers already trained. 4. Tally self-reported levels of expertise. Block teachers adequately trained to requests for more courses.	These questions serve to provide background information and a base for projected planning.	Findings summarized & reported—major discrepancies should be noted.

Evaluation Question	Collection Procedure	Analysis Procedure	Evaluation Criteria	Procedure for Making Judgment
4. Are the computer training workshops useful?	C. Post-activity surveys D. Interviews with teachers	Tally acquired skills. List in decreasing order. Tally used skills. List in decreasing order.	New skills should be mentioned by 75 percent of participants.	If not, consult trainers to rework courses.
a. What skills do teachers acquire?				
b. Do they use skills in their classroom? At home?		Block usefulness according to various courses.	Courses not listed as useful should be reviewed.	
c. Are courses perceived as useful?		Compare hardware & software used in classrooms to courses offered.	Correlation should be at least .5.	
d. Matched to existing hardware & software?			Courses should be offered at all levels of expertise.	
e. Matched to existing levels of skill?		Compare self-reported skill levels to levels offered.	75 percent should be favorable (3 or above).	
f. Workshops long enough? Thorough enough?		Analyze questions regarding issues listed (e,f,g) by using a 1-5 scale. Look for large discrepancies (1's, 5's).	Dissatisfaction problems, etc., should be noted.	Trainers should be given information.
g. Trainers adequate?				
h. Teachers satisfied?		Summarize interview findings in narrative form. Look for themes, perceptions of satisfaction.		Summarize.

Evaluation Question	Collection Procedure	Analysis Procedure	Evaluation Criteria	Procedure for Making Judgment
5. Should computer related services be offered?	A. Records analysis	Evaluator lists requests from district personnel & compares to teacher requests & to actual offered services.	There should be a high correlation (.5 or better) between items.	Summarize.
a. What services exist?				
b. Should they?				
c. Should they be modified?	C. Surveys	Compare requests from needs assessment to actual services.	Individual requests should be mentioned.	
d. What requests does OCTC get?				
e. What do district curriculum people offer now?	D. Interviews	Evaluator lists suggestions and needs mentioned by teachers. Tallies requests.		
f. What do they want OCTC to offer?				

Reporting Summary

The evaluation of the computer training component of the Oswego County Teacher Center covers four months, from February 1988 to May 1988. The May deadline is necessary to ensure adequate time for OCTC to conduct and analyze survey and needs assessment results before the Program and Communication Specialist sets up summer offerings, workshops, etc., to be determined by evaluation results. For staff members of OCTC, many opportunities for informal reporting exist and will frequently be utilized in the normal performance of the evaluator's job. Formal report will be completed on a set schedule, and those deadlines are also indicated.

Event	Date/Frequency	Format	Nature/Scope of Content	Audience
Informal meeting with Coordinator	February 16	Meeting over coffee	Discuss evaluation plan	OCTC Coordinator
Liaison update	End of February, prior to data collection	Memorandum	Announce upcoming evaluation, request assistance in data collection, information on distributing & collecting survey instrument.	Building liaison
Initial report	February	Oral report by OCTC Coordinator	Status & planning report, request for assistance.	CAI Committee
Preliminary information release	February/March (First month of data collection)	Centerline (newsletter) article	Explain purpose of upcoming data collection instruments, solicit cooperation, support, input.	General OCTC membership (all Oswego County teachers/administrators)
Mid-year report	End of March	Printed outline listing objectives, activities, progress	Progress, status, completion of objectives to date.	State Education Department
Progress updates	Bi-weekly at staff meetings/March-May	Oral synopses	Progress, preliminary findings, next steps	OCTC Coordinator

Event	Date/Frequency	Format	Nature/Scope of Content	Audience
Progress updates	Monthly, regularly scheduled committee meetings/March-May	Brief, written summaries with by oral briefing	Progress, preliminary findings, next step	OCTC Coordinator, Program Committee Executive Committee, CAI Committee
Final report: summary revision	By end of May	Written report with oral summary, Q&A session	Review of study, present data, conclusions, interpretations, recommendations, implications	OCTC Coordinator, Program Committee Executive Committee, CAI Committee
Final report	May 30	Written report with appendices, instruments	Review of study, present data, conclusions, interpretations, recommendations, implications, fuller data reports	OCTC Coordinator, Executive Committee Governing Board, all committees
Final report: abstract	End-of-year report May 30	Press release, news article in Centerline (June), written summary to SED	Review of study, present data, conclusions, interpretations, recommendations, implications	State Education Department/ teachers

The evaluation director will be the Oswego County Teacher Center Program and Communication Specialist, OCTC Coordinator will assist in a consultant's role when feasible. The Computer-Assisted Instruction (CAI) Committee will be asked for feedback when appropriate. An outside consultant will be hired for design review and analysis and interpretation assistance. One of two secretaries at OCTC will be available as needed to perform data entry duties. The other secretary will be available as needed to tabulate survey results and format data in a comprehensive package. The printing department at BOCES will copy, collate, and process reports as an in-kind contribution to the Teacher Center.

Evaluation Work Plan	Person Responsible	February	March	April	May
A. Design the Evaluation					
- develop focus of evaluation	Evaluator	1 (2/1-2/5)			
- draft design	Evaluator	1.5 (2/2-2/5)			
- review draft	Consultant & Coordinator	1 (2/8-2/12)			
- revise	Evaluator	.5 (2/8-2/12)			
- review	Coordinator	.5 (2/8-2/12)			
- produce copies of final plan	Secretary	.5 (2/15)			
B. Develop Procedures & Instruments					
- create master schedule	Evaluator	.5 (2/15)			
- draft survey questions	Evaluator	.5 (2/16)			
- review survey questions	Consultant/Coordinator/CAI Committee	.5 (2/17-19)	.5(2/17-2/19)	.5(2/17-2/19)	.5(2/17-2/19)
- revise survey	Evaluator	.1 (2/19)			
- print survey	Printing/BOCES	.1 (2/22)			
- field test survey	Evaluator	1 (2/23-2/26)			
- review & revise current post-activity survey	Evaluator	.2 (2/17)			
- print post-activity surveys	Printing/BOCES	.1 (2/22)			
- design interview questions	Evaluator	.5 (2/18)			
- schedule interviews	Evaluator	.5 (2/19)			
- schedule computer time	Evaluator	.1 (2/19)			

Evaluation Work Plan	Person Responsible	February	March	April	May
C. Information Collection					
– send out liaison update	Evaluator, Secretaries	.05,.1 (2/22-2/23)			
– send out surveys	Secretaries		.1 (2/29-3/1)		
– distribute post-activity surveys	Evaluator		.05 (3/7-3/25)	.05 (4/11-4/22)	
– tabulate surveys	Secretary		1 (3/25-4/1)		
– tabulate post-activity surveys	Secretary		.1 (3/25)	.1 (4/22)	
– interview teachers	Evaluator		4.5 (3/7-3/11,	4/11-4/14)	
– do records analysis	Evaluator & Secretary		2.5 (3/1-3/4,	.5 (4/11-4/14)	
– interview district curriculum personnel	Evaluator		4.0 (3/28-3/31)		
D. Analyze Information					
– analyze surveys	Evaluator			1 (4/4)	
– analyze post-activity surveys	Evaluator			.5 (4/25)	
– analyze records	Evaluator			1.5 (4/15)	
– analyze interview records	Evaluator		.5 (3/31)	.5 (4/25)	
– review analysis	Consultant				1 (5/1-5/5)
E. Reports					
– Liaison update	Evaluator & Secretary	.25 (2/22-2/23),	.25 (2/22-2/23)		
– Initial report	OCTC Coordinator	.1 (2/18)			
– Preliminary information release	Evaluator		.1 (2/29-3/1)		
– Mid-year report	Evaluator		.1 (3/31)		
– Progress update	Evaluator		.5 (3/16,3/30 4/13,4/27,5/11)		
– Progress update	Evaluator		.3 (3/5,4/17,5/14)		
– Final report preparation	Evaluator, Secretary, Printing				2 (5/9-5/13), 1.1 (5/16-5/25),.5(5/31)
– Final report presentation	Evaluator				.5 (5/31)

Evaluation Budget

The Evaluation Director is employed as the Program and Communication Specialist for the Oswego County Teacher Center (OCTC) and would conduct an evaluation of this sort as part of her normal job function. She shares the time of two full-time secretaries with the OCTC Coordinator. This budget includes their salary even though this evaluation would be perceived as part of their assigned duties. Normally, the printing department at BOCES, which is the LEA (Local Educational Agency) for OCTC, absorbs the cost of printing materials for OCTC as an in-kind contribution to the Teacher Center. The BOCES mail courier is also available to avoid the cost of mailing reports, etc., so there is also no charge for that. A cost is included for these services here, however.

Personnel	Actual	Contributed
Evaluator 25.8 days @ $150/da		3,870.00
Secretary 3.75 days @ $37.50/da		140.62
Consultant 2.5 days @ $175/da	437.50	
Coordinator 1.6 days @ $175/da		280.00
Subtotal	437.50	4,290.62

Travel and Mileage Reimbursement

Mileage for interviews 500 mi. @ .22/mi.	110.00	
Meals (5 lunches)	25.00	
Subtotal	135.00	

Materials and Supplies (Printing, paper, postage costs are contributed by BOCES.) If not contributed:

Surveys--printing & postage (2,000 @ .30/ea)	600.00
Post-activity surveys--printing & postage (60 @ .30/ea)	45.00
Final report--printing and postage (100 @ 1.00/ea)	100.00
Final report summary (20 @ .25/ea)	5.00
Final report abstract (2,000 @ .10/ea)	200.00
Subtotal	950.00

TOTAL	$ 572.50	$5,240.62

38

Meta-Evaluation

A. Standards Considered Not Applicable or Marginally Applicable

<u>B3 Cost Effectiveness</u>. Although the evaluation will provide information for planning and will involve time and effort of Teacher Center staff, actual cost in terms of dollars and cents is not an issue. The secretaries and evaluator already conduct evaluations as part of their routine activities and additional funds will not be spent, except nominally to cover the cost of the consultant, mileage, lunch, and postage. Printing reports and surveys are normally an in-kind contribution from BOCES.

As a matter of fact, the state requires teacher centers to evaluate their programming and assumes that monies will be spent to this end. Since the Program and Communication Specialist is taking an evaluation course at her own expense to enhance her skills as an evaluator, the state is saving money that would be used to pay for increased consultant time and for the additional time the Center Coordinator would have to spend evaluating the computer training component herself.

<u>C1 Formal Obligation</u>. Since this will be an internal evaluation conducted primarily by staff members as part of the normal function of their jobs, a written agreement will not be needed. The evaluator (also the Program and Communication Specialist) will report on the design and progress of the evaluation to the Coordinator and the executive and program committees and a group memory (minutes) will be kept of major agreements and understandings. A formal contract would be superfluous in this context.

Since the external evaluators we plan to hire as consultants have already contracted with us in the past to help with evaluations and since $437.50 is a relatively small contract, we will continue the practice of agreeing verbally to contractual obligations and paying for these consultants' services through a purchase order sent out by the business office at the BOCES that is our LEA.

<u>C4 The Public's Right to Know</u>. This is basically an internal evaluation designed to provide data useful in improving the computer training component of the Teacher Center's programming. The issues of public safety and the right to privacy are not really applicable in this particular formative study, but they would not be ignored should they arise. The findings would, of course, be available to all interested parties, but the primary purpose is to help the Coordinator and the Program and Communication Specialist plan for the next year's computer training workshops and related services that do not really impact the general public.

B. Standards that are Applicable and that Have Been Well Provided for in the Evaluation.

A1 Audience Identification. Since this is an internal evaluation conducted by teacher center staff, this is an ideal situation to ensure that all appropriate audiences have been identified and their needs have been accounted for. The Program and Communication Specialist is well aware of who will use the evaluation results and how to rank-order them, who is being studied, and who will be affected by the results. To the greatest extent possible, the evaluator has planned through meetings, reports, etc., to meet the information needs of these audiences so that the evaluation creates a positive response and the full utilization of data to improve programming in the county. Great effort has gone into identifying the crucial audiences for this evaluation.

A8 Evaluation Impact. In conjunction with the standard listed above, evaluation impact has been well provided for. It is important that there be follow-through by audience members and that the findings be utilized to improve, expand, or maintain existing programming that works. After all, this is primarily a formative evaluation of the computer training component of the Teacher Center operations.

Since the evaluator will support the Coordinator in effecting programming changes based on the evaluation findings, a direct line has already been established to ensure evaluation impact. Through the planned reporting schedule and through informal meetings with key audience members, the evaluator will help these audience members assess the results of the evaluation and fully utilize these data to improve programming.

B2 Political Viability.

To some extent, political viability is important in this evaluation. The Teacher Center services nine school districts and BOCES. Care must be taken to provide equitable service to all districts, regardless of size and location. To inadvertently overlook administrators or district curriculum personnel in one district during the course of the evaluation could disrupt the data collection procedure and destroy the final impact. Second, other groups offer similar services in the area of computer training. The CAI Committee should be actively involved in this study to ensure that the evaluation design is optimally useful and that the resultant changes can be mutually coordinated and efforts not duplicated. Care must be taken to identify and collaborate with all contributing audiences.

C. Standards that are Applicable and Not Yet Well Provided for in the Evaluation

A4 Valuational Interpretation. This extremely important standard has not yet been well provided for in the sense that the evaluator is not completely sure how to assess the data collected in the evaluation. At this time, interpretation of findings will be viewed as a collaborative effort involving the Coordinator, the consultant, and members of various contributing audiences. Since the bases for value judgments are not clear at this time, great care must be taken during the evaluation to foster the application of this standard.

C2 Conflict of Interest. Some conflict of interest exists in any internal evaluation. Since the primary evaluator is also the person responsible for the programming of the computer training component of the Teacher Center, it is possible that evaluation results could be biased. Initial efforts to avoid this include good audience identification, close contact with an outside consultant, and an excellent working arrangement with various Teacher Center committees and the Coordinator. Maintaining an awareness of possible problems should help the evaluator develop methods to deal with this conflict should it arise.

D9 Analysis of Qualitative Information. Due to the nature of the collection process for qualitative data, it is often impossible to plan ahead how to summarize and present the data collected except in a generalized manner. While this poses planning problems, it offers the exciting possibility of discovering new information that had not been considered by the evaluator. With quantitative data analysis, one knows what one is looking for. But in open interviews and in unobtrusive procedures, one isn't always sure. Greater flexibility and the ability to respond in an unbiased way are crucial. Therefore, the evaluator must try to confirm and verify information whenever possible. I will seek a consultant's help with qualitative analysis, but my lack of experience will undoubtedly hamper the information gathering process, i.e., unstructured interviews, records analysis, and so on.

HANDOUT 3: Assignments Checklist

Assignment 1: Program Selection

General comments
___ 1. not in required format
___ 2. exceeds specified page length
___ 3. poorly written

Purpose of program
___ 4. not clearly or completely stated
___ 5. confuses purpose of program with purpose of
         evaluation
___ 6. assumptions not made clear
___ 7. abbreviations not explained

Clients of program
___ 8. clients of program confused with clients of
         evaluation
___ 9. lacks specific detail--"company employees" vs.
      "salespeople and marketing personnel with less than
      one year's experience"

Purpose of evaluation
___ 10. identified <u>what</u> is being evaluated, not <u>why</u> (e.g.,
         "modification of syllabus" vs. "modification of
         syllabus in order to decrease teaching time and
         increase test scores")
___ 11. identified <u>how</u> evaluation is being done not <u>why</u>
         (e.g., "interview teachers before and after new
         program is in place")
___ 12. purpose not possible with time, resources,
         technology available
___ 13. vague terms such as "needs," "improve," "assist,"
         (e.g., "determine if program meets student needs"
         --what kinds of needs?--emotional, social
         materials, support?)
___ 14. purpose not relevant, judging from description of
         program

Basic operation
___ 15. information presented not relevant to evaluation
         purpose (e.g., "purpose is to examine materials and
         their implementation in order to make
         improvements", but basic operation description does
         not include information on present materials
         implementation)
___ 16. important information missing (e.g., scope of
         program, timeframe, budget, locale, management
         procedures, materials, personnel)

Assignment 2:   Focus Summary

General comments
___ 1.   not in required format
___ 2.   exceeds specified page length
___ 3.   poorly written

Object focus
___ 4.   repeat of basic operation in Assignment 1 with no additional information or detail provided--description lacks sufficient detail
___ 5.   major focus not identified
___ 6.   secondary focus not identified
___ 7.   focus not related to purpose of study
___ 8.   scope of evaluation is too large/too small

Purposes
___ 9.   primary purpose not identified
___ 10.   secondary purpose not identified
___ 11.   identified _what_ is being evaluated, not _why_ (e.g., "modification of syllabus" vs. "modification of syllabus in order to decrease teaching time and increase test scores")
___ 12.   identified _how_ evaluation is being done not _why_ (e.g., "interview teachers before and after new program is in place")
___ 13.   purpose not possible with time, resources, technology available
___ 14.   vague terms such as "needs," "improve," "assist," (e.g., "determine if program meets student needs" --what kinds of needs?--emotional, social, materials, support?)
___ 15.   purpose not relevant, judging from description of program

Audience
___ 16.   major clients not identified
___ 17.   importance of audiences not indicated
___ 18.   important stakeholders or audiences missing
___ 19.   "audience," "stakeholders," and "clients" confused
___ 20.   clients of evaluation confused with clients of program

Contextual factors
___ 21.   important contextual factors missing
___ 22.   importance of contextual factors not identified
___ 23.   factors identified with no explanation of how they may influence evaluation

Assignment 3:   Question Summary

General comments
____ 1.   not in required format

Primary questions
____ 2.   too few or too many major questions listed
____ 3.   questions not listed by significance or chronology
____ 4.   questions not comprehensive, only concern part of the evaluation's focus
____ 5.   questions do not relate to the evaluation's purpose
____ 6.   secondary questions do not relate to primary questions
____ 7.   important questions are missing, given purpose of evaluation
____ 8.   questions semantically too complicated, need to be simplified

Audience
____ 9.   specific audience interest in question is unclear
____ 10.   confuses data sources with audiences wanting information
____ 11.   does not sufficiently differentiate audience information needs

Why question is important
____ 12.   importance not related to evaluation's purpose
____ 13.   importance not related to audiences indicated
____ 14.   confuses how information will be used with why it is important

Assignment 4:   Question/Procedure Matrix

General comments
____ 1.   not in required format

Collection procedure
____ 2.   too few or too many collection procedures
____ 3.   missing important procedures (e.g., unobtrusive measures)
____ 4.   confuses data collection with analysis procedures (e.g., "time series" is analysis)
____ 5.   asking respondents who do not have information
____ 6.   using weak information source, better data available from another source
____ 7.   procedure not appropriate for respondents
____ 8.   procedure vague (e.g., "discussion with teacher")
____ 9.   procedure impractical or obtrusive
____ 10.   information collected for primary question from only one source
____ 11.   procedure collects information on too few or too many questions

_____ 12.   missing possible cross-referencing of data (e.g., have both teachers and participants rate the participants' level of satisfaction and compare data)

_____ 13.   using multiple collection procedures inappropriately (e.g., no new information gained by using multiple collection procedures)

Assignment 5:   Procedures Summary

General comments
_____ 1.   not in required format

Schedule
_____ 2.   unable to determine exactly when data will be collected: dates, day of week, time of day, chronological sequence

_____ 3.   vague (e.g., "interview three each week". Does that mean interview two a week until all 12 have been interviewed, or interview same two each week, or ...?)

_____ 4.   inappropriate data collection schedule

Respondents
_____ 5.   confuses data collector with information sources

Sample
_____ 6.   number of respondents unclear

_____ 7.   missing criteria for selection (e.g., "eight teachers", which eight?)

_____ 8.   proposed sample would present obvious bias

Assignment 6:   Analysis and Interpretation of Data

General comments
_____ 1.   not in required format

How analyzed
_____ 2.   analysis method vague (e.g., "content analysis," "summarize ratings," "analyze data")

_____ 3.   better descriptive procedures needed (e.g., means, ranges, frequencies)

_____ 4.   ranking or rating scales are needed

_____ 5.   missing opportunities to block data (e.g., is there a difference in attitude between freshmen and sophomores?)

_____ 6.   failure to interrelate data: comparisons, relationships not examined

Criteria
___ 7.   no criteria indicated
___ 8.   criteria questionable or justification is unclear
(e.g., "acceptable is 3 or above on 6 point scale"
- how determined?)
___ 9.   missing valuable information by examining only
frequency counts or averages

Procedure to make judgment
___ 10.   no procedures specified
___ 11.   "evaluator will present findings to client" as
standard reply is not informative
___ 12.   lack of clarity about how data will be used

Assignment 7: Reporting Summary

General comments
___ 1.   not in required format

Event
___ 2.   too many or too few reporting events; utility vs.
cost
___ 3.   no introductory meetings with those who are
involved in evaluation
___ 4.   not sensitive to political issues (e.g., first
meetings about evaluation are scheduled with staff
instead of client)

Date/frequency
___ 5.   not enough time for event (e.g., two days to design
five reports)
___ 6.   interim meetings with client or audiences not
scheduled, preliminary data not shared
___ 7.   dates not coordinated (e.g., press release before
presenting results to the client)

Format
___ 8.   inappropriate format or content for audience (e.g.,
parents presented with technical report)
___ 9.   does not take advantage of variety of possible
formats (e.g., graphics, executive summary, oral
report)

Scope/content
___ 10.   content inappropriate to audience
___ 11.   does not take advantage of information gathered
from other sources
___ 12.   does not maximize reporting of same information to
multiple audiences

Audiences
___ 13.   neglects important audiences (e.g., audiences identified in Assignment 2)
___ 14.   inappropriate distribution of reports
___ 15.   assumes there is general interest in work when may not be
___ 16.   assumes a formal meta-evaluation report is needed when may not be

Assignment 8:   Management Plan: Personnel

General comments
___ 1.   not in required format

Tasks
___ 2.   task breakdown too detailed or not detailed enough
___ 3.   tasks not categorized
___ 4.   tasks listed chronologically, not by task group
___ 5.   missing tasks (e.g., pilot test instruments, train team to use instruments)

Personnel
___ 6.   personnel for given task not specified
___ 7.   personnel grouped: impossible to tell who in the group performs what task
___ 8.   inappropriate personnel for task

Days/dates
___ 9.   calendar dates of work missing
___ 10.   level of effort (number of work days) missing
___ 11.   working three days in two-day time period (e.g., 3/2-1 through 2-2)
___ 12.   weekends and holidays are overlooked
___ 13.   total work time exceeds the time available in week/month, for given personnel
___ 14.   starting date is inappropriate
___ 15.   not enough time indicated for task

Assignment 9:   Management Plan: Budget

General comments
___ 1.   not in required format

Categories
___ 2.   major categories missing
___ 3.   important charges within categories missing
___ 4.   mismatch between work planned and budget (e.g., paying staff for four months although actual work time is much less)
___ 5.   personnel in management plan are not accounted for in budget

How computed
___ 6.   computation of costs not indicated
___ 7.   total cost presented without adequate explanation
___ 8.   missing major expenditures indicated in plan (e.g., videotape, or postage for returning mailed survey)
___ 9.   costs estimated too high/too low
___ 10.   contributed, in-kind, or external support should be summarized but indicated separately
___ 11.   errors in mathematical computations

Assignment 10: Meta-evaluation Summary

General comments
___ 1.   not in required format
___ 2.   poorly written

Standards
___ 3.   weak explanation of why identified standard is not applicable
___ 4.   identified standard as "not applicable", but then explained how it has been well-accounted for
___ 5.   weak explanation of how standard has been well provided for (e.g., identify audience - audiences listed with no indication of how audiences were identified)
___ 6.   no explanation of how design would be changed to take into account standards which apply but have not been provided for
___ 7.   misinterpret standard (e.g., conflict of interest)
___ 8.   missing important standards

2

CONCEPTUALIZING EVALUATION: THE KEY EVALUATION CHECKLIST

Karen E. Kirkhart   Michael Scriven
Syracuse University   University of Western Australia
School of Social Work   P. O. Box 69
117 Brockway Hall   Point Reyes, CA 94956
Syracuse, NY 13244-6350   In the US: 415/663-1511
(315) 443-5574   In Australia: 011-61-9-386-2568

This teaching activity is based upon Scriven's (1983) Key
Evaluation Checklist (KEC). The checklist is a conceptual tool
to identify key dimensions of any evaluative study. It includes:

1. Description
2. Client
3. Background and content
4. Resources
5. Consumer
6. Values
7. Process
8. Outcome
9. Generalizability
10. Costs
11. Comparisons
12. Significance
13. Recommendations
14. Report
15. Meta-evaluation.

This activity presents and illustrates the basic dimension
of the KEC, gives the students hands-on exercises in which to
apply the concepts, and then ties the conceptual framework to the
stepwise process of evaluation planning and implementation.

The Key Evaluation Checklist is not a set of linear steps
for planning an evaluation. Rather, it is a blueprint for
identifying issues, concepts and dimensions that are relevant to
a number of different steps in planning and carrying out

evaluation. Using the KEC to map out these key issues, concepts, and dimensions is an iterative process; that is, students will go through the checklist more than once, moving back and forth among checklist categories, as they raise questions, identify issues, and come to a clearer understanding of what is to be evaluated and of the evaluation process itself.

MATERIALS

Handout 1: Example: Key Evaluation Checklist

PROCEDURES

1.   Introduce the Key Evaluation Checklist

Write the 15 elements of the KEC on the blackboard (or on a flipchart if board space is limited). It helps to have all 15 elements visible to the class throughout the session to assist in cross-referencing elements. As summarized above, the major points to be made in introducing the checklist are:

a.   It provides a list of key components or ingredients that are necessary and relevant in thinking about **any** evaluation; it does not provide procedural steps for implementing an evaluation. (Depending on the level of class being taught, you may use a recipe analogy here: the KEC provides the list of necessary ingredients but not the procedures for assembling them into a final product.)

b.   It may be used either to **plan** an evaluation (as illustrated here) or to **do** an evaluation (i.e., as the criterion for judging the merit or worth of something). We use a planning example in introducing the KEC because it is easier to grasp the elements in that context.

c.   Many iterations are involved in using the KEC. One must go through it at least two or three times to flesh out even a preliminary evaluation plan, letting the content unfold and using the KEC categories to help organize it. It is not a linear process, although students may choose to go through the elements in linear order in the first review of the checklist.

d.   The 15 elements of the KEC are not independent of one another. They sometimes overlap or are inter-related in particular ways, as illustrated in the example that follows.

2.   Present an Example

Using the example handout, review each element of the KEC,
presenting the definition and illustrating its application. For
the initial application it is useful to pick an evaluand familiar
to all students; therefore, we typically use the class in which
they are enrolled. (This is also consistent with the consumer
orientation of the KEC, since students can then reflect on the
evaluand from the consumer perspective.) Also, it is helpful to
begin with an evaluand that is a program having some sort of
service delivery component. This permits direct application of
the full range of KEC components in a way that beginners find the
most straightforward.

In reviewing each KEC element, emphasize (1) whether that
element refers to a component of the evaluand, the evaluation, or
both, and (2) what the similarities and relationships and among
the elements. In grouping the elements for review, we begin with
the first six (bracketing them on the board) labeling them
informally as "Mapping the Territory" in that they are
descriptive, information-gathering elements. The next five we
then consider as a group, "Posing Evaluative Questions," followed
by the final four, "Bringing it all Together." Review the
example handout to illustrate each component of the KEC,
highlighting the points that are made at the top of each section.

3.   Assign an Application Exercise

Use a blank KEC worksheet[1] to give students an opportunity to
apply the concepts of the KEC to a new problem situation. This
may be done individually or in groups, in class or as outside
homework. Begin by assigning a common example so that the
answers can be reviewed in class. Design a problem statement
that relates to the background or interests of your students. It
will help if students are familiar with the type of program to be
evaluated. Some problem statements we have used include:

a.   Day care. The West Side Day Care Center has experienced a
      drop in enrollment in the preschool program. A number of
      parents have withdrawn their children to enroll them in
      other centers in the community. Concerned about the
      enrollment decline, the advisory board orders an evaluation
      of West Side's preschool program to determine its strengths
      and weaknesses and provide recommendations for improvement.

----
[1]   A blank copy of this worksheet is not shown due to space
      limitations. Readers may reconstruct an approximation of
      this worksheet by deleting the sample responses shown in
      italics from the example handout presented as Handout 1.
      The KEC components are shown in bold print in the handout.

52

The County Child Care Council will provide a consultant to conduct the study, and the Day Care Board has budgeted $75 for supplies and related expenses.

b.   Education. Times are tough in Skokie, Illinois. The school budget must be cut, and some of the school board members are out to ax the band. Others think this would be a very serious mistake. Hearing of your expertise in evaluation, the superintendent of schools phones you for help. She asks you to develop a plan for the evaluation of the band program, outlining the major considerations that such an evaluation would need to address. You have a budget of $100 or so and a little released time. The evaluation must be done within a 90-day period. The design must be done within ten days.

c.   Mental health. The Crestview Mental Health Center has sponsored a series of community education activities in the past year on "The Challenges of the Family." Workshops, discussion groups, and information and referral services addressed such topics as "Communicating with your Teenager," "Maintaining a Happy Marriage," "Managing Family Finances," and "Dealing with Substance Abuse." The executive director has asked the agency's assistant director to put together an evaluation of this program using persons from inside and outside the agency. The assistant director can work up to one-third time on the evaluation; other team members would be volunteering their time. A modest budget for expenses is provided.

Provide each student with a blank KEC worksheet with the common problem statement written in on the first page. Make clear what you expect the finished product to look like (for example, we ask only that each student make notes on his/her worksheet from which he/she can speak in subsequent class discussions. We do not require any formal write-up at this point, although that could be an adaptation). When the students have completed the exercise, review illustrative answers and respond to questions that have come up while working on the assignment. (The review can be conducted orally or with the assistance of visual cues such as writing sample answers on the board, overhead transparencies, or enlarged "worksheet" pages of a flipchart).

When the group exercise has been carefully reviewed, give students an opportunity to apply the KEC to a problem of their own choosing. Ask each student to form an individual problem statement. (We have them submit their statements on 3x5-inch cards so we can review them during a break in class to make sure they are starting off in the right direction.) Have them work through their problems as a homework assignment, using a blank KEC. (We use this as an ungraded homework assignment and tie it to some other aspect of the course for which a grade is assigned --e.g., an exam question on the KEC or a final paper that centers around an evaluation proposal.)

Questions on the individual applications should be answered in class, but it is not necessary to review the full content of each student's product. Application of specific KEC components may be shared with the class to illustrate particular issues or problems in evaluation. (With students' permission, keep a file of sample applications to guide future students).

4.   Integrate the KEC with the Process of Evaluation.

As a conceptual framework, the KEC will prove useful at many stages in the evaluation process. Since beginning students of evaluation are often eager to grasp the procedural steps of planning and carrying out an evaluation, it is important to help them make this connection to the KEC. Using whatever procedural framework best fits the content area of your evaluation course, indicate how the KEC can contribute to each step of the evaluation process.

DISCUSSION

These materials were first developed for instructing school administrators in Nova University's National Ed.D. Program for Educational Leaders. That program is especially challenging for instructors since student contact in evaluation is limited to three six-hour lectures delivered at monthly intervals, and students work independently and in study groups to master content. Beginning in 1986, we began to design curriculum materials to guide students in their independent work. The KEC example handout is a part of that series. The version presented here was developed for use in an introductory graduate level evaluation course for master's students in social work.

The KEC materials are extremely flexible in their application. They have been used successfully with both masters and doctoral students. They can be used as the basis for one or two three-hour class sessions or an intensive workshop. Pieces of the material may be adapted for briefer time periods. The KEC may also be used as an organizing framework for an entire course, paired with supplementary readings to flesh out issues and topics. The KEC is especially useful in a "models-oriented" course, as it provides a basis for comparing and contrasting models of evaluation research.

BACKGROUND READING

Rossi, P. H., & Freeman, H. E. (1985). Evaluation: A systematic approach. (Third edition). Beverly Hills, CA: Sage Publications.

It is helpful to use a basic introductory evaluation text such as this one to flesh out issues and topics raised by the KEC. The text is useful to (1) discuss certain topics in more detail, (2) present alternative or contrasting perspectives on selected topics, and (3) connect the KEC to procedural steps in conducting evaluation.

Scriven, M. (1981). <u>Evaluation thesaurus</u>. (Third edition). Inverness, CA: Edgepress.

This is the reference text in which the KEC is introduced and in which the related terms and concepts are explained.

HANDOUT 1:   Example: Key Evaluation Checklist

The purpose of this Example is to illustrate the application of the Key Evaluation Checklist (KEC) to a real-world problem. Following each set of instructions as they appear on a blank Worksheet, there are notes that illustrate how each KEC item may be applied. The intention here is to be illustrative rather than exhaustive; that is, not all relevant information has been noted. You may well find yourself expanding on the sample answers as you walk through the example.

Problem Statement

***   Briefly describe a circumstance or situation in which evaluation is needed or might be useful in your work. Include a statement of:

a.   what is to be evaluated (evaluand)
b.   impetus for the evaluation (why do it?)
c.   intended use of findings

Note that this is a <u>brief</u> statement of the evaluation problem you wish to undertake. It is intended to serve only as a starting place, so it does not need to be complete or detailed. As you work through the KEC, you will be fleshing out these and many other important aspects of the evaluation.

> *As a graduate level instructor, I am concerned about my instructional effectiveness. I want to evaluate both my teaching and the curriculum in order to revise and improve my introductory evaluation course. I'll use the KEC to plan the components of this evaluation.*

Description

*** Write a neutral description of what is to be evaluated (the evaluand). It will help you to build a full description if you include:

a. nature and operation (What bounds, constitutes, or defines that which is to be evaluated?)
b. function (What does the evaluand <u>do</u>?)
c. delivery system (How does it do it?)
d. support system (How does it <u>continue</u> to do it?)

*** On your first pass through the KEC, sketch out the description, answering these four questions to the best of your current knowledge of the evaluand. Often you may not know certain descriptive information. Use a separate blank sheet of paper to note these questions to be asked or issues clarified in order for you to have a complete, neutral description of the program. Note also who you might ask to get this information, and how you might go about gathering it.

*** As you go through the KEC and later as you gather more complete information, refer back to this checkpoint and modify or refine your description, updating it to make the final product as complete and neutral as possible.

a. **Nature and operation**. *The evaluand is my introductory evaluation course. This evaluand includes (1) the graded assignments, (2) student preparation, (3) assigned readings, (4) my classroom instruction, and (5) student evaluation.*

b. **Function**. *The class fulfills several functions. It instructs students in the logic of evaluation. It stimulates me, the instructor, to new ideas regarding evaluation. It employs me. It prepares students to be intelligent consumers of evaluation.*

c. **Delivery system**. *Knowledge of evaluation is delivered to students by (1) instruction by the professor, (2) peer instruction (group work and interaction among students), (3) outside readings from the texts and library reserve, and (4) homework assignments.*

d. **Support system**. *Many persons and organizations provide support to make the class possible. The University schedules space and equipment and handles student enrollment. The bookstore makes required texts available for purchase. A commercial copy center makes recommended journal articles available for purchase. Support staff prepare and duplicate the course syllabus and handouts. Families of students adjust their schedules and use of resources so that students can enroll and attend.*

Client

Definition: Person/agency for whom an evaluation is formally done; the person/agency who commissions the evaluation.

*** First, define who the client is to be for this evaluation. This will be the primary person/agency to whom the evaluator is accountable in reporting the results. Is the client the initiator of this evaluation? If some other person/agency initiated the evaluation, it should be noted.

*** Second, list other persons/groups who will have an interest in the evaluation and will be consumers of the evaluation results. These are the stakeholder audiences. (In listing the stakeholder audiences, make sure that you have considered those with particular interests in the evaluand, such as its consumers, its providers, its instigator, and/or its inventor.)

Client:

The client of this evaluation is me, the instructor responsible for the course being evaluated (the evaluand).

Initiator:

In this case, I am also the initiator of this evaluation. No one else asked me to do it; I want to do it for my own benefit.

Stakeholder audiences:

Other persons who will be interested in the results include: fellow instructors who teach in the research curriculum area (of which this course is a part), the Dean of my school, students and graduates of the M.S.W. program who are or were consumers of the evaluand, colleagues in the American Evaluation Association's Topical Interest Group on Teaching Evaluation.

Background and Context

<u>Definition</u>:   Circumstances that do or may influence the outcome
of the evaluand and/or evaluation.

*** Make two lists here--one for circumstances that will affect
the <u>evaluand</u> and one for circumstances that will affect the
<u>evaluation</u>. Note some items may appear on both lists, since some
background issues that affect the evaluand will also affect its
evaluation.

Background & Context of EVALUAND	Background & Context of EVALUATION
- *History of the introductory evaluation course and of previous instructors*	- *Previous types of student feedback requested on this course*
- *Reputation of the course among students, faculty colleagues*	- *This is a* **formative** *evaluation to help improve my course*
- *Instructor evaluation by students at the end of the semester*	- *Instructor evaluation by students at the end of the semester*
- *Curriculum organization i.e., how this fits into the research curriculum and into the student's areas of specialization*	- *The evaluator is* <u>*internal*</u> *to the system being evaluated*
- *Student admission requirements and course prerequisites*	- *Qualifications of the evaluator*
- *Instructor qualifications*	- *Stakeholder audiences in the evaluation*

Resources

Definition: The sources of support or means available to carry out the evaluand and to conduct the evaluation.

*** Make two lists here also--one for resources available to the evaluand and one for resources available to the evaluation. Start with resources that are actually being used or have already been allocated to the evaluand and evaluation. Then try to think more broadly and add potential resources that one might draw upon to support the evaluand and/or its evaluation.

Resources for use by EVALUAND Resources for use by EVALUATION

Actual Resources

Resources for use by EVALUAND	Resources for use by EVALUATION
- Instructor time	- Previous instructors' notes and records
- Student time	- Student feedback
- Money budgeted by the university	- Research curriculum colleagues to give feedback
- Facilities	- Evaluator time
- Books, materials	- Support staff to prepare and duplicate instruments
- Faculty colleagues to provide guest lectures	- Graduate assistant assigned to the course
- Field placements to provide relevant experiences	

Potential Resources

Resources for use by EVALUAND	Resources for use by EVALUATION
- Former students as tutors	- Observers to critique classes
- Exchanges with other universities	- Former students to provide follow-up information
- Additional field placements	- An external evaluator

Consumer

<u>Definition</u>:   First, list all persons who are consumers of the evaluand.

***   List all persons who are consumers of the evaluand. Make sure to identify all <u>true consumers</u>, i.e., recipients of the program who are impacted <u>either</u> directly or indirectly.

<u>Directly impacted consumers</u>

-   *Students in the M.S.W. program*

<u>Indirectly impacted consumers</u>

-   *Spouses of M.S.W. students*

-   *Families of M.S.W. students*

-   *Work colleagues of M.S.W. students*

-   *Field instructors at students' field placements*

***   Second, double-check to make sure that all those you have identified as true consumers are <u>recipients</u> of the program, as opposed to <u>providers</u> of the program. If you have listed providers, delete them above, and list them separately below.

<u>Providers of the evaluand who are impacted by it</u>:

Faculty colleagues; Dean of the School of Social Work

Now you should have a complete picture of all those impacted by the evaluand--direct and indirect consumers plus providers.

Values

Definition: The standards of merit or worth that underlie the
               evaluation, making it more than mere description.

The merit or worth of a program can be defined in terms of
consumer needs, consumer wants or preferences, professional
standards, program goals, logical analysis, or believed standards
of merit. Each of these represents a different set of values.

*** First, determine what values will form the basis of this
     evaluation. (Check all that apply.)

     [X]   Consumer needs
     [X]   Consumer wants
     [ ]   Professional standards
     [X]   Program goals and objectives
     [X]   Logical analysis
     [X]   Judged or believed standards of merit
     [ ]   Other_____

*** Second, for each set of values you have identified, clarify
      whose values are represented. (For example, which consumers
      will have their needs or wants represented? Whose values
      are reflected in the program goals?)

*** Third, list the content of these values, if known, or if
      unknown to you, how will you ascertain them in designing the
      evaluation? (For example, you may be able to list
      applicable professional standards, it they exist, but judged
      or believed standards of merit among the stakeholder
      audiences may be trickier to identify.)

Consumers' needs and wants. *The consumers whose needs and wants I will
address are those students who are presently participating in my introductory evaluation
course and those students who completed the course last year under my instruction. Some
student needs are already known (e.g., needs of students to master evaluation knowledge for
the examination and for subsequent application; needs of students for examples relevant to
their field placement settings); others I must ascertain through a needs assessment. Some
student preferences or wants are already known (e.g., students prefer a varied class format
during the course); others must be learned from student feedback (a wants assessment).*

Program goals and objectives. *These represent the values of faculty
colleagues in my school and in the research curriculum area in particular. To identify the
full range of goals and objectives. I would inspect all available goal statements in written
program descriptions plus interview key persons (e.g., chairs of program specializations for
which this is a required course) to get a more complete picture.*

Logical analysis. *This would largely reflect my own values regarding the content
and process of the course. I would look at current practices, analyze how instructor and
student time is spent, and detect logical inconsistencies or gaps.*

<u>Judged or believed standards of merit</u>. *This reflects the informal norms within my school as well as my own beliefs regarding what constitutes good instruction (e.g., instructor preparation, accessibility to students.*

Process

<u>Definition</u>:   The <u>operation</u> of the evaluand.

In drawing evaluative conclusions, some of the variables that you may judge are "process phenomena"--elements of the evaluand's operation first identified descriptively under KEC-1. Here you are selecting which particular aspects of process you will attend to in judging how well the evaluand was implemented. There are three kinds of process phenomena to consider:

a.   those that are part of the evaluand,
b.   those that are part of the context or environment of the evaluand, and
c.   those that represent immediate or concurrent effects of the evaluand.

*** List below the <u>process</u> variables that the evaluation will address in each of these three categories.

<u>Evaluand</u>	<u>Context</u>	<u>Immediate effects</u>
Attendance	*Adequacy of facilities*	*Student satisfaction with course*
Timing, pacing of the course	*Availability of materials*	*Instructor satisfaction with course*
Clarity of handouts	*How well this course fits with the rest of the curriculum in student's program of study*	
Factual correctness of lectures		

Outcome

Definition: Post-treatment effects.

It is useful to think of outcomes associated with the evaluand as falling along a chronological continuum. The immediate outcomes are those that occur concurrent with the intervention. You identified some of these already when you considered the Process checkpoint. The intermediate outcomes occur at or soon after the conclusion of the intervention. Finally, long-term outcomes represent effects of the evaluand that are expected to occur at some future point in time.

*** First, list the outcomes that are intended to occur as a result of the evaluand. List immediate, intermediate, and long-term outcomes.

Immediate	Intermediate	Long-term
Student satisfaction	*Student passes final exam in course*	*Student applies evaluation skills on the job*
Student knowledge of terms, concepts	*Student ability to critically evaluate concepts*	*Student continues to read & use evaluation information*

*** Now, consider possible unintended outcomes that might occur as a result to the evaluand. These unintended outcomes may be either positive or negative, and they can occur at any point in time. Next to each unintended outcome, write a (+) or (-) to note whether it is a positive or negative potential outcome.

Unintended Outcomes

Student meets a colleague who share a special content interest (+)	*Knowledge of evaluation enables student to write a grant proposal (+)*	*Student receives job promotion based in part on evaluation expertise (+)*
Field performance suffers due to time spent studying evaluation (-)	*Failure to achieve desired grade leads to loss of self-esteem, depression (-)*	*Grant proposal is funded, bringing recognition & new opportunities (+)*

To help you think of all the possible outcomes, review your list of impactees (direct and indirect consumers, plus providers) from the Consumer checkpoint. For each of these populations, consider the variety of effects that might occur: cognitive, affective, psychomotor, health, social, environmental.

Generalizability

Definition: The potential or versatility of the evaluand,
               applied to other circumstances.

In addition to judging the merit or worth of a particular
evaluand, it is often relevant to consider its generalizability
to other persons, places, times, and versions. Would you expect
the evaluand to be equally effective under other conditions?

*** List below the questions it would be important to consider
concerning the generalizability of the evaluand. The questions
should concern the use of the evaluand with other people, in
other places, or at other times. In addition, questions might be
raised considering modified versions of the evaluand.

Important Questions to Consider

1.   How well can the process used in the regular M.S.W. program generalize to students in the
      advanced standing program? (People)

2.   How well will the outcomes observed with family mental health students generalize to
      students in the health concentration? (People)

3.   Could my course work with honors undergraduates as well as with master's students?
      (People)

4.   Would the course work as well in an off-campus site? (Places)

5.   Could the sequencing of the course within students' program of study be varied? (Time)

6.   Could the sequencing of the topics within the course be altered? (Versions)

7.   Could the frequency of meetings be altered? (Times)

8.   Could this material be presented as computer assisted instruction for individual study, using
      the microcomputer laboratory? (Versions)

66

<u>Costs</u>

<u>Definition</u>:   What is used up or given up to operate the
                        evaluand.

There are a great number of costs of different kinds
<u>potentially</u> associated with any given evaluand. The object of
this checkpoint is to identify what costs are pertinent to this
evaluand. To do this, you will need to consider: (a) who will
incur the costs, (b) what kinds of costs will there be, and (c)
when will they be incurred? (You may wish to think of organizing
this checkpoint in a matrix format.)

*** First, list <u>who</u> will incur the costs. Again, it will be
helpful to refer to your list of impacted groups (Consumer
checkpoint).

*** Second, for each payer group you've identified, list the
different <u>types</u> of costs that will be incurred. You will want to
consider <u>at least</u> three types of costs for each payer group:

1.   Money costs--things that must be purchased or funds
      that must be expended to operate the evaluand (e.g.,
      personnel or supplies).

2.   Non-money costs--other things that get "used up" in the
      conduct of the evaluand (e.g., time and energy).

3.   Opportunity costs--the value of the forsaken
      alternative, i.e., what could have been done with the
      monetary or non-monetary resources had they not been
      spent as they were on the evaluand.

*** Third, review each cost to note <u>when</u> it will be incurred --
before the evaluand begins (B), at the start-up (S), during
operation (O), or at the termination or wrap-up of the evaluand
(T).

<u>Costs to students</u>:

1.   <u>Money costs</u> -- Tuition (B); Books (S); Transportation, meals, (and possibly lodging) to
      attend classes, study groups (O)
2.   <u>Non-money costs</u> -- Energy (O); Enthusiasm (O); Time (O); Pride or self-esteem (e.g., if class
      performance is lower than expected) (T)
3.   <u>Opportunity costs</u> -- What you could have done with money had you not spent it on tuition
      (B)? What you could have accomplished during the time spent commuting to and from
      classes (O)?

(Example would continue with other impacted groups...)

Comparisons with Alternative Options

Definition: Identification of <u>critical competitors</u>--those options producing similar or better effects for less costs or better effects for about the same cost.

You may have judged the process and outcome of the evaluand to be worthwhile, but you must still raise the question, "Is the <u>best</u> use being made of less resources?" The comparison with alternative options challenges the status quo to propose even better potential ways to meet consumer needs.

***   First, list all the <u>critical competitors</u> to this evaluand that you are aware of or that have been previously proposed.

***   Second, think hard to try to expand your list by adding hypothetical options that might also work. Be creative and expansive in your thinking.

List of Critical Competitors

1.   *Individual mentorship*

2.   *Programmed written instruction*

3.   *Traditional text plus workbook for individual or group work*

4.   *Videodiscs*

5.   *Computer-interfaced telecommunications*

6.   *Field-based instruction, utilizing field placements and instructors*

7.   *Conference-format intensive training over several consecutive days*

68

Significance

Definition: The <u>synthesis</u>, or overall sum total, of all preceding considerations.

At this point in the evaluation, you will bring together all of the information you have collected to make an overall judgment of the merit or worth of the program. This is a lot of information to synthesize, so you must stop and plan out what dimensions of evaluand process or outcome you are going to pay the most attention to, the relative importance of each dimension, and the merit or worth of each separate dimension according to your chosen criteria. You may do this quantitatively or qualitatively; either literally or figuratively you are essentially compiling a "flexible weighted sum."

***   First, list each of the <u>separate evaluand dimension</u> (process, outcome, generalizability, costs,and comparison with critical competitors) that you will judge in reaching an overall evaluation of the merit or worth of the evaluand.

***   Second, indicate the <u>relative importance</u> of the dimensions (either) through a numerical weighing or description).

***   Third, make a <u>judgment of the merit</u> of each dimensions (either via a performance score or verbal description).

***   Fourth, weight each dimension's performance according to its value and bring together all of these judgments of the evaluand (multiply and sum).

Dimension	Importance		Merit		
A. *Student satisfaction*	8	x	9	=	72
B. *Student exam performance*	8	x	7	=	56
C. *Lecturer preparation*	10	x	10	=	100
D. *Curriculum*	10	x	8	=	80
					308

(In this example, both importance and merit were weighted on a 10-point scale. Using the importance weights shown above, the maximum possible performance score is 360; thus, the session earned 86 percent).

NOTE: There will be important "no-compromise" requirements of the evaluand that would <u>override</u> the balanced synthesis described above.

***   List below some possible "no-compromise" requirements for this evaluand.

Ethical (non-sexist, non-racist) behavior on the part of the instructor.

Recommendations

Definition: Remedial actions.

*** First, are <u>recommendations</u> desired from this evaluation?

    [X]   Yes
    [ ]   No
    [ ]   Unclear (Return to Client for clarification).

*** Second, are <u>recommendations</u> justified based on the results?

    [X]   Yes. Results are clear and provide sufficient
           information to make recommendations.

    [ ]   No. Results are clear, but there is insufficient
           information to make recommendations.

    [ ]   No. Results are inconclusive.

*** Third, if warranted, what recommendations will be made?

Recommendations

When this evaluation was carried out, information gained clearly indicated ways to improve the class. For example, recommendations over several semesters' evaluation included:

- *Reduce the total required readings to be more selective in identifying a core curriculum.*

- *Develop worksheets to accompany key chapters to facilitate student use of text material.*

- *Revise the assignment instructions so that all students have a clear understanding of what is expected.*

- *Develop more efficient ways of covering core material in class so that there is time left to cover other relevant topics.*

- *Expand use of supplemental readings so that students are exposed to a broader view of evaluation, including methods.*

- *Encourage use of student study groups to complete assignments and prepare for the examination.*

70

Report

The results of the evaluation (and appropriate recommendations) will be reported to the <u>client</u> and to many, if not all, of the <u>stakeholder audiences</u>. In order to communicate results effectively, you will want to tailor the reports to the particular interests and other characteristics of the audiences. This means that while an overall written report is available for inspection, there will likely be multiple briefer versions presented, often in innovative non-written formats.

***   First, list all audiences (client and stakeholders) to whom the findings will be reported.

***   Second, for each audience, consider <u>which findings</u> will be of greatest relevance/interest.

***   Third, for each audience, consider <u>what type of report vehicle</u> will be most effective.

Audiences

<u>Client</u> (myself, as instructor) will be interested in all aspects of the findings. For my personal use, I would prepare summary tables of major results and recommendations. No formal written report would be required.

<u>Students</u> would be interested in the major findings of the needs assessment and of the full evaluation. They would also be interested in the recommendations for improvement. A useful format might be an executive summary sent to the graduate student organization to report orally at a meeting and discuss. Graduates could be informed via an alumni newsletter.

<u>Faculty in the research curriculum area</u> would likely have a general interest in the evaluation plus a particular interest in recommendations relevant to their classes. A written summary to be discussed at a curriculum area meeting would be a good vehicle.

<u>Dean</u> would receive a summary of the evaluation in my annual faculty report.

<u>Professional colleagues</u> in the American Evaluation Association could be informed via a paper or poster session at the annual meeting or a written summary in **Evaluation Practice**.

Meta-Evaluation

Definition: The evaluation of the evaluation itself, either
              formatively, during planning and implementation,
              or summatively, at the end before disseminating
              the final report.

As with any evaluation, a number of different methods could
be used in planning and conducting the meta-evaluation. To make
sure that no important aspects of the evaluation are overlooked,
one of the most useful tools is again the KEC.

*** Apply the KEC to the evaluation you have just designed:

1.   Describe the evaluation.
2.   Identify the client(s) of the meta-evaluation.
3.   Identify the background and context of the evaluation
     and of the meta-evaluation.
4.   Identify the resources available to the evaluation and
     meta-evaluation.
5.   Who are the consumers of the evaluation?
6.   What values underlie the meta-evaluation?
7.   What conclusions can be drawn about the evaluation
     process or implementation?
8.   What conclusions can be drawn about the results of the
     evaluation?
9.   How generalizable are the results of the evaluation?
10. What costs were involved in conducting the evaluation?
11. What alternate types of evaluation might have been
     performed? How do these compare with what was done?
12. What is the overall significance of the evaluation?
13. What recommendations will the meta-evaluation make
     regarding the evaluation?
14. Report the meta-evaluation.

Applying the KEC to your evaluation plan gives you an
opportunity to pull all your notes together and double-check the
feasibility, accuracy, utility, and propriety of your intended
evaluation. Answering the KEC meta-evaluation questions will
provide a pretty good overall summary of your design, with its
strengths and weaknesses.

Applying the KEC to your completed evaluation provides a
summative look at its strengths and weaknesses and suggests
improvements to be made in future evaluation efforts of this
kind.

3

JOURNAL WRITING IN EVALUATION

Egon G. Guba

The term project consists of a journal keeping activity from which summaries of the "state of the student's mind" about evaluation is derived about halfway through the term and again at the end. The class jointly derives criteria by which these statements can be assessed; they are also asked to write a one-page self-assessment of their constructions based on those criteria. The intent is to get the students started on developing their own unique construction of evaluation, and get them in a posture to continue seeking out improvements.

PROCEDURES

The journal should be kept on a class-to-class basis, that is, an entry should be made in the journal for each class session. THEY MUST BEGIN WITH THE VERY FIRST SESSION. Students must equip themselves with an 8 1/2x11-inch bound journal. (One with hard covers that lies flat when closed is ideal.) For each class they make an entry that summarizes as well as they can their present thoughts and ideas about evaluation. They date the entry. Each new entry should update what they have written so far, noting any changes in their thinking, any new ideas, and particularly, any principles which they believe should guide the evaluator in carrying out an evaluation. The journal should exhibit what some have called progressive subjectivism, that is successive entries should be more sophisticated and informed than earlier ones. Students are advised to imagine themselves as anthropologists who have decided to study a land in which an activity totally foreign to their culture--evaluation--occurs on a day-to-day basis. Their task is to catch the meaning and spirit of that activity.

About halfway through the term, they must prepare a statement (no longer than five double-spaced pages) that summarizes where their thoughts are at that time, based on the journal entries they have made thus far. At this point, some class time is spent having each student say, in five to ten minutes, "where their heads are" about evaluation. Within a few days they should bring to class a sufficient number of copies of their statements so that each class member and the instructor can have one.

Their task is then to read all other statements and, on the basis of that reading, propose a series of criteria that they believe are appropriate to judging their quality. Class time is devoted to the presentation and refinement of these individual lists into a master list. They then are asked to write a statement (no more than one single-spaced page) in which they apply the agreed-upon criteria to their own statement. They give this one-page critique to the instructor. This critique is not intended so much to render a judgment about what they've written as to set an agenda for continuing refinement and improvement in their constructions.

At the end of the course they are asked to write a second statement, also not to exceed five double-spaced pages, and a one-page assessment thereof. Those two items together with their journal are called for on the last day of class. The agenda for improvement based on this second critique specifies what they will do to continue growing after the class is over.

DISCUSSION

The two statements, the critiques, and the journals (which they continue to keep) provide a good assessment not only for the student himself or herself but for the instructor as well. I have never been able to document the quality of my teaching as well as I can from these statements. So I find also that I need give no examinations, a fact that frees and empowers the students in ways I would not have thought possible.

It is essential that they begin on this task at once and work at it faithfully. If they have questions or problems in connection with doing it, they are encouraged to raise these in class so that everyone can benefit from whatever may be negotiated in response.

4

FIELD EXPERIENCES IN EVALUATION COURSES

Michael Morris

Incorporating meaningful field experiences into program evaluation courses is a continuing challenge for instructors. This out-of-class activity describes the process of providing for such an experience in a one semester, 13-week course for master's level students in either community psychology or industrial/organizational psychology.

Examples of actual projects that have been conducted during the course include: (1) an analysis of the educational outcomes experienced by undergraduates who had received special support services from the university after having been placed on academic probation due to low grades, (2) a program-monitoring evaluation that examined the procedures followed in processing applications for admission to the graduate school, and (3) a needs assessment, jointly sponsored by union and management, in which the university's blue-collar employees were surveyed in order to identify quality-of-work-life issues that were outside the boundaries of the collective bargaining agreement between the two parties.

PROCEDURES

Pre-course Preparation

Approximately two months before the course begins, the instructor sends a memorandum to a wide variety of administrative units within the university (e.g., academic departments, the alumni office, the counseling center), inviting them to submit requests for evaluation assistance. Because the instructor cannot assume that all recipients of the memo are familiar with evaluation research, a brief description of the various types of evaluation is included.

The requests are screened for their general acceptability and follow-up calls are made in response to all written submissions. (Some individuals simply phone in their requests.) Projects that would primarily consist of having students analyze pre-existing sets of data are usually judged to be unacceptable. In most cases these data sets have been "lying around" the department or division for some time with no action having been taken, a fairly reliable predictor of low commitment to the evaluation project on the part of the decision-makers involved. In addition, such projects do not provide students with an opportunity to develop and implement a data-collection strategy, an important evaluation task.

Most requests are for needs assessments or program monitoring projects, with a few focusing on the evaluation of program outcomes. So far there have been no proposals for cost-benefit or cost-effectiveness analyses. In view of the fact that these topics are not discussed until late in the evaluation course, a lack of requests in this area is probably all to the good.

First Class Meeting

The list of potential evaluation projects is distributed to all students. In addition to the campus-based projects, there are typically one or two off-campus projects included on the list. These latter proposals are from settings that the instructor has contact with in a professional or volunteer capacity, and are generated through a much more informal process than the on-campus requests.

Before the Second Class Meeting

Students form teams of two or three and submit their project preferences to the instructor. To avoid placing an undue burden on project sponsors, the students are instructed to refrain from contacting the sponsors during this period. Instead, sufficient details are given to the students in written and oral project descriptions to enable them to make enlightened choices.

Employed students who do not wish to participate in one of the listed projects can satisfy the field requirement by doing a program evaluation where they work. Prior to the second class they must give the instructor a brief description of what they plan to do. The criteria for judging the acceptability of these proposals are the same as those used for other projects.

Second Class Meeting

Project assignments are announced. In most cases student teams get their first choice, and in no instance has a team ever been assigned to a project that was lower than its second choice.

Before the Third Class Meeting

Student teams are expected to meet with their project sponsors to begin negotiating the specifics of their evaluations. Because the teams only have one week in which to schedule and hold these meetings, the instructor encourages sponsors to be as accommodating as possible when first contacted by the team.

Third Class Meeting

Teams share with the rest of the class the results of their initial meetings with project sponsors. Problems and issues are brainstormed, and various action strategies are discussed.

By the Fifth Class Meeting

Teams submit written evaluation plans to me and their project sponsors. These plans discuss in detail the focus and purpose of the evaluation, as well as the procedures to be followed in carrying it out (including a timetable). The resources required for the project are set forth, along with an analysis of any ethical issues raised by the project.

If the evaluation plan is submitted late, the grade received by the team suffers significantly. This policy motivates teams to confront rather than avoid problems when designing the evaluation. Because of the shortness of a 13-week semester, procrastination in developing a plan can easily have fatal implications for the plan's implementation. Stringent time frames are a reality frequently encountered by practicing evaluators, and students are almost certainly better off if they learn this fact sooner rather than later.

By the Twelfth Class Meeting

Teams submit final reports to the instructor and the project sponsors. The format for the report can vary widely depending on the nature of the project. Once again, a significant grade penalty is assigned if the report is late.

Before the Thirteenth Class Meeting

Teams are expected to meet with sponsors to review and discuss the final report. These meetings occasionally lead to one or two follow-up sessions after the course is over.

Thirteenth Class Meeting

Teams share with the rest of the class the results of their wrap-up meetings with project sponsors. The overall structure of the field work component of the course is discussed and critiqued by the class as a whole, and recommendations for change are solicited. And the end of a very strenuous semester is celebrated with refreshments provided by the instructor and the students.

DISCUSSION

Project sponsors and students have consistently rated their involvement in the field work experience positively. Four characteristics of the approach contribute to its success so far: projects are client-driven, small-scale, regulated by strict deadlines, and use on-campus settings. Some limitations of this approach include: most outcome-oriented evaluations, as well as those involving cost-benefit or cost-effectiveness analysis, are simply not feasible within such a short time frame. Also, the methodologies the students employ are usually not very high-powered in terms of design or quantitative sophistication.

BACKGROUND READINGS

Patton, M.Q. (1986). Utilization-focused evaluation. (second edition). Beverly Hills: Sage.

Posavac, E.J., & Carey, R.G. (1985). Program evaluation: Methods and case studies. (second edition). Englewood Cliffs, NJ: Prentice-Hall.

Sudman, S., & Bradburn, N.M. (1982). Asking questions: A practical guide to questionnaire design. San Francisco: Jossey-Bass.

5

IDENTIFYING THE EVALUATION AND ITS USEFULNESS

Frederick K. Richmond
F. Reid Willis
Kathleen L. Nazar
Keith L. Douglass
Dawn M. Fye
Joan M. Gibson

This exercise represents the first step in a logical thought process of selecting, collecting, and interpreting information to help managers make choices or decisions about their program, their staff, or clients who are receiving their services. Generally, managers have certain questions for which they want answers and they need or request information to supply the answers. In applied settings like state government, managers must zero in on pertinent data that specifically answer their questions.

All managers have recurring questions about programs and want to use their resources efficiently, so all managers have the need to use evaluation to support their management activities. The three major reasons to evaluate are:

1.   To determine whether implementation occurred according
     to plans.

2.   To answer key management questions:
     a)   To reduce uncertainty in decision making.
     b)   To weigh alternatives before making decisions.

3.   To make efficient use of limited resources:
     a)   To be accountable.
     b)   To be in a proactive rather than reactive position.

Managers must also address the question of usefulness of the evaluation information. Evaluation is particularly useful:

-when the manager has the ability to influence change either through authority over his/her own unit, or through advocacy with peers or supervisors.

-when the significance or usefulness of anticipated evaluation information outweighs anticipated evaluation costs (based on the judgment of the manager).

-when the manager has questions about the program (what works well, what doesn't work well, why it does or does not work well).

-when the program has a clear purpose and direction.

-when managers agree on what the program is trying the achieve. If there are vast discrepancies in perceived goals, evaluation cannot occur.

Under the above conditions, program expectations (goals) are clear and the manager is in a position to ask questions and request information about program performance, and to use this information to manage and improve the program.

This exercise is designed to provide the student with the opportunity to identify various evaluations that could be conducted based on the "Shucks Unlimited Case" and to determine how these evaluations would be useful to the manager in this case.

MATERIALS

1.   Shucks Unlimited Case
2.   Shucks Unlimited Case: Instructor Answer Sheet

PROCEDURES

The instructor would first explain the concepts of selecting questions, reasons for evaluating, and usefulness of evaluations (as described previously in the Concept section). Students would then be instructed to read the Shucks Unlimited Case and to answer three questions:

1.   What are the questions the manager would want to answer in this situation?
2.   Why would the manager want the answers?
3.   How can the manager use each answer?

Small group discussions can then occur for 30 minutes, followed by whole class discussion for 15 minutes. Each group should select a spokesperson to review the evaluation activities identified by the group. The instructor can help identify the similarities and differences.

DISCUSSION

This activity was used in a workshop on program evaluation for managers in the Pennsylvania Department of Public Welfare (DPW). Evaluation activities within the DPW reflect the decentralized organizational structure, and the very different requirements and constraints on managers of income transfer programs, state-operated facilities, county-based grant and contract programs, and licensure programs.

HANDOUT 1: Shucks Unlimited Case

Shucks Unlimited is a Pennsylvania producer and distributor of various types of hybrid corn. Competition among distributors of seed corn in the state has become increasingly intense during the past five years. Poor profits and high interest rates have stifled any expansion attempts to date; however, interest rates have recently begun to decline.

Because of poor profits, Shucks management has become increasingly concerned about sick leave taken by some employees. The personnel manager in Region III reports that a small group of sales personnel have been calling in lately claiming to have contracted a rare human version of the Northern Corn Leaf Blight. Morale at Region III and headquarters seems to be low.

Choosing corn hybrids is one of the most important things many farmers do each year. Studies have shown that there can be over 100 bushels per acre difference between some hybrids under exactly the same conditions. Because of the tremendous difference in yield potential among hybrids, harvestable yield remains the most important criterion in hybrid selection for most farmers. Other criteria are also considered. The switch to earlier planting has made cold tolerance an increasingly important factor. Germinability (the capacity to germinate and grow normally) and seedling vigor are critical to the grower. Resistance to disease as well as standability are also important hybrid characteristics to consider.

Last month, members of the Shucks laboratory developed a new variety of 90-day corn. Lab staff are extremely excited about this development. In fact, they believe that this new variety of corn will outperform the leading 90-day hybrids presently on the market. The Shucks lab, however, has been known to make mistakes.

The president of the company has asked for an unbiased appraisal of the performance of the new variety of hybrid corn vs. the leading 90-day hybrids presently on the market. The Corn Division has one full growing season to perform this appraisal and has access to Shucks test fields throughout the state. Shucks staff will plant the test plots to specification for planting depth, seed spacing, planting date, and so forth.

Shucks Unlimited Case: Instructor Answer Sheet

Task: Identify various evaluations that could be performed.

1. What are questions the manager would want to answer in this
    situation?

Possible answers (non-exhaustive):

    What is the "Shucks" market image for corn among farmers?

    How would interest rates affect Shucks' money borrowing
    power?

    Why are Shucks' profits low?

    What can we expect in sales for Shucks during the next two
    years?

    How does Shucks' new hybrid compare with the leader for:
    -yield?   -seedling vigor?
    -cold tolerance?   -resistance to disease?
    -germinability?   -standability?

    How should the new hybrid be sold on the market and when?

    What are the problems with staff turnover and morale and how
    do they affect productivity?

2. Why would managers want answers and how would the answers be
    used?

Possible answers (non-exhaustive):

    To determine accurately whether the new product is better
    than products previously developed or the competition's
    products.

    To develop a marketing and sales strategy for the new
    product.

    To develop a competitive pricing structure for the new
    product in light of competition and changing interest rates.

    To identify ways of increasing sales and improving
    productivity of sales personnel.

    To determine if the existing management structure needs to
    be changed in order to resolve Region III personnel
    problems.

6

EVALUABILITY ASSESSMENT

Pauline E. Ginsberg

Even experienced evaluators will occasionally find themselves in
a situation where they wonder why they ever agreed to take on a
project, a situation where the prospect of completing a
particular evaluation and seeing their work utilized looks dim.
If this can happen to experienced individuals, how much more
likely it is to happen to novices! Hence a careful evaluability
assessment before entering into a project can prevent many dead-
end efforts. Although experienced evaluators may do informal
evaluability assessments based upon their prior efforts, students
should be taught to follow a more formal procedure.

MATERIALS

Current newspapers and news magazines including the students'
local paper(s) and the campus paper.

PROCEDURES

1. Prepare

Students should be asked to read and bring to class examples of
functioning programs in the form of clippings from current
newspapers and news magazines. If the class is small or the
instructor has some favorite examples, it is helpful for the
instructor to contribute to this effort as well.

2. Review and Discuss

Briefly review the criteria for establishing that an activity
does, in fact, constitute a program. Discuss what is necessary
in order for a program to be evaluable. Posavac and Carey (1985,

p. 36) refer to six criteria. Campbell (1979, p. 84) is   t h e source of a seventh.

> a. It must have a well-developed theoretical base.
> b. It must have sufficient resources.
> c. It must be ready for substantial implementation.
> d. It must have realistic goals and expectations.
> e. Relevant data must be available or collectible.
> f. It must be implemented as planned.
> g. The desired evaluation must focus upon program alternatives rather than the performance of individual administrators.

3. Screen

Review each of the clippings, discarding those describing programs that are clearly not evaluable. For those that remain, identify the information still needed in order to assess the evaluability of the program.

The exercise can be ended at this point or continued to complete a full evaluability assessment. If the latter is chosen, the following procedure is suggested.

4. Organize

Form work groups by asking each student to rank the remaining local programs in order of preference. Work groups should include four to six people who are given class time to organize themselves to obtain missing information about their program from written sources and/or interviews with program staff (hence the emphasis on local programs).

5. Obtain Information

This step should be completed by students outside of class in accordance with the division of labor agreed upon in their work groups.

6. Share

Work groups should meet separately so that members can exchange information. Because most of my students have jobs and are unable to find a meeting time outside of class, I provide a portion of a class period for this activity.

7. Summarize

Students may submit written evaluability assessments and/or present the completed evaluability assessment orally to the class. When I used this exercise in the past, I did not ask for a written report but only an oral presentation to the class. The next time, in addition to the oral group effort, I will ask for a written summary from each individual. This way I will be assured that all members of the class understand the material and they will gain more practice in writing.

DISCUSSION

This activity was used during the spring of 1988 in the course "Program Evaluation," an upper level course offered by the Psychology Department of Utica College, an undergraduate campus of Syracuse University. Utica is a small community where many students already hold responsible positions in human service agencies. Others will do so upon receipt of their bachelor's degrees.

Hence it is often they who will be deciding when an evaluation is to be done, by whom it will be done, and how to respond to its findings. For this reason, it is important to make the program evaluation course as practical as possible-- including as much field experience as feasible.

Although it is possible to ask students to complete this exercise individually rather than having them work in small groups, I have a strong preference for the latter approach particularly when it involves field experience. I recommend this approach for two reasons. First, it is more realistic. Most evaluation work is done in groups. Second, it is efficient. A student who interviews one person for this assignment and learns the results of three other students' interviews from them not only improves his or her communications skills and ability to work as a team but also saves time for other assignments.

BACKGROUND READING

Campbell, D.T. (1979). Assessing the impact of planned social change. Evaluation and Program Planning, 2, 67-90.

Posavac, E.J., & Carey, R.G. (1985). Program evaluation: Methods and case studies, (second edition). Englewood Cliffs, NJ: Prentice-Hall.

7

EVALUATION QUESTIONS AND METHODS

David A. Dowell

The underlying concept of this activity is to stimulate students to think through problems and come up with creative and thoughtful solutions to choosing the evaluation questions and method. The students are given the following choices of methods: needs assessment, social experimentation (a.k.a. impact assessment), cost-effectiveness, management information systems, nominal group/delphi, quality assurance, literature review, personnel evaluation, expert review (a.k.a. illuminative evaluation), and systems evaluation.

MATERIALS

1. Definition of terms
2. Scenarios

PROCEDURES

The students are instructed to read the definition of terms, and any areas of confusion are discussed. They are then told that they will be reading a series of scenarios designed to illustrate many of the principles and techniques of program evaluation. In many or even most of the exercises, the limits of space make it impossible to provide the detail that would be necessary to define a situation fully. As a consequence, for many of the exercises, there is not a single right answer. Rather, the exercises are intended to stimulate the student to think through the problems and come up with creative and thoughtful solutions. Their success is measured not by whether their answer agrees with a single standard but by whether they understand thoroughly the logic of their answer and whether this logic is thoughtful and compelling.

The students are required to read a narrative case study and develop a solution to the problem posed. Students may respond in writing, orally in groups, or both (preferred). For each scenario, they are asked to (1) state one or more answerable evaluation questions that address the information needs of the agency, (2) choose one or more useful evaluation methods, and (3) describe the strengths and weaknesses of the methods they have identified as possibly appropriate. They are then shown an example of a scenario and an appropriate answer (shown in Handout 2: Scenarios).

DISCUSSION

Since the exercises cover a broad range of topics in program evaluation, an expert discussant is necessary. Students are learning by solving case problems and always have numerous questions. The use of the case study method makes the abstract concepts of evaluation much more concrete.

This exercise is merely one of a series that the author has used extensively in teaching the program evaluation course. Topics for which he has developed similar exercises include:

1.   Models of program evaluation
2.   Evaluation questions and methods
3.   Measurement
4.   Reliability
5.   Design of social experiments I
6.   Design of social experiments II
7.   Validity threats
8.   Ethics and evaluator roles
9.   Management information systems
10. Cost-finding, cost-effectiveness, and cost-benefit analysis

BACKGROUND READING

Posavac, E.J., & Carey, R.G. (1985). Program evaluation. Englewood Cliffs, NJ: Prentice-Hall, Inc.

HANDOUT 1:   Definition of Terms

1.   NEEDS ASSESSMENT: Methods for determining the existence, magnitude, and priority of needs for services in a particular area or among a particular population.

2.   SOCIAL EXPERIMENTATION: (a.k.a. IMPACT ASSESSMENT OR OUTCOME RESEARCH):   Methods for determining the impact of services upon clients or the impact of program activities upon communities using experimental tools adopted from laboratory social psychology.

3.   COST-EFFECTIVENESS: A set of methods for determining the cost of producing program outcomes. Cost-effectiveness is based upon and requires social experimentation methods plus accounting methods.   Closely related concepts are COST-FINDING, an accounting technique, and COST-BENEFIT, which converts outcomes or benefits to dollars (or "utiles").

4.   MANAGEMENT INFORMATION SYSTEMS: Record-keeping systems that aid managers in making program decisions. MIS systems are usually computerized.

5.   NOMINAL GROUP/DELPHI: Techniques for soliciting input from experts or concerned individuals for purposes of setting goals or arriving at increased consensus about issues.

6.   QUALITY ASSURANCE: Methods for assuring that services are provided in keeping with standards for those services. QA involves having a team of professionals review individual cases and identify those which may not be receiving quality services.

7.   LITERATURE REVIEW: Searching the literature for evidence about program effectiveness, usually done for purposes of planning services or as a pre-evaluation step.

8.   PERSONNEL EVALUATION: Evaluation of the performance of a particular program staff person.

9.   EXPERT REVIEW (a.k.a. ILLUMINATIVE EVALUATION): Inviting an expert in the field to visit a program for purposes of suggesting improvements or making a judgment about program quality.

10.   SYSTEMS EVALUATION: This method involves gathering information about the program's internal operation including such issues as the assignment of responsibilities, goal setting, goal assessment, communication, paper flow, and decision making. A systems evaluation is usually based on interviews with the staff and board.

In addition, there are broad categories of evaluation approaches known as "formative" and "summative" evaluation. Formative evaluations are undertaken for purposes of program improvement. Summative evaluations are undertaken for purposes of deciding whether programs are a success. Formative evaluation is often an expert review or MIS, and summative is often a social experiment---but not always.

HANDOUT 2: Scenarios

DIRECTIONS: For each of the scenarios below, (1) state one or more answerable evaluation questions that address the information needs of the agency, (2) choose one or more useful evaluation methods, and (3) describe the strengths and weaknesses of the method(s) you have identified as possibly appropriate.

SAMPLE EXERCISE: The local halfway house for women works with adult criminal offenders. They provide refuge, counseling and support, and some skills training. The director believes that the program is a success, and would like to demonstrate that belief to her funders.

ANSWER: An answerable evaluation question would be "What is the criminal behavior of women after going through the halfway house compared to very similar women who did not have that service?" This is a situation for social experimentation. The only convincing evidence for a program of this sort will be information about the subsequent criminal histories of the women who went through the halfway house compared to another program or to another group who received no halfway house services.

(In fact, just such a study was carried out in Long Beach, California, using FBI crime statistics. It showed that the women who went through the Hoffman House were significantly less likely to commit future crimes compared to non-halfway house women.)

EXERCISES

1.   A local community mental health center director is interested in expanding services into a new problem area: substance abuse. However, the director is uncertain of the need for substance abuse services in the communities in the center's catchment area.

2.   The local mental health center provides a very large volume of services in the inpatient and outpatient programs. The center director is worried about maintaining quality of services but is not sure how that might be done.

3.   Funding is getting tight for private, nonprofit mental health agencies. The center director often finds him/herself in a position of defending the agency to funders and political persons. He/She would like to have current statistics about the agency but, typically, available statistics are six months to a year old.

4.   The state department of mental health services is experiencing a funding crunch. Because of it, state officials want local programs to operate in the most efficient manner possible. In the area of services to chronic patients, there are several possible approaches used

across the state including hospitalization, partial hospitalization, and aftercare. For each there is some evidence of effectiveness. How might the state choose the most useful approach or approaches?

5.   The local nonprofit women's shelter has operated with few problems for several years. Recently, however, staff have been increasingly hostile to one another. Their hostilities all seem to center on work-related issues including accusations of unfair workloads, competition over work responsibilities, blaming for program foul-ups, and work not completed. The director is at a loss to reduce their hostilities.

6.   The university counseling center includes a dozen professionals who operate more or less independently and democratically. Recently, there has been increased disagreement among them about how to allocate resources among new and ongoing programs. The director's best idea is to vote. Do you have another idea?

7.   The chair of the Department of Psychology is concerned about the teaching effectiveness of one of the faculty members. There are rumors of missed classes, unfair grading, and disorganized lectures. Rumors are not adequate evidence for the chair to act. What should she/he do?

8.   The local community mental health center had recently been given responsibility for day treatment of a group of chronic patients. The staff have never done day treatment before and need information as to how to proceed.

9.   The local early education center (Head Start) seems to be functioning well but the director would like to determine if quality can be improved. She has a low budget for this activity, $500; what might be a method to use?

10.   The State Department of Mental Health has just received an augmentation of $1 million. The State Psychological Association is pushing the idea of using the money for school-based and community-based prevention programs. The State Medical Association wants to use the money for hospital-based treatment of the severely mentally ill. Outline a strategy to resolve this dispute.

8

ALTERNATIVE EVALUATION DATA COLLECTION TECHNIQUES

James S. Long

The emphasis here is on alternative evaluation data-gathering techniques. That emphasis is placed within the context of alternative evaluation research designs.

I have used this activity with county extension agents in a noncredit, inservice education course. Alternative data-gathering techniques are introduced through a matrix; one dimension represents the settings (individual, group, community) in which extension faculty work with learners; the other dimension depicts the nature of the transaction when gathering evaluation data--reactive, nonreactive, interactive.

With their graduate degrees, for instance, in agriculture and home economics, most of our county agents are familiar with experimental research designs. I introduce other designs and endeavor to relate the choice of evaluation data gathering technique to an appropriate evaluation research design.

More specifically, the "settings" referred to above, include, for example:

- Individual, one-to-one contacts such as a home or farm visit, telephone consultation with a business manager or personal correspondence with a county government official.

- Group contacts such as a meeting of the county 4-H council, a workshop with the weed control board, or a seminar with the economic development committee.

- Community contacts as through a public forum, a weekly column in a local newspaper, or a radio spot.

For the second dimension of the matrix--the "transactive environments"--the nature of the transactions could be:

- Reactive, in which the extension agent asks predetermined questions and clientele respond, as when we use mailed surveys or telephone interviews with fixed choices;

- Nonreactive, in which the extension agent unobtrusively listens and observes systematically as when doing a content analysis of public records or photographing a "before" and "after" series.

- Interactive, in which the extension agent and constituency, through dialogue, progressively and collaboratively evolve the question and data. A conversation or a focused group interview, for instance, often produces new, more refined, questions and more precise evaluation data appropriate to the criteria important to each stakeholder.

MATERIALS

I ask agents before the "clinic" to send me copies of their earlier evaluations and their plans for upcoming evaluations. I make available the matrix (see Handout 1) and samples of instruments.

PROCEDURES

1. Individually, agents working in a county send earlier evaluations and future plans to me.

2. I tentatively categorize their data gathering techniques within the framework of the matrix, as seen for instance, in Handout 1.

3. I feed back my perceptions to the group of agents in that county; we discuss my categorizations.

4. I introduce other alternatives to illustrate "cells" and techniques new to the agents.

5. We assess the alternatives in a preliminary way.

6. Then we take a break and, maybe, plan a new evaluation with an agent or two.

DISCUSSION

1. I use agents' experiences to familiarize myself with their educational programs, their evaluations, and with the participants themselves.

2. I go to a county and meet with the group of agents there.

3. I acknowledge the evaluations that participants have done.

4. Avoid critiquing earlier efforts; encourage agents to assess their evaluations and to identify what they'd want to try next time.

5. Introduce yet other alternatives; then, perhaps, appraise a technique within the context of a broader array of types of alternatives.

6. Allow "soak" time--a half-day to reflect, introduce alternatives, assess them relative to their work in continuing education.

7. Be available to consult about an immediate need.

BACKGROUND READINGS

Patton, M.Q. (1987). Creative evaluation. Newbury Park, CA: Sage Publications.

Agents' annual plans, evaluation plans and evaluations themselves.

Graduate research design and methods courses from which the "students" could review their notes.

HANDOUT 1:   Data Gathering Techniques

The Setting

Transactive Environment	One-to-One	Group	Community
Reactive	-Interview	-"Continuum"	-Newspaper poll
	-"Jellybeans"	-Show of hands	-
	-"SNickers"	-	-
	-	-	-
Nonreactive	-Behavior checklist	-Process observation	-Document analysis
	-Video recording	-	-
	-	-	-
	-	-	-
Interactive	-Coaching	-Focused group interview	-Forum
	-"Interview-a-Partner"	-Delphi	-Talk show
	-	-Nominal group	-
	-	-	-
	-	-	-

Illustrations of Evaluation Data-Gathering Techniques

"Jellybeans." This worked well with youth when we wanted to assess whether "bowl" activities were "too easy," "just right," or "too hard." We counted out a fixed number of jellybeans, placed the same number in each of three cups, the cups having been labeled "too easy," "just right," or "too hard." We asked each 4-H'er to take one jellybean from the cup that best described how he/she felt about that activity. A sweet reward for giving us evaluation data!

"SNickers." A retrospective technique, utilizing a Likert-type scale. Immediately after a skills-building workshop, we asked each participant (professionals), on an achievement scale for each workshop objective, to write an "S" where they started and an "N" where they are now. In addition, we asked open-ended questions: "What helped?" and "What next?" In this way, we gathered data about (1) self-perceived changes in competence, (2) the learning activities to which we could most attribute the changes, and (3) new, more advanced, learning activities for future workshops.

"Continuum." A physically active technique during which members of a small group place themselves along a strip of masking tape on the floor, with one option printed on easel paper at one end of the tape and a contrasting option at the other end. For instance, "direct marketing for raspberry growers near Seattle" could be a "good" or a "bad" idea. The marketing seminar participants could place themselves along the continuum depending upon their opinion. That indication of opinion near the end of a seminar could be used to evaluate the seminar.

In addition, the activity could be used to raise "Why?" questions; the discussion (an interactive group technique) could also be used to collect a new level of evaluation evidence: for example, are the reasons based on empirical evidence from the seminar or just speculation?

Process Observation. Let's say we're teaching new 4-H "ambassadors" (junior leaders) some concepts about conducting meetings. We could ask an extension agent or an adult volunteer leader or even one of the ambassadors themselves to serve as process observer--to note the extent to which ambassadors followed effective meeting procedures--confirming the agenda, guiding a process to introduce ideas, allowing for open discussion, reaching a decision, recording the action. The extent to which the trainees adopted suggested procedures could be evidence to evaluate the leadership training.

Coaching. A lot of coaching goes on in teaching individuals to use microcomputers. There's a lot of telling, showing, hands-on practice, feedback, reviewing, questioning, speculating about "What if...?" What proves effective with one individual may be different from a teaching strategy helpful for another individual.

Coaches pick up cues--formative evaluation evidences--and use them to adapt their teaching strategies.

Interview-A-Partner. In one instance, participants from the Class of 1984 were paired with members of the Class of 1985. Given a set of open ended questions, they interviewed each other about their training, their use of the training and suggestions for training the Class of 1986. The interaction produced vivid recollections about the training and its field applications (or misapplications!) and hard-hitting, pointed suggestions for improving the training.

Forum. Our college conducted a round of open community forums to listen to residents' perceptions of our research, teaching, and extension programs. Folks spoke out (!) and, in doing so, offered information to help us evaluate our college's tripartite mission.

9

ESTABLISHING EVALUATION BOUNDARIES

John C. Ory and Larry Braskamp

This class activity is part of an undergraduate educational psychology course in evaluation methods. The course begins with a review of various models or approaches to evaluation, including Objectives-Oriented, Management-Oriented, Consumer-Oriented, Adversary-Oriented, Naturalistic-Oriented approaches (as described in Worthen and Sanders' Educational Evaluation, 1987). Following the review of approaches, the course focuses on "doing evaluation," taking the students from planning an evaluation to improving the utilization of findings.

This class activity serves as a bridge between the units on approaches to evaluation and planning an evaluation. The activity requires students to (1) demonstrate knowledge of the various approaches to evaluation, and (2) begin thinking about the scope of work required in planning an evaluation.

MATERIALS

Handout 1: Evaluation Scenario and Questions

PROCEDURES

The class is divided into groups of three or four students. The attached evaluation scenario and set of questions are distributed to the groups. Each group is assigned a major evaluation model or approach and asked to respond to the evaluation questions as would followers of the given approach. For example, students assigned a Management-Oriented approach may answer the questions using the CIPP approach to evaluation. The students are given approximately 30 minutes to work together on the questions before the instructor reads some of the questions aloud and asks for group responses.

DISCUSSION

Having the groups present their answers orally to the class helps educate students who had difficulty understanding a particular evaluation approach. The instructors' two goals for the activity are usually achieved, i.e., we learn of our students' level of understanding about the evaluation approaches and the students are impressed by how much work goes into planning an evaluation. Additionally, the students enjoy "acting" as Robert Stake or Michael Scriven as they respond to the evaluation questions.

BACKGROUND READING

Worthen, B., & Sanders, J. (1987). Educational evaluation. New York: Longman.

HANDOUT 1:   Evaluation Scenario and Questions--Rita School District

A pilot reading program is being planned in the Rita School District, located in a Midwestern city of 70,000. The reading program is designed to help third graders identified as poor readers based on test scores and teacher evaluations. Approximately 100 third graders in four diverse elementary schools will be assigned a personal tutor in September 1988. The tutors will be seniors in high school who will be involved in a program that permits students to combine community service and course work for credit. The seniors will be expected to go to the elementary school of their assigned third grader one and one-half hours, three days a week. One teacher (to be called the project director) will be assigned to administer this program that will include a short training session to familiarize the seniors with the tutorial approach to be used and to supervise the program during the first year. The Rita School District is funding this project with the understanding that, if successful, this program will be integrated into the school curricula.

It should be noted that the Rita School District has previously co-sponsored a federal grant that investigated the naturalistic study of teacher intervention. As a result, the district has received a considerable amount of positive public relations. It should also be mentioned that the local teacher association has refused to endorse the new reading program.

QUESTIONS

1.   Why should an evaluation be undertaken?

2.   Which audiences should be addressed prior to building the evaluation design?

3.   What would be the role of the evaluator?

4.   What evaluative information can be collected?

6.   How should the evaluation be planned and designed?

7.   What methods and techniques will be used to collect information?

8.   From what individuals, if any, would you obtain reactions about the program?

9.   How should the evaluation data be analyzed and integrated?

10. What should be included in the evaluation reports?

11. To whom would the evaluation reports be made?

12. What are some of the possible "general policies" of the school district that may influence the selection of evaluation criteria?

13. How would you like the evaluation efforts to be used?

14. To what extent would the evaluator be involved in management of the program? Is decision making based on evaluation results?

15. What would be the importance of the objectives in the evaluation of the program?

16. Do you foresee any possible barriers to the implementation of the evaluation? If so, how can they be avoided?

10

ALTERNATIVE MODELS FOR EVALUATION

James W. Altschuld
Phyllis M. Thomas

Most evaluation courses and workshops at some point deal with evaluation models such as those proposed by Stufflebeam, Stake, Kirkpatrick, Brinkerhoff, and others. While models or persuasions, as they are termed by Borich (1983), often overlap, they also differ in regard to how the evaluation enterprise is viewed and how programs are evaluated. Students generally struggle to gain an initial understanding or appreciation of these similarities and differences unless they are provided with hands-on opportunities to apply a model (or models) to program situations.

In this activity students are individually assigned different combinations of an evaluation model and a program scenario. They then plan an evaluation for the scenario from the perspective of the model. Each student works independently on a homework assignment, completes a worksheet, and brings copies to the next class session. Students are then organized into small groups in which the scenario is common to every group member, but each has used a different model to plan the evaluation. Through review, discussion, and synthesis of evaluation plans, students begin to grasp the essential features of evaluation models, their assumptions, similarities and differences, and advantages and disadvantages.

MATERIALS

1. Six summaries of evaluation models, each one approximately one page in length. (See Handout 1 for an example.)

2. Six program scenarios, each one generally a paragraph in length. (See Handout 2 for four examples.)

3. Directions for Scenarios/Models Assignment Worksheet. (See Handout 3.)

4. Worksheet for Scenarios/Models Assignment. (Not included here, due to space limitations.)

5. A deck of assignment slips or cards, each with a different number-letter combination as follows: 1A, 1B, 1C, 1D, 1E, 1F,...6A, 6B, 6C, 6D, 6E, 6F. (See PROCEDURES below.)

PROCEDURES

1. Establish the background necessary for the exercise -- teach the evaluation models. Before using the activity, assign readings and teach the evaluation models such as those proposed by Cronbach (1963), Stake (1967), Scriven (1969), Stufflebeam (1971), Kirkpatrick (1960, 1983), Tuckman (1979), Brinkerhoff (1983, 1987), Wholey (1979), Owens (1973), Guba and Lincoln (1983), Patton (1978), and so forth. We suggest spending five to eight hours of class time on this material.

Models provide the historical background for the field as well as examples of approaches to evaluation. Reading assignments may be drawn from evaluation textbooks, journal articles, and/or conference papers. One-page summaries of evaluation models are used during the class to serve as guides for lecture and discussion. In-depth details for planning evaluations are covered in a later course.

2. Select the models and scenarios for the activity and prepare the assignment slips. Decide which scenarios and models you will use for this activity. The optimal number of scenarios and models depends on the number of students in the class. We generally assign each student a unique scenario/model combination. Thus, for a class of 36 students, we might use six scenarios with six models (6 x 6 = 36 unique assignments). You would need to adjust the number of scenarios and models for a larger or smaller class. (See the DISCUSSION section for further details).

Code each scenario with a number and each model with a letter. In our example, the scenarios are coded 1-6 and the models are coded A-F. Use these codes to prepare the deck of assignment slips.

3. Initiate the scenarios/models homework assignment once the models have been presented. During class, explain that for homework each person will be working independently to plan an evaluation of one program scenario from the perspective of one evaluation model. Also explain that you will be assigning the

scenarios and the models by having students count off by an appropriate number or by using some other system. Distribute the assignment slips in random fashion.

Explain that the number on each assignment slip corresponds to the number of the scenario. The letter corresponds to an evaluation model (however you have coded the models).

Distribute appropriate handouts/resource materials and provide instructions for the homework. Ask each student to complete the worksheet and bring seven copies of his/her work to the next class.

4. Conduct the scenarios/models activity during the next class session after the homework is completed (approximately one hour is required). Form the class into small groups, a separate group for each scenario assigned. In our example, six groups are formed in the following arrangement:

Group 1 - Six individuals each with an assignment slip--
    1A, 1B, 1C, 1D, 1E, 1F--where 1 represents the common
    scenario 1 and A-F represent different evaluation models.

Group 6 - Six individuals each with an assignment slip--
    6A, 6B, 6C, 6D, 6E, 6F--where 6 represents the common
    scenario 6 and A-F represent different evaluation models.

Ask each group to appoint a spokesperson/moderator. Provide instructions for the small group process:

Distribution of homework (five minutes). Each person in the group and the instructor should receive a copy of six different evaluation plans for the common scenario (based upon six different models).

Silent review (15-20 minutes). Each group member should silently review the work of others.

Small group discussion (20 minutes or more). Each small group moderator should lead a discussion of the assumptions made about the scenario and seek group consensus on a set of reasonable assumptions.

This should be followed by an open, free-flowing discussion of the models, assumptions, how they were applied to the scenario, pros and cons, suitability of each model for the scenario, and so on.

Small group closure (10-15 minutes). The group will then synthesize across models and plan an evaluation of the scenario for presentation to the class.

Reconvene the class into a large group. Ask selected group moderators to describe: their scenario; related assumptions made by the group; models that seemed to fit well and those that did not; and the evaluation approach synthesized by the group. Pose questions to the group, invite the rest of the class to comment, and lead a discussion of the evaluation approaches.

DISCUSSION

This activity has been used for nearly five years in several workshops and in a graduate course entitled "Introduction to Educational Evaluation." The course is the first one in a six-course evaluation program offered in the College of Education of The Ohio State University. Students consistently have found the activity helpful in promoting their understanding of evaluation models.

Helpful Hints

1. This activity is designed to provide a beginning understanding of evaluation models. Model summaries and scenarios are deliberately brief to prevent students from becoming lost in details. Discussions of costs, implementation, and so on, are reserved for later classes.

2. The brevity of scenarios encourages students to make assumptions about the entity being evaluated. Discussions focus on the need to check out assumptions and make them explicit.

3. Good timing is critical to the success of this activity. It must be structured to fit the class period.

Variations of the Activity

1. The number of scenarios and models can be adjusted for a larger or smaller class. For example, for 24 students, you could use six scenarios with four models or four scenarios with six models (6 x 4 or 4 x 6 = 24 assignments). A third option would be to use five scenarios with five models (5 x 5 = 25 assignments) and have one assignment slip left over. We mention the third option because the class size is not always convenient for dividing groups evenly or for using all assignment slips. Be prepared to be flexible, and be ready to rearrange groups at the last minute to accommodate student absences.

2. The activity can be repeated with each student assigned a new scenario and model, or initial assignments could include multiple scenarios and/or models.

3.   Each scenario/model combination can be assigned to two
     students, each working independently on the homework (a form
     of replication).   In class, two independent small groups
     would be formed to discuss each scenario. Thus, if you used
     three scenarios you would have six groups. After the small
     group discussion has been completed, the groups with the
     same scenario would join forces and compare their
     assumptions and evaluation plans. We have used this
     variation in a large class where we wanted to concentrate
     efforts on a few selected models. (Assignment slips must be
     set up to accommodate the "duplicate" assignments.)

4.   A two-phase group process can be used. First a small group
     can be formed for each evaluation model (group A, B, etc.)
     with each group member having a different scenario. Group
     discussion would focus on the applicability of the common
     model to the different scenarios. After 15-20 minutes,
     students would change seats and form groups with the common
     scenarios, but different models. This variation has the
     advantage of allowing students to clarify the essential
     features of the assigned model before comparing it to
     others.

BACKGROUND READING

Borich, G.D. (1983). Evaluation models: A question of purpose
     not   terminology.   Educational   Evaluation   and   Policy
     Analysis, 5(1), 61-63.

Guba, E.G., & Lincoln, Y.S. (1983). Effective evaluation:
     Improving the usefulness of evaluation results through
     responsive and naturalistic approaches. San Francisco:
     Jossey-Bass Publishers.

Worthen, B.R., & Sanders, J.R. (1987). Educational evaluation:
     Alternative approaches and practical guidelines. White
     Plains, N.Y.: Longman, Inc.

HANDOUT 1: Stufflebeam's Evaluation Model

FOUR TYPES OF EVALUATION

	CONTEXT EVALUATION	INPUT EVALUATION	PROCESS EVALUATION	PRODUCT EVALUATION
OBJECTIVE	Defining the operating context, identifying and assessing needs and opportunities; diagnosing problems underlying the needs and opportunities.	Identifying and assessing system capabilities, available input strategies, and possible implementation strategies.	Identifying or predicting defects in the procedural design or implementation; providing information for process decisions; maintaining a record of procedural activities.	Relating outcome information to objectives, context, input, and process information.
METHOD	Describing and comparing actual and intended inputs and outputs, comparing probable & possible system performance; analyzing causes of discrepancies between actualities & intentions.	Describing and analyzing available human and material resources, solution strategies, & procedural designs for relevance, feasibility and economy.	Monitoring potential procedural barriers & remaining alert to unanticipated ones, obtaining information for process decisions, and describing the actual process.	Defining & measuring criteria associated with objectives, comparing these with predetermined standards or comparative bases, interpreting outcomes in terms of context, input and process information.
RELATION TO DECISION MAKING IN THE CHANGE PROCESS	Deciding upon the setting to be served, goals associated with meeting needs for planning changes.	Selecting sources of support, solution strategies, & procedural designs for structuring changes.	Implementing & refining the program design & procedure, for effecting process control.	Continuing, terminating, modifying, or recycling a change activity, linking the activity to other major phases of the change process.

*Adapted from Stufflebeam (1971), Educational evaluation and decision making.

HANDOUT 2:   Program Scenarios

1. A large city school system has become concerned about the progress of elementary students in mathematics. They have noticed, via normed test scores, major deficiencies in number systems, moving place values, beginning set concepts, and complex addition. Based upon these findings and the perceived need to improve they have proposed and implemented a program that contains the following features: an analysis of the entire K-6 mathematics program; the development of short competency-based mathematics tests; the development of classroom teacher materials, and an inservice program.

2. The understanding of careers has been studied nationally with the results indicating that most secondary students (middle, junior high, and senior high school) do not have a good grasp of career options or even what their parents do on the job. A national center has developed a set of career-oriented games, simulations, individual activities, and small group activities for integration into various subjects (e.g., English, mathematics, social studies) and for use in a nonsubject-related manner. The materials are flexible and come with inservice programs designed to help teachers and administrators facilitate the use of the materials and to provide additional career exploration activities. The latter might include career fairs, invited speakers, and field trips.

3. Apathy! Apathy! Apathy! were the moans of the Joneses (a husband-and-wife teacher team) as they considered their weary bones one day at the junior high school. What to do? What to do? What to do? Then it came to them--AIRS (Apathy Intensity Reduction Scheme). Their plan included: student activities (arts, crafts, games) twice a week; a teacher costume day on Halloween; a teacher-to-teacher birthday luncheon exchange (e.g., served at school by candlelight); a teacher buddy or help system; a school treasure hunt with clues posted daily on the bulletin boards.

4. A suburban school district has recently become concerned about the degree to which students are falling behind in their classroom assignments and the high rate of failure in grades 7-10. They are studying the problem and looking into potential causes: the nature of the curriculum; lack of preparation; the number of (too many?) assignments; the fit between student ability levels and the curriculum. They are also considering solution strategies such as: cross-age tutoring with older students tutoring younger ones; pairing of students (those with strong skills and weak skills) within classrooms, allotting some end-of-period time for study in class. The district definitely will be deciding upon and then offering some programs to address the problem.

HANDOUT 3: Directions for Scenarios/Models Assignment Worksheet*

Step 1.   Read all of the scenarios.

Step 2.   On the worksheet record the evaluation model and program scenario that have been assigned to you.

Step 3.   List any assumptions you are making about your scenario. Assumptions might deal with such factors as: duration of activities to be evaluated; nature of activities to be evaluated; types of materials used in the program. Use the attached worksheet.

Step 4.   List the main points of the evaluation model.

Step 5.   List key features of the scenario.

Step 6.   On scrap paper, design as full and complete an evaluation plan for the scenario as you are able--you are only limited by your creativity. For the time being, don't worry about evaluation costs. Remember that your evaluation plan should be based upon the model assigned to you. Summarize your model-based plan on the worksheet.

Step 7.   List the advantages and disadvantages of your model-based evaluation plan. What is good about it? What is missing from it?

Step 8.   Review the other evaluation models. List any other models that might be useful for your scenario and reasons why.

Step 9.   Bring seven copies of your worksheet to the next class session.

Step 10. This is an individual assignment that will be shared with others in a group situation. By individually generating ideas and then discussing them in small groups, it is hoped that more ideas will be generated, and further that the collective result will be greater than the sum of the parts.

*The worksheet that is normally attached is not shown here due to space limitations.

11

PLANNING A DISCREPANCY-BASED EVALUATION

Joseph P. Caliguri

In the day-by-day world of organizational life, students have little time for reflection on what they are about in terms of demands, pressures, tasks and responsibilities. Almost constantly, students are confronted with minor problems demanding quick decisions but usually with symptoms of problems that necessitate a systematic approach to resolution.

The following format has been used as a problem-solving project for students, whether the focus is on personal or professional growth goals. The format encompasses the fundamentals of planning under the rubric of "intelligent preparation for action" and resolution of identified problems, needs or deficiencies. Congruence analysis focuses on the evaluator's search for discrepancies between what was intended and what occurred. It asks whether what was intended occurred. Were the observed antecedent conditions congruent with those that were expected? Did the teacher carry out the project plan? Were the intended outcomes achieved and were there additional effects?

The students should develop the following competencies:

-To acquire basic knowledge about planning fundamentals.

-To acquire experiential understandings about planning as a process and a product or outcome.

-To acquire initial skills in developing a clear and coherent plan by demonstrating the interrelatedness of the four fundamental steps of planning depicted in the planning format as a prelude to implementation of the plan.

-To acquire formative evaluation skill in terms of modifying a plan during its implementation or conditions, restraints, or unanticipated events occur that necessitate adjustments.

-To acquire summative evaluation skill in terms of aligning appropriate evaluation measures with stated goals to assess the degree to which goals have been achieved.

MATERIALS

1. Overhead transparency of the planning format.

2. Reprints of the planning format for class dissemination. (Handout 1).

3. Examples of completed projects by students for dissemination to new students after an instructor has done initial project work.

4. Grading criteria as established by the instructor for the project work.

PROCEDURES

1. Instructor explanation of planning format utilizing an overhead transparency.

2. Planning format disseminated to class with examples of students' completed projects when they become available after an initial semester's work.

3. Instructor meets with students in a one-to-one conference if class is small. In larger class sizes, instructor can meet with groups of students numbering four, five, or six, to assist students in identifying problems and developing a plan.

4. Time frames are then established within the course time table for intermittent assessment of project work and closure date for typed reports.

DISCUSSION

The discrepancy-based evaluation approach was used in one school district that had invested in classroom computers for teachers' instructional use. A computer coordinator position was created to train teachers for computer instruction. A computer coordinator selected from the ranks with experience in computer instruction utilized the action learning project format to create a training plan for implementation--identification of the discrepancy, development of goals to correct the discrepancy, devising the timetable and activities for accomplishing the goals, and identifying evaluation measures to assess how well the training goals were accomplished. A follow-up evaluation plan was also devised by the coordinator to assess the impact of training on the teachers' use of computer instruction in the classroom.

HANDOUT 1: Planning Steps in Course Action Learning Project

<u>Step 1</u>. Identify and describe the <u>discrepancy</u> or <u>discrepancies</u>. Discrepancies are <u>needs</u>, <u>deficiencies</u>, <u>problems</u>. In the statement of the problem, you are describing and documenting what is wrong (e.g., students are not learning quickly enough). Teaching methods are ineffective, or we lack appropriate instructional materials and equipment.

> Problem--a deviation from an expected standard, level
>   of performance, or goal.

> Problem finding--identifying deviations/needs/deficiencies.

> Multidimensional or large problem--can be broken down
>   into subproblems.

<u>Initial Stage of Action Learning Project</u>

> You find the problem.
> The problem is finding you--Stray Cat Theory.

<u>Step 2</u>. Develop goals <u>from the discrepancies</u> or needs you have described.   Goals are statements of intent to correct the problem, needs, or deficiency. (See shopping list reference.)

<u>Step 3</u>. Devise a program or activities which will accomplish the goals you have formulated for the project. Include a calendar or timetable that will show when the activities will be done, who will do them, how they will be accomplished, and how long it will take.

<u>Step 4.</u> Identify evaluation measures or techniques that you match to the goals to show you how well you have accomplished the goals.

<u>Three Basic Questions</u>

Where Am I Going?--Discrepancies or needs or problem spelled
        out. Goals developed from Step 1.

How Am I Going To Get There?--Program or activities/timetable,
        and so on from Step 3.

What Difference Does It Make?--Evaluation or results
        from selection of evaluation techniques used to measure
        accomplishment of goals (Tests/instruments/surveys/
        questionnaires/interviews/observation reports/logs/case
        studies/inventories). You should also check the
        literature on evaluation in the university or other
        accessible libraries.

Step 5.   Recycle the plan based on the experience and plan modifications identified for subsequent implementation   if the situation necessitates follow-through.

A CATEGORIZED "SHOPPING LIST OF VERBS
USEFUL FOR MAKING GOALS MORE PRECISE

SIMPLE TASKS	STUDY SKILLS	ANALYSIS SKILLS	SYNTHESIS SKILLS	GENERAL APPLCTN
				Arts & crafts:
attend	arrange	analysis	alter	
choose	attempt	appraise	change	
collect	categorize	combine	design	assemble
complete	chart	compare	develop	blend
copy	cite	conclude	discover	brush
count	circle	contrast	expand	build
define	classify	criticize	extend	carve
describe	compile	deduce	generalize	color
designate	consider	defend	paraphrase	construct
detect	diagram	evaluate	predict	crush
differentiate	document	explain	propose	cut
discriminate	find	formulate	question	dab
distinguish	follow	generate	rearrange	dot
distribute	formulate	induce	recombine	draw
duplicate	gather	infer	reconstruct	drill
find	include	paraphrase	regroup	finish
identify	itemize	plan	rename	fit
imitate	locate	present	reorganize	fix
indicate	map	save	reorder	fold
isolate	organize	shorten	rephrase	form
label	quote	structure	restate	frame
list	record	switch	restructure	grind
mark	relate		retell	hammer
name	reproduce		rewrite	handle
note	return		signify	heat
omit	search		simplify	illustrate
order	signify		synthesize	make
place	sort		systematize	melt
point	suggest			mend
provide	support			mix
recall	underline			mold
repeat	volunteer			nail
select				paint
state				paste
tally				pat
tell				position
underline				poor
				press
				procedure
				roll
				rub
				sand
				saw
				sculpt

A CATEGORIZED "SHOPPING LIST" OF VERBS
USEFUL FOR MAKING GOALS MORE PRECISE

GENERAL APPLICATIONS (cont.)

Drama:	Language:	Mathematical:	Music:	Physical:
act	abbreviate	add	blow	arch
clasp	accent	bisect	bow	bat
correct	alphabetize	calculate	clap	bond
cross	argue	check	compose	carry
direct	articulate	compound	conduct	catch
display	capitalize	compute	finger	chase
emit	edit	count	harmonize	climb
enter	print	derive	hum	coach
exit	pronounce	divide	mute	coordinate
express	punctuate	estimate	play	critique
leave	read	extrapolate	pluck	float
move	recite	extract	practice	grip
pantomine	speak	graph	sing	hit
pass	spell	group	strum	hop
perform	state	integrate	tap	jump
proceed	summarize	interpolate	whistle	kick
respond	syllabicate	measure		knock
show	translate	multiply		lift
start	type	number		march
turn	verbalize	plot		perform
	write	prove		pitch
		reduce		run
		remove		score
		solve		skate
		square		ski
		subtract		skip
		tabulate		somersault
		tally		
		verify		

II QUALITATIVE METHODS IN EVALUATION

12

NATURALISTIC INTERVIEWING

Jennifer C. Greene

Naturalistic Interviewing is designed as an in-class, small group discussion activity. The activity is oriented around key issues that arise when conducting open-ended, unstructured qualitative interviews within a naturalistic evaluation framework. These key issues include interviewer training, bias and reflexivity, respondent motivation, recording data, and sources of distortion in interviewing. Each small group of students discusses one of these issues as it is manifested in a specific evaluation context, namely, an evaluation of a statewide program to combat drunk driving. After their discussion, all groups share their "results" with the whole class, typically invoking further discussion. This activity focuses on methodological issues, not rationales for or techniques of interviewing. Thus, it is appropriately scheduled toward the end of a course unit on naturalistic, qualitative interviews.

MATERIALS

Handout 1 contains an outline of the <u>issues</u> relevant to naturalistic interviewing, a description of a hypothetical <u>evaluation context</u>, and directions for group activities.

PROCEDURES

Handout 1 is largely self-explanatory. The major steps involved in its implementation and specific leader/instructor responsibilities are outlined below. These steps and responsibilities are consistent with general guidelines for in-class, small group activities.

   1.   <u>Introduce activity</u>.   The leader should introduce this activity as an opportunity for class members to address in

some depth key issues associated with naturalistic interviewing. These issues have surfaced in both prior readings and class discussions about interviewing. To facilitate the task, the issues will be discussed in the context of a specific hypothetical (or actual) naturalistic evaluation.

2. Review activity. The leader should briefly review with the whole class the first two sections of the activity: Issues and Evaluation Context. This review should mainly ensure that all class members share a common understanding of these sections.

3. Outline tasks. The leader should then outline the actual tasks of the activity, as presented in the third Activity section of the handout, Parts I and II. For these tasks, the class will be divided into six small groups (numbering three to six members each). Each group will be assigned one of the issues identified in the first section of the activity. And, as indicated, each group's task for Part I of the activity will be to:

a.   develop several specific examples of how their issue might manifest itself in the drunk driving program evaluation context (i.e., the nature of the "problem");

b.   suggest several specific strategies or procedures for addressing this issue in this context (i.e., suggested "solutions" to the problem); and

c.   prepare a group report to the whole class and, time and interest permitting, start off this report with a two to three-minute role play illustrating one of the points the group would like to make.

Possible guiding questions for each group's discussion are offered in the remainder of the handout. Part II (on mixed methods) is self-explanatory.

4. Small group work. The leader should allocate about 20 minutes for the small group discussions and preparation of their reports to the whole class. During this time, the leader should circulate among the groups, listening, helping any group that's stuck, offering suggestions, etc.

5. Group reports for Part I. Each group should then be allocated about five minutes to report their "results" to the rest of the class. Further discussion among the whole class should be encouraged, as time permits.

6. Class discussion for Part II. Ideas and issues generated in relation to Part II (mixed methods) can be discussed at the end of this activity among the class as a whole.

   7. Summary. Upon completion of the activity, the leader
should summarize key points made, including unresolved questions
and issues.

DISCUSSION

Clearly this activity could be implemented with a different set
of issues and/or a different evaluation context and/or more or
less time for each of its parts.

   The naturalistic interviewing activity has been used (most
recently in Spring 1988) in an intermediate graduate level course
on qualitative research and evaluation methods. This course is
part of a program evaluation graduate curriculum offered by the
Department of Human Service Studies at Cornell University.
Enrollment in this course has risen in recent years to about 25,
representing multiple fields across the university, e.g.,
nutrition, education, rural sociology, psychology, human
development, and agricultural economics.

BACKGROUND READING

Deuzin, N.K. (1978). The research act: An introduction to
   sociological methods. New York: McGraw Hill, ch. 4.

LeCompte, M.D., & Goetz, J.P. (1984). Ethnographic data
   collection in evaluation research. In D.M. Fetterman (ed.),
   Ethnography in educational evaluation. Beverly Hills, CA:
   Sage, pp. 37-59.

Patton, M.Q. (1980). Qualitative evaluation methods. Beverly
   Hills, CA: Sage, ch. 7.

HANDOUT 1: Activity for Naturalistic Interviewing

Issues

Some of the key issues raised in our discussion of naturalistic qualitative interviewing are the following:

1. Can the naturalistic evaluator be trained? If so, what kinds of training would be most useful? If not, what implications does this have for the naturalistic approach to evaluation, including the match of evaluator characteristics to study site?

2. The act of naturalistic inquiry is an act of symbolic interaction, and the evaluator is a part of the context being studied. Understanding the context thus includes understanding one's own role in it, as well as the individual filters or lenses through which one views the world. What specific strategies can facilitate this understanding (or how do we "practice reflexivity")?

3. In qualitative interviewing, what are some responses to concerns about motivating the respondent or addressing the question, "What's in it for the respondent?" How can interviewers achieve a degree of "muted equality" necessary for eliciting trustworthy information?

4. In qualitative interviewing, what issues are raised by the options of tape recorders versus note taking? Can we offer any guidelines to facilitate this choice?

5. Sources of distortion in qualitative interviewing include (a) misinterpretation of language; (b) respondent inability/unwillingness to discuss certain things; (c) respondent falsification of information (e.g., via social desirability, memory gaps, reactivity, ulterior motives); (d) interviewer bias and subjectivity; (e) lack of parity, trust, rapport in interviewer-respondent relationship; and (f) context of interview. What strategies can we employ to assess the degree and nature of distortion and to get underneath it if necessary? When might such strategies not be necessary?

6. What role can/should naturalistic qualitative interviewing play in combination or as "mixed" with post-postivist quantitative methods in evaluation and applied research designs?

Evaluation Context

Imagine you are the naturalistic evaluator of a statewide program in Alabama established to combat drunk driving. This program, which has been in operation for three years (and therefore has stabilized), includes four main components: (a) training of police officers to detect indicators of drunk driving and to administer sophisticated "breathalyzer" tests on the spot; (b) training of bartenders in when and how to refuse service to customers who've "had enough"; (c) stiff and consistently applied fines and sentences (i.e, no plea bargaining allowed) for first-time and repeat offenders; and (d) an ongoing mass media campaign to inform and alert the public about this program.

For various reasons, you have decided to begin your evaluation by interviewing recent offenders/drunk drivers who've been caught. Your initial major purpose for these interviews is to elicit descriptions of the actual drunk driving incidents of these offenders, as well as their knowledge and perceptions of the program.

Activity

Part I: Issues 1 - 5. The tasks for each group are to translate or apply your general issues to the specific Alabama drunk driving program evaluation context outlined and:

1. develop several specific examples of how this issue might manifest itself in this context (i.e., the nature of the "problem")

2. suggest several specific strategies or procedures for addressing this issue in this context (i.e., suggested "solutions" to the problem)

3. prepare a group report to the whole class and, time and interest permitting, start off your group report with a two to three-minute role play illustrating one of the points you'd like to make.

Some possible guiding questions for each group follow. You're also encouraged to think about these questions from the perspective of you as the evaluator.

Group 1 - Issue 1 (Training)

* What particular characteristics, qualities, qualifications are likely to be important in a naturalistic evaluator in this context? And why?

* Are these characteristics, and so on, "trainable"? If so, or if not, what are the implications?

Group 2 - Issue 2 (Reflexivity)

* What particular characteristics of a naturalistic evaluator and of her/his role in this context are likely to be important candidates for reflexivity? And why?

* How could an evaluator be reflexive about these?

Group 3 - Issue 3 (Respondent motivation)

* What are possible barriers or obstacles to respondent (guilty offender) motivations for sharing trustworthy information in this interview context?

* How could a naturalistic interviewer address such barriers?

Group 4 - Issue 4 (Recording interview data)

* In this specific interview context, what are the advantages and disadvantages of taping versus notetaking?

* What would you recommend and why?

Group 5 - Issue 5a-c (Distortion in interviewing)
Group 6 - Issue 5d-f (Distortion in interviewing, cont'd)

* What are some specific, probable examples of each source of distortion in this interview context?

* What cues might be present to indicate that certain respondent information was not trustworthy?

* What strategies could an interviewer use to get underneath or behind this distortion?

Part II: Issue 6. The task for all groups here is to translate or apply Issue 6 to this specific evaluation context and to generate one answer (among many possible ones) to the question posed by the issue.

13

CRITICAL ISSUES IN PARTICIPANT OBSERVATION

Jennifer C. Greene

As with all qualitative data gathering techniques, inherent in participant observation are methodological issues of strategy, as well as issues related to values, ethics, and politics. The methodological issues include contextual limits to genuine participation, the dual and sometimes conflicting nature of the participant and observer roles, and resource considerations. The more value-laden issues in a participant observation context include the meaning of informed consent and the ethics of covert observation, the politics of alignment and nonalignment, and the risks of genuine participation. On all of these issues, reasonable people disagree.

This class discussion activity is intended to surface many of these issues and to engage students in some initial reflection about their own positions on them. The discussion is based on a handout listing nine participant observation scenarios. The issues represented in each scenario are as follows:

1.   What are some inherent <u>limits to genuine participation</u> in evaluation/research contexts (e.g., due to demographic, cultural, and other differences between the inquirer and members of the setting being studied)? What are the ethics of those participant observation roles that involve "complete" participation and <u>covert or hidden observation</u>?

2.   When is a participant observer justified in directly intervening in a setting? What are relevant ethical and political limits, if any, to <u>participation as intervention</u>?

3.   In what ways and in what contexts can participation as <u>involvement</u> undermine or challenge observation as <u>detachment</u>?

130

4.   In what ways and in what contexts can observation as detachment undermine or challenge participation as involvement?

5.   Under what circumstances, if any, are deception and covert observation ethically justifiable?

6.   What does a participant observer do with his/her own political sympathies in a given context? What are the benefits and risks of both alignment and nonalignment with a particular group in an inquiry context?

7.   What are the trade-offs between deep and broad participation, or between intensive participation with one group in a setting versus less intensive participation with multiple groups? Are these necessarily mutually exclusive?

8.   Is "going native" an important methodological risk for the participant observer? An important personal risk? Why or why not?

9.   What variations of the participant observer role can fit within the limited resources of most evaluation contexts? Is very minimal participant observation (e.g., a two-day site visit) really worth it?

MATERIALS

A copy of the discussion handout is attached.

PROCEDURES

This class discussion was designed for use at the very beginning of a "unit" on participant observation (PO) in a course on qualitative evaluation methods. Students should have some familiarity with the issues in this discussion, from the assigned readings on PO and/or from other methodological discussions in class.

The procedures for implementing this activity are quite straightforward:

1.   The instructor introduces the activity as a discussion about critical issues in PO and reviews the three questions at the top of the handout, repeated below.

For each of the following naturalistic inquiry scenarios please address these questions:

a.   Do you agree or disagree with the researcher's or evaluator's actions?
b.   If you agree, why? What's your rationale or justification? If you disagree, what would you do

differently and for what reasons?
c.   What more general issues, concerns, or challenges in participant observation does this scenario illustrate?

2.   Students are given approximately 15 to 20 minutes to review each scenario with respect to these three questions. Dividing students into small groups of four to five each works best for this purpose. Alternately, students can conduct this part of the activity with their neighbor or by themselves. Whatever strategy is used, the instructor should circulate among the students, answering questions and prompting discussion.

3.   Then the class reconvenes as a whole and the instructor leads a whole group discussion on each scenario with respect to the questions identified. At the end, the instructor provides some closure by reviewing the critical issues that surfaced. (Listing these on the blackboard during the course of this whole class discussion is a helpful strategy.)

Depending on time available,this activity can be tailored for part of a class (e.g., 30 minutes) or for a whole class (e.g., 60-90 minutes).   For example, the scenarios could be divided among groups of students for a shorter activity. And the small group as well as the whole class discussion can be shortened or lengthened to fit multiple time parameters.

DISCUSSION

Among the many variations possible for this discussion activity are these two: (1) At the beginning of the whole class discussion, tally on the blackboard students' agreement/disagreement answers to handout question 1.   Such tallies quickly indicate which scenarios have consensus, which have strong minority views, and which are more controversial. Discussion could then be focused on the latter. (2) During the whole class discussion, encourage students to share additional examples of the issues identified from their own experience or substantive fields.

BACKGROUND READING

From the syllabus for this course, the following are the readings for the unit on participant observation.

Bogden, R.C., & Biklen, S.K. (1982).   Qualitative research for education. Boston: Allyn and Bacon, ch. 3, pp. 73-93.

Denzin, N.K. (1970).   The research act. New York: McGraw-Hill, ch. 7.

Filstead, W.J., (ed.) (1970).   Qualitative methodology.   Chicago: Rand McNally, chs. 12, 13, and 14.

132

Lincoln, Y.S., & Guba, E.G. (1985).   <u>Naturalistic inquiry</u>.
    Beverly Hills, CA: Sage, ch. 10, pp. 273-276 [course text].

Patton, M.Q. (1980).   <u>Qualitative evaluation methods</u>.   Beverly
    Hills, CA: Sage,   ch. 6 [course text].

HANDOUT 1:   Critical Issues in Participant Observation

For each of the following naturalistic inquiry scenarios, please address these questions:

1.   Do you agree or disagree with the researcher's or evaluator's action?
2.   If you agree, why? What's your rationale or justification? If your disagree, what would you do differently and for what reasons?
3.   What more general issues, concerns, or challenges in participant observation does this scenario illustrate?

A.   A sociologist/ethnographer interested in the culture of Southern, urban U.S. blacks "becomes black" (through skin dye, facial make-up, wig) and journeys South for several months of living and working.

B.   During his ethnographic study of Boston's Italian neighborhood (<u>Street Corner Society</u>), William F. Whyte recounts his observation that one member of the Norton street gang (Long John) was experiencing physical symptoms (headaches) reflecting a loss of status in the group. To address this problem, Whyte suggested a "social therapy" to Doc (his key informant), who followed Whyte's advice. Long John regained some status within the group, and his headaches went away.

C.   An evaluator of an educational/rehabilitation program for incarcerated juvenile delinquents became a volunteer "Big Sister" to one of the youth and developed a sustaining personal relationship with her.

D.   Another evaluator of this educational/rehabilitative program for incarcerated juvenile delinquents withdrew from the study because his nephew was one of the youths involved and he had a close, personal relationship with this young man.

E.   An evaluator of a community-based, conflict mediation program decided first to experience the program as a client. With the help of a cohort, she fabricated a dispute and, together, they sought help from the program, posing as disputants.

F.   An evaluator of a teacher training program learns of a long-standing, bitter dispute between the teachers' union and the administrators in the district. The evaluator's own sympathies are with the union and he decides to use his expertise, and the evaluation, to promote and advance the union's position.

G.   An ethnographer interested in the culture of rural high schools in the United States today befriends and develops key informants exclusively from the older, home-town members of a highly factionalized faculty.

H. An evaluator of a community development project in Zaire leaves the evaluation team to join the project as a full-time community leader.

I. An evaluator of an irrigation project in Sri Lanka opts for two one-week observational visits to each of two selected communities, because the U. S. Agency for International Development (USAID) has allocated only eight months for the study.

14

NATURALISTIC DATA COLLECTION: CASE STUDY DISCUSSION

Jennifer C. Greene

The naturalistic, qualitative data collection instrument of choice is the human inquirer himself or herself, complete with his/her own individual strengths and weaknesses, world views, and values. Thus, learning about qualitative data collection entails not only apprehension of what constitutes a good open-ended interview question, how to record observational field data, and the like, but also appreciation of the value-ladenness and concomitant need for reflexivity that permeate naturalistic inquiry. Thus, learning about qualitative data collection invokes a rather large span between theory and practice.

To help students cross that span, one vital instructional tool is practice and feedback, e.g., via field-based assignments. A second instructional tool is critical analysis of case study material. This discussion activity falls in the latter category. It is designed to help students see and critically evaluate a concrete set of naturalistic data collection strategies used in an applied inquiry setting.

MATERIALS

Reading

Marotto, R.A. (1986). "Posin' to be chosen": An ethnographic study of in-school truancy. In D.A. Fetterman and M.A. Pitman (eds.), Educational evaluation: Ethnography in theory, practice, and politics, Beverly Hills, CA: Sage, pp. 193-211.

Handout

The handout for this activity briefly reviews Marotto's study and then quotes two of his major conclusions, followed by a list of discussion questions. The quotes are relevant to several of the discussion questions, specifically those about bias, values, and reflexivity.

PROCEDURES

This discussion activity was designed for use toward the end of class units on qualitative data collection (interviews, observation, document review) in a course on qualitative evaluation methods. The activity can be a relatively brief discussion or a more extensive review and analysis of data collection issues, depending on time available and implementation procedures. Obviously, students need to have read the case study ahead of time. A highly organized instructor could also share the handout in advance of the activity.

The implementation procedures are straightforward:

1. The instructor introduces the activity as a review of naturalistic data collection issues via a critical discussion of a case study.

2. Students are then given approximately fifteen to twenty minutes to discuss among themselves answers to the discussion questions posed. Dividing students into small groups of four or five each works best for this purpose. Alternately, students can conduct this part of the activity with a neighbor or by themselves. Whatever strategy is used, the instructor should circulate among the students, answering questions and prompting discussion.

3. Then the class reconvenes as a whole, and the instructor leads a whole class discussion loosely organized around the discussion questions. At the end, the instructor provides some closure by summarizing the major points made.

Sample, though not necessarily exemplary, answers to the discussion questions on the handout are as follows:

1. What may have contributed to Marotto's effectiveness or ineffectiveness as a "participant as observer?"

The author should have commented more explicitly on this issue in his description of methods. This information is needed in order for the reader to make an informed judgment about the quality of the observational data. Possibly relevant factors here include the demographc characteristics of the researcher, his experience as an ethnographer, his familiarity and prior experience with the cultures of schools, and key characteristics of his ethnographic style.

2. In addition to interviews and observations, how might documents and records have been used?

Important historical and contextual information may have
been available from (a) individual student school files over the
last five to ten years, (b) school board meeting minutes over the
last few years, (c) stated school rules and policies. For
example, a review of these documents may have yielded information
on the historical patterns underlying the Brothers' current
behavior and on the overall culture of the school.

3. Marotto's case study is filled with quotes. How do you
think he recorded his data?

Again, this should have been clearly described in the
methods section. Marotto probably used some combination of a
tape recorder and memory, the latter perhaps enhanced by his
experience as an ethnographer and by his extensive time on site
(or prolonged observation).

4. What personal biases, views, opinions might Marotto have
brought with him to the study? Any clues as to whether he was
appropriately "reflexive" about these?

Marotto states up front that the disportionate number of
minority suspensions in this school was the "idea base that
guided the entire study." This idea base clearly reflects some
important values about racism, e.g., the rate of school
suspension should not be different for different racial groups.
In addition, Marotto seeks to understand this phenomenon by
probing primarily for an emic understanding of the culture of the
Brothers. This also reflects a set of values, including perhaps
a suspicion of institutional racism in the formal system of the
school.

Marotto says virtually nothing in this article about these
value issues nor about any efforts to be reflexive. Thus, the
reader has little information on this aspect of data quality.

5. Were Marotto's "sympathies" with the Brothers, with the
school system, both, or neither? Does it matter?

(See sample response to 4. In addition--)
Marotto's sympathies seemed to be clearly with the Brothers.
He portrays the Brothers more as victims of an unresponsive,
uncaring system than as deviants from it. And, yes, this "slant"
to this ethnography matters a great deal. It provides the
foundation for the kinds of conclusions reached in the sample
quotes on the handout. A different "slant" would yield very
different conclusions.

6. What ethical issues might be present in this context?

Examples here include (a) informed consent of participants
for data collection and reporting (especially because Marotto
used names and pictures versus disguising the identities of his
respondents), (b) if and how Marotto shared with the Brothers his

138

own views about their culture and its dead-end future prospects, and (c) if and how Marotto shared with the school system his recommendations and rationale for change.

DISCUSSION

This activity is readily adaptable to a different case study and/or different discussion questions. The value of this activity lies in student understanding and critique of important naturalistic data collection issues as they are manifested in a given case study. To realize this value, the instructor needs to keep the small group and especially the whole class discussions targeted and focused on these key issues and concerns.

BACKGROUND READINGS

Relevant chapters from the texts for this course are:

Lincoln, Y.S., & Guba, E.G. (1985). <u>Naturalistic inquiry</u>. Beverly Hills, CA: Sage, ch. 10, pp. 267-288.

Patton, M.Q. (1980). <u>Qualitative evaluation methods</u>. Beverly Hills, CA: Sage, chs. 6,7.

Selected other readings on data collection from the course syllabus are:

Adler, P.A., & Adler, R. (1987). <u>Membership roles in field research</u>. Qualitative Research Methods Series 6. Beverly Hills, CA: Sage.

Denzin, N.K. (1978). <u>The research act</u>. New York: McGraw-Hill, chs. 4,7.

LeCompte, M.D., & Goetz, J.P. (1984). Ethnographic data collection in evaluation research. In D.M. Fetterman (ed.), <u>Ethnography in educational evaluation</u>. Beverly Hills, CA: Sage.

Whyte, W.F. (1984). <u>Learning from the field</u>. Beverly Hills, CA: Sage, chs. 2,3,4,6,7.

HANDOUT 1:   Naturalistic Data Collection

Context

In "Posin' to be chosen," ethnographer Richard Marotto describes
the "in school truancy" behavior of a small group of black males,
dubbed the Boulevard Brothers, in a Buffalo, New York high
school. His description includes the inside or emic perspective
of this phenomenon and the school system's response to it.
Marotto spent two semesters at the high school plus some time
outside the school with the Boulevard Brothers in a participant-
as-observer role. Marotto concludes his discussion with several
interpretations and recommendations about how the school should
change its response to the Brothers' in school truancy:

> As long as we ignore or censor discussion of "gamin-ship" in
> our educational system--because skin color is compounding
> the issue--we will protect and perpetuate its destructive
> influence in our urban secondary schools. The syndrome
> described in this chapter is really the "testing games" and
> other street behavior of the tough, lower class Black
> adolescent males. These streetcorner testing games are
> manifestations of survival and coping techniques and norms
> that are well established features of the Brothers'
> streetcorner society....These games by their nature are
> manipulative, and [their] purpose is to play upon teachers'
> fear, ignorance, or apathy so as to shift the balance of
> power in the school into certain students' favor....We need
> to sharpen our understanding....it behooves us to get our
> diploma in street knowledge.

> A second response requires one to go beyond just knowing how
> to stop deviant behavior. The Brothers have to be made
> aware of their culpability and the need to change their
> dysfunctional behavior patterns in school....More
> specifically, students of the street have to learn that (1)
> engaging in streetcorner behavior in order to impress one's
> peers is not appropriate in every context, and (2) using
> racism, insensitive teachers...irrelevant
> curricula...suspensions...on which to blame their deviant
> antics is not facing the "cold-blooded" fact that they are
> responsible for their own actions.

Discussion

1.   What may have contributed to Marotto's effectiveness or
     ineffectiveness as a "participant as observer?"

2.   In addition to interviews and observations, how might
     documents and records have been used?

3.   Marotto's case study is filled with quotes. How do you
     think he recorded his data?

4. What personal biases, views, opinions might Marotto have brought with him to the study? Any clues as to whether he was appropriately "reflexive" about these?

5. Were Marotto's "sympathies" with the Brothers, with the school system, both or neither? Does it matter?

6. What ethical issues might be present in this context?

7. Other issues and concerns?

15

"TRUSTWORTHINESS" IN NATURALISTIC INQUIRY: AUDIT TRAILS

Jennifer C. Greene

Of continuing debate within the evaluation community are issues related to the quality, rigor, or "trustworthiness" of qualitative evaluation results and conclusions.   This debate stems in large part from the legitimized "subjectivity" of qualitative inquiry and from its common lack of "objective" numbers and statistics.   The debate's issues include philosophical concerns about the nonfoundational nature of qualitative inquiry (and thus the impossibility of any universal criteria for judging quality; Smith, 1984); more value-laden and political concerns about which criteria to use (e.g., Pearsol, 1987); and methodological issues of how to demonstrate quality in qualitative inquiry.

A prominent strand in this debate is Lincoln and Guba's original (1981, 1985) and more recent (1986) formulations of trustworthiness criteria and of recommended strategies to assess satisfaction of these criteria for qualitative inquiries.   Their original trustworthiness criteria parallel traditional inquiry standards as follows: credibility is the qualitative analog for internal validity, applicability for external validity, dependability for reliability, and confirmability for objectivity.   Among the strategies proposed to assess satisfaction of these criteria is the meta-evaluative external audit.   Akin to a fiscal audit, a qualitative evaluative audit is intended to assess the dependability or professional soundness of a study's methods and the confirmability or groundedness of its results and conclusions in the data collected.   A major requirement for an audit is the evaluator's maintenance of an audit trail throughout the study.   This trail, which documents all methodological activities, processes, decisions, and rationales, is what an external auditor reviews for purposes of assessing the study's dependability and confirmability.

This   class   discussion   activity   is   intended   to   provide students with concrete examples of the various components of an audit trail and to encourage their critical reflection on the value of the audit concept.

MATERIALS

This activity is based on a hypothetical evaluation context, presented in Handout 1. This handout has three main sections:

1. Context--brief descriptions of the evaluand and the major evaluation focus

2. Status--evaluation activities conducted and sample extracts from an audit trail to date

3. Questions--target questions for discussion

PROCEDURES

This activity was designed as part of a "unit" on quality or trustworthiness in a course on qualitative evaluation methods. The activity can be a relatively brief discussion or a more extensive analysis of trustworthiness issues, depending on time available. Students should have done the reading ahead of time.

The implementation procedures for this activity are straightforward.

1. The instructor introduces the activity as practice and review of the audit concept. The handout is also briefly reviewed.

2. Students are then given approximately five to ten minutes to think about their responses to the discussion questions, either by themselves or in quiet discussion with a neighbor. Alternately, students could be divided into groups of four or five and given a longer time period for a small group discussion of the questions. During this time, the instructor should be alert to students' needs for clarification or direction.

3. Then, the instructor leads a whole class discussion loosely organized around the discussion questions. At the end, the instructor provides some closure by summarizing the major points made.

Sample, though not necessarily exemplary, answers to the discussion questions on the handout are as follows.

1. What else should be in your audit trail thus far?

For both the document review and the interviews--
rationale or intended purpose for this method,
sampling strategy and rationale,

methodological comments on data quality,
analytic strategy and rationale,
other emerging themes from this method,
ideas for further data collection generated from this method.

For both methods and/or across methods--
reflexive comments on evaluator's biases,
how they might be manifested in data collected,
and how they might be tracked in the future.

2.   What would you do next in this evaluation?

Interview another purposive sample of both mid-term and short-term (or new) program participants both to assess the similarity of their perceptions with those of the long-term participants and to generate additional themes of importance.

Review documents and/or interview staff to assess the nature and extent of program changes since the beginning.

3.   How would you record this decision in your audit trail?

To illustrate for the interviews, one strategy would be to call these "Interview Set 2" and, on a page with this heading, write:

* Purpose: (a) to assess whether mid-term (two- to four-year) and short-term (< one year) program participants have similar overall perceptions of the program as long-term (five-year) participants; and (b) to generate additional themes about participants' overall program experiences.

* Rationale: Program experiences and perceptions may vary with longevity in the program.

* Sampling strategy: From a list of current participants, randomly select six mid-term and six short-term participants.

* Rationale: At this point in the study, there is no further information on which to select interviewees; six was chosen because that's the number of long-term participants interviewed and because it's large enough to reveal possible similarities and differences in perceptions but also small enough to conduct this initial evaluative phase reasonably quickly.

4.   What uses could be made of your audit trail or why maintain one?

Though there are no "right" answers here, one useful contrast for discussion is the audit as a meta-evaluative procedure externally conducted near the end of a study versus the audit as a self-monitoring, "quality control" process effected via the maintenance of an audit trail throughout the inquiry.

DISCUSSION

This activity has worked best for me as a short, succinct
discussion. A more elaborated version of this activity, however,
could include a lively debate about the overall value and worth
of the audit concept.

BACKGROUND READINGS

<u>Major Reference</u>

Lincoln, Y.S., & Guba, E.G. (1985). <u>Naturalistic inquiry</u>.
    Beverly Hills, CA: Sage, ch. 11, Appendices A and B.

<u>Referenced in This Write-Up</u>

Guba, E.G., & Lincoln, Y.S. (1981). <u>Effective evaluation</u>. San
    Francisco: Jossey-Bass.

Lincoln, Y.S. (1986). The development of intrinsic criteria for
    authenticity: A model for trust in naturalistic researches.
    Paper presented at the Annual Meeting of the American
    Educational Research Association, San Francisco.

Pearsol, J.A. (guest ed.) (1987). Special feature: Justifying
    conclusions in naturalistic evaluation. <u>Evaluation and
    Program Planning</u>, <u>10</u>, 307-358.

Smith, J.K. (1984). The problem of criteria for judging
    interpretive inquiry. <u>Educational Evaluation and Policy
    Analysis</u>, <u>6</u>, 379-391.

HANDOUT 1:
"Trustworthiness" in Naturalistic Inquiry: Audit Trails

Context

You are the evaluator of a local "homebound elderly visitors'
program." In this program, trained volunteers spend at least two
hours a week visiting a homebound older person. The volunteers
are asked to make a commitment of 12 months' participation when
they sign up. The program has been in operation for five years
and serves approximately 50 older people at any one time.

The focus of your evaluation is on the impact or effects of
this program on the homebound elderly, primarily in the area of
opportunities for and quality of social interaction.

Status

To date in your evaluation, you have reviewed recent program
reports and proposals and conducted personal interviews with the
six participants who have been in the program since the beginning
(i.e., a purposive sample).

Part of your "audit trail" consists of the following
emerging themes or working hypotheses developed thus far:

* The importance of the weekly visit seems to vary
  considerably among these older people. For some, it is "the
  highlight of my week and has been for the last five years,"
  while others report forgetting about it until the visitor
  actually arrives.

* Program materials emphasize the principle of
  "individualization" in program implementation, encouraging a
  wide variety of activities during the visits according to
  the needs and interests of the individual older person.
  Participant interviews reflected this variety. However, as
  suggested by the first theme, the matching of activity to
  individual needs may not always be appropriate.

* An undercurrent in the interviews was a separation of the
  visit from the visitor. The discussions focused on the
  visit, rather than the individual who did the visiting.
  Perhaps this reflects some "lack of rapport" or "fear of
  attachment" or "insulation against attachment."

Questions

1. What else should be in your audit trail thus far?
2. What would you do next in this evaluation?
3. How would you record this decision in your audit trail?
4. What uses could be made of your audit trail or why maintain
    one?

16

QUALITATIVE DATA ANALYSIS AND INTERPRETATION

Jennifer C. Greene

Miles and Huberman's 1984 "sourcebook" presents a wide-ranging, creative set of ideas and strategies for analyzing qualitative evaluation/research data. A major message of this sourcebook is that important themes and especially patterns in a set of qualitative data can be effectively discerned, interpreted and reported via the use of displays. Matrix displays, in particular, are advocated for higher-order analyses of patterns in a set of descriptive results.

Examples of the matrix displays presented in this sourcebook include both descriptive and explanatory matrices, single-site and multiple-site matrices, those with both ordered and categorical dimensions, and two-way to N-way matrices. Entries in matrix displays include direct quotes from the data, data summaries, inquirer explanations, frequencies, and ratings or judgment.

This class activity is designed to give students practice in qualitative data analysis using Miles and Huberman's ideas about matrix displays.

MATERIALS

This activity is based on a hypothetical evaluation context presented in Handout 1. This handout includes four major sections:

1.   Program context--a brief description of the evaluand

2.   Evaluation context--presentation of the major evaluation question and a brief listing of the naturalistic evaluation methods used

148

3.   "Final" category system for self-perceptions program outcome
     --results of a descriptive analysis of the data relevant to
     program participants' self-perceptions, presented as four
     major themes (The descriptive analysis here involved
     iterative data coding and development of a category system;
     see Lincoln & Guba, 1985, for this data analysis strategy.)

4.   Further analysis via matrices or other displays--the target
     questions for this activity, e.g., "What kinds of
     matrices/displays might help further understand
     relationships of these [self-perceptions] data to program
     components, activities, processes?"

PROCEDURES

This class activity was designed for use toward the end of a
"unit" on data analysis in a course on qualitative evaluation
methods. Students should have done the relevant reading in Miles
and Huberman ahead of time.

     The procedures for implementing this activity are
straightforward.

     1.   The instructor introduces the activity as practice in
using Miles and Huberman's matrix display ideas for qualitative
data analysis. The handout is reviewed with the students, in
particular to ensure that they understand the third section
presenting the hypothetical descriptive results.

     2.   Students are then divided into small groups of three to
five each and asked to respond to the discussion questions
identified by generating as many different matrix displays as
possible in the time allotted. About 20 minutes works quite well
for this small group discussion part of the activity. During
this time, the instructor should circulate among the groups,
answering questions and prompting creative thinking.

     3.   The class then reconvenes as a whole, and each group in
turn is asked to share one or two of the displays they generated.
As appropriate (e.g., for complicated displays), group
representatives can put their displays on the blackboard for
easier review. The instructor should focus discussion of each
display thus shared around what questions it could answer, what
patterns it could reveal, or what value it could have for this
hypothetical evaluation context. The instructor should also
provide some closure to the discussion by summarizing the major
points illustrated.

     This activity could be shortened (e.g., by assigning each
group a different discussion question or by reducing the time
allotted for the small group or whole class discussions) or
lengthened (e.g., via more time allotted or by adding further
questions).

149

Sample, though not necessarily exemplary, answers to the
discussion questions on the handout are as follows.

*   What kinds of matrices/displays might help further
     understand:

1.   Interrelationships Among These Self-Perceptions Data?

A two-way matrix crossing the four self-perception themes with
each other and entering (a) actual data instances where the two
themes represented by a given cell co-occur or are cited
together, (b) frequencies of the number of participants for whom
both themes represented by a given cell were recorded, or (c)
evaluator judgments about contingencies among the four themes.

	Self-worth	Physical self-concept	Self-confid-ence	Self-control
Self-worth				
Physical self-concept				
Self-confidence				
Self-control				

2.   Relationships of These (Self-Perceptions) Data to Program Components, Activities, Processes?

The obvious response here is a kind of Miles and Huberman
"effects matrix," crossing program elements with the four major
self-perceptions themes. Matrix entries could then again include
(a) raw data (e.g., participants' own attributions of a self-
perception outcome to a particular program element), (b)
frequencies of such attributions, or (c) evaluator-judged
attributions or contingencies.   Such a matrix could most
importantly reveal patterned links between program components and
outcomes, as illustrated in the following hypothetical matrix of
attributional frequencies (albeit much more clearly than is
likely in "real life").

	Self-worth	Physical self-concept	Self-confidence	Self-control
Program residence	30		1	10
Program counseling	2	3	25	15
Program education		26	1	10

Note: Total N=35, but not all participants reported all four self-perception outcomes.

3.   Relationships of These (Self-Perceptions) Data to Other Characteristics of Participants?

Matrix possibilities here include two-way to multiple-way crosses of the self-perception themes with such participant characteristics as current versus former participant, demographics, and data related to other participant perceptions or outcomes.

If important patterns are revealed in these kinds of displays, the results could be further used to develop a Miles and Huberman "causal network" or flowchart depicting higher-order relationships among participant characteristics, program experiences, and program outcomes.

4.   Relationships of These (Self-Perceptions) Data to Other Program "Outcomes" (Represented in Other Phenomenological Perspectives, Views of Meaning)?

Again, an obvious response here is a matrix crossing self-perception themes with themes/categories representing other program outcomes.

Another idea here is a Miles and Huberman "time-ordered matrix" linking participant perceptions of program effects to time in the program. This kind of display could reveal important interrelationships among program outcomes and between outcomes and program experiences.

| | Month in program | Years post-program |
	1 2-4 5-8 9	1 2-4 5-7 8-10
Self-perceptions outcomes		
Psychological adjustment outcomes		
Life adjustment outcomes		
Other outcomes		

DISCUSSION

Time permitting, a useful capstone to this activity is to engage students in some critical reflection on the value of Miles and Huberman's display message for qualitative data analysis. A key issue in such a discussion would be the contrast between Miles and Huberman's self-avowed "soft-nosed logical positivism" and the phenomenological bases for most qualitative approaches to inquiry.

BACKGROUND READINGS

Lincoln, Y.S., & Guba, E.G. (1985).   Naturalistic inquiry. Beverly Hills, CA: Sage, ch. 12.

Miles, M.B., & Huberman, A.M. (1984).   Qualitative data analysis: A sourcebook of new methods. Beverly Hills, CA: Sage, especially chs. 3,4,6,7 (pp. 215-230), 8.

HANDOUT 1:   Qualitative Data Analysis and Interpretation

The program being evaluated is a Tompkins County live-in residence program for pregnant teenagers during their pregnancy through the birth of their child.   The program has three major components: (1) the residence itself (a place to be with peers and to be taken care of); (2) psychological/emotional counseling; and (3) education regarding pregnancy, childbirth, relevant nutrition issues, and parenting.

Evaluation Context

Major evaluation question: To what extent and in what ways does the program help participants deal successfully with their pregnancy, especially in terms of their (1) self-perceptions, (2) psychological and emotional adjustment, and (3) longer term "life adjustment" (i.e., education, work, marriage and family)?

Major methods used to collect information on participants' perspectives.   They include   (all naturalistic)   on-site observation,   interviews   with   current   participants   (n=25), interviews with purposive sample of former participants (n=10), all in their mid to late twenties).

"Final" Category System for Self-Perceptions Program Outcome

Four major themes, represented in four "slightly fleshed out" categories:

1.   Basic self-worth, feeling accepted as a person

* Nearly all current participants spoke of the importance of feeling accepted "just as I am" in the residence.   This acceptance allowed them to let down their defenses, "take off my mask," and "stop pretending all day long about everything to everyone."   This acceptance seemed to provide a basic, elemental measure of self-worth.

* Without exception, the ten former participants spoke about their experience in the program as a "safe harbor to weather the storm," a place that provided reassurance, protection and "caring about me as a person."

2.   Physical self-concept

* Many current participants highlighted a reversal in their "physical self-concept" or perceptions of their bodies-- from feelings of hatred and betrayal to positive, proactive beliefs in the importance of taking care of themselves physically.

3.   Self-confidence

* About half of the former participants spoke about their

program experience as follows: "Early pregnancy is not an experience I'd wish on anyone, but it did help me to grow stronger, learn that I was the only one who could be responsible for my life. So, I had to take charge."

4.   Self-direction, control

*   Most of the remaining former participants (those not referred to under "self-confidence") reported that they "seem to keep making mistakes, though not always the same ones" [only one said she'd had a second teen pregnancy]. They said they often felt confused about what's right and seemed to be lacking in direction and belief in themselves.

*   For some of the current participants, their self-reflections were strongly marked by feelings of control and self-direction. "I've learned I have to take charge of my life and I've learned, I think, that I can do it."

*   Most of the other current participants expressed continuing anxiety and fear about the future, uncertainty about their relationships with their parents and how, when, and if they'd be able to go back to school.

Further Analysis via Matrices or Other Displays

What kinds of matrices/displays might help further understand:

1.   interrelationships among these self-perceptions data?
2.   relationships of these data to program components, activities, process?
3.   relationships of these data to other characteristics of participants?
4.   relationships of these data to other program "outcomes" (represented in other phenomenological perspectives, views of meaning)?
5.   other?

17

WRITING AND INTERPRETING ETHNOGRAPHIC PROTOCOLS

Helen B. Slaughter

This teaching activity is based on methods for training observers
to conduct naturalistic, or ethnographic nonparticipant
observations of classroom interaction. It is based on work by
(1) Tikunoff, Berliner, and Rist (1975) on ethnographic methods
used in the Beginning Teacher Evaluation Study, (2) Evertson,
Emmer and Clements (1980) on writing verbatim narrative accounts
of classroom processes, (3) Johnson and Gardner (1979) on methods
for training classroom ethnographers to assist in collaborative
research, (4) Gump (1980) on the ecological observation of
classroom contexts, and (5) Slaughter and Chilcott (1981) and
Slaughter, Haussler, Franks, Jilbert and Silentman (1985)
regarding the writing and interpretation of observational
protocols for use in team, multisite ethnographic evaluation.

Observation is part of an entire fieldwork cycle that has
been variously described as naturalistic evaluation by Guba and
Lincoln (1981), or ethnographic evaluation by Bogdan and Biklen
(1982). There is no one "standard" approach to naturalistic
observation, but there are commonalities among most methods
describing themselves as qualitative or fieldwork-based.
Teachers of evaluation may want to refer to a special issue of
the Anthropology and Education Quarterly (1983) on the teaching
of fieldwork to educational researchers.

The methodology described in this chapter will relate to
steps regarding the observation process, taking field notes,
writing protocols, and beginning preliminary analysis through the
use of ethnographic summaries. This method has been used
successfully by the author to train ethnographic research
assistants for three qualitative and ethnographic multisite
evaluation research studies, and to train students in a graduate
course on qualitative research methods in education.

MATERIALS

Example of a protocol and an ethnographic summary used in classroom a ethnographic study (see handout 1).

PROCEDURES

1. Purpose

Establish the purpose of writing protocols as part of an evaluation research study. Observations resulting in protocols produce first level or raw data of classroom events that may be relevant to the overall purpose of an evaluation, such as documenting methods used and/or providing empirical evidence to support claims about the attitudes and responses of the participants toward an educational program or innovation. The method described here emphasizes the development of highly specific, detailed accounts of the context and the ongoing social and linguistic interaction of participants in the classroom situation. It deliberately separates the reporting of ethnographic observational data collected during the fieldwork stage, and the interpretation of the meaning and significance of those data for theorizing and/or other evaluative purposes. Observers are trained to write descriptive and value-neutral protocols in the protocol proper, and to also analyze, interpret, and hypothesize about the data in a separate ethnographic summary written as soon as the protocol is completed. When in the classroom, ideas that come to mind about the "meaning" or "significance" of an episode or happening may be entered in parentheses as "observer comments," but care must be taken not to lose sight of ongoing events.

2. Theoretical Base

Develop a theoretical basis for guiding ethnographic observation in the classroom. Simon (1985) argues that it is important that ethnographic evaluations, including observation, be based on a theoretical framework of questions, assumptions to be questioned in the field, and searching for information needed for the evaluation. In other words, although flexible and amendable to change as determined by conditions found at work in the field, educational ethnography needs to be theory based, as well as theory generating. However, ethnographic observation needs to be conducted in a non-judgmental, open, and unbiased manner. Chilcott (Slaughter and Chilcott, 1981) found that an important part of training teachers, or others in classroom observation methods, was to help teachers recognize and curtail their judgments of the merit and worth of the teaching they were observing, and to look for larger patterns of interaction. Through reading sample ethnographies, writing descriptions of videotaped classroom events and comparing notes, and discussing the limitations of videotaped data, novice ethnographers began to understand the difference between the world view of the education profession and that of anthropology. This was done by constantly reminding students "through specific illustrations drawn from their observations of the <u>cultural baggage</u> which they were carrying which was biasing their observations" (Chilcott, 1981). One of the reasons for developing a two-tiered method, separating the protocol from the ethnographic summary, is to provide an opportunity for observers to articulate their feelings as well as their questions about what is going on in the summary.

3. Observing in the Classroom

Maximize observational time. When entering the classroom have it prearranged with the teacher that you will be taking notes and will be primarily in an observer role. Also mention that you may informally interact with students from time to time, but that you will make every attempt to fit into the background and not interfere with the on-going course of classroom events. You will first orient yourself to the physical and social context of the classroom and try to get an idea of the natural activity units that occur during the observational period which may be a class period, or longer. Try to have a list of student names beforehand and learn to identify students as soon as possible. Find a place to sit in the classroom where you can adequately see the whole room, or the small group activity you are observing, without interfering with the teacher's "space" or being too prominently in view of the whole class. In other words, try to be unobtrusive. However, do not be afraid to move around the room to observe different kinds of activities. Over the days that you observe, students will pay less and less attention to your presence, especially if you have taken care not to become a "helper" or too active a participant in the room.

As soon as possible begin taking running notes of classroom events, including verbatim notes of teacher-student, and peer verbal interaction that is related to the focal area of the study. If at all possible, identify the speakers by name or initial. Although pseudonyms will be used in your final report, it is confusing to use them during the study. (It also makes it hard to use the data in teacher interviews when pseudonyms are used prematurely). If at all possible, tape record during the time that you are in the classroom. Take time beforehand to be sure that you handle the recording process smoothly as this can be distracting to students. Note the time approximately every five minutes, (this helps you to remain alert), and also note the beginning and ending of the natural activity units or events occurring during the observational period.

In taking notes in the classroom, record only material that would not be offensive if it were read by students or the teacher. Make a mental note of other material and add it to your

field notes later when you are writing up the protocol or
ethnographic summary. Sometimes students will come up to you and
ask what you are doing. Tell them that you are interested in the
learning activities in the classroom and are writing down notes.
If a student wants to talk to you during an important
observation, tell the student you are busy doing your "work"
right now but that you'll talk to him or her later.

The purpose of the field notes is to provide documentation
for a description and interpretation of the process, a
documentation that at the time it is being recorded may seem to
be of little value or significance to the study. In ethnography,
the significance of certain types of events or interactions may
not "emerge" from the data until a certain period of time has
been spent in the site. Sometimes the significance of an event
may not be apparent until after it is noticed that similar or
different kinds of things are going on at other times, or in
other sites. Therefore, the observer must "get to it" in taking
detailed field notes and give the study time to develop more
focused and relevant research questions over time. This method
is especially useful in capturing insights into student responses
to instruction and other factors affecting the classroom learning
climate. Therefore, avoid an overemphasis in your note-taking on
teacher talk. Move around the room, and try to obtain samples of
peer interaction during group or independent learning time.
While your primary mode of operation is that of a neutral
observer, from time to time interact selectively with students,
asking what they are doing or asking them to explain some
assignment to you. Depending on the purpose of the study, a
great deal can be learned from verbally interacting with
students as well as with teachers.

4. Protocol Writing

Prepare the narrative overview and the protocol. Write up your
field notes soon after leaving the classroom. If at all
possible, complete the protocol before re-entering the classroom
to do another observation or to interview the teacher. It is
estimated that it will take three or more hours of write-up time
for every hour in the classroom to produce protocols of adequate
quality and detail. The protocol should, as much as possible,
reconstruct the events observed while in the classroom; both your
field notes and memory are used in this process. In most
research writing, events are told in the past tense and we have
found that protocols are often more easily readable when written
in past tense. Use a transcript format for including dialogue in
the protocols as this makes both writing and reading the
protocols easier. Not all tape recorded material will be entered
into the protocol because of time constraints; however, try to
provide examples of different kinds of speech events and long
enough sequences of interaction that one can "read between the
lines" in interpreting the significance of events. Remember that

the protocol provides the kind of raw data that can be used to generate or to test hypotheses. Include drawings or examples of student work where relevant to the observations.

Carefully mark all pages of the protocol with date, time, classroom site, page number, and make a second copy of all protocols when they are finished. Protocols are confidential data: keep them in a secure place. For more refined indexing of protocol data, all lines can be numbered; if this proves cumbersome, then all paragraphs can be numbered. The protocol "overview" is a cover sheet for the protocol summarizing the main things that were observed, perhaps referring the reader to specific pages; it can be useful in locating certain kinds of observations that you may want to organize later in the study. It is written, of course, after you have completed the protocol.

5. The Ethnographic Summary

Struggle with the interpretation and index the data. After the protocol is completed, the ethnographer writes an interpretation of the observation. This may include positive or negative feelings about what is happening in the site, or study, and hunches about what might be important to look at in more depth in future observations. As the study progresses, the ethnographic interpretations become more data-based and theory-based, and may begin to resemble final reports where interpretation and examples of data from observations are interspersed. These analyses, with their references to specific pages and lines in the protocol, are invaluable in synthesizing data, refining the observations in the ongoing study, and writing the final report. They are an essential and important step in the method as one can become "entrapped" in the descriptive detail of the study and lose sight of its purpose and scope. They are also difficult for many novices to write, especially those with little social science background. It is extremely helpful for students to present some data to the class and engage in discussion with peers and the instructor about the meaning of the data in writing up the ethnographic summary.

6. Validating the Protocol through Teacher Interviews

The two-part protocol can be helpful as a tool for sharing data with teachers, data that can be deepened in its interpretation through mutual dialogue, without prematurely interjecting evaluative judgments into the research process since the ethnographic summary is not shared. It may be useful, relatively early in a study, to share at least one classroom protocol with the teacher to demonstrate the neutral character of the observation process. However, be careful to conduct this interview as an interested researcher and do not become prescriptive or confuse this evaluation research process with clinical observation or other forms of supervision.

160

DISCUSSION

The activity of conducting a single classroom observation and
writing a protocol and ethnographic summary has been a
requirement for students enrolled in the Spring of 1987 and 1988
in the course "Qualitative Research Methods," an introductory
course for master's and doctoral students in the College of
Education and other social science graduate students at the
University of Hawaii. After writing up their protocols, students
share some of their data and tentative hypotheses with the class
and elicit feedback from their peers. Some students decide to
conduct a series of observations in completing the major paper
for the course.

BACKGROUND READING

Bogdan, R.D., & Biklen, S.K. (1982). Qualitative research
    for education: An introduction to theory and methods.
    Boston: Allyn and Bacon.

Evertson, C.M., Emmer, E.T., & Clements, B.S. (1980). Report of
    the methodology, rationale and implementation of the junior
    high classroom organization study. (R & D Rep. No. 6100), R
    & D Center for Teacher Education, the University of Texas at
    Austin, February.

Guba, E., & Lincoln, Y. (1981). Effective evaluation. San
    Francisco: Jossey-Bass.

Gump, P.V. (1980). Observation--of persons and contexts. Paper
    presented at the annual meeting of the American Educational
    Research Association, Boston, MA.

Johnson, N.K., & Gardner, D.H. (1979). Toward a prototype for
    training classroom ethnographers. Paper presented at the
    annual meeting of the American Educational Research
    Association, San Francisco, CA.

Simon, E.L. (1986). Theory in education evaluation: Or, what's
    wrong with generic-brand anthropology. In D.M. Fetterman
    and M.A. Pitman, (eds.), Educational evaluation:
    Ethnography in theory, practice and politics. London:
    Sage.

Slaughter, H., & Chilcott, J. (1981). Classroom ethnographic
    study of an activities-based supplemental mathematics
    program. Paper presented at the annual meeting of the
    American Educational Research Association, Los Angeles, CA.

Slaughter, H.B., Haussler, M.M., Franks, A.S., Jilbert, K.A., &
    Silentman, I.J. (1985). Contextual differences in oral and

written discourse during early literacy instruction. Paper presented to the Annual Meeting of the American Educational Research Association, Washington, D.C.

Tikunoff, W.J., Berliner, D.C., & Rist, R.C. (1975). Special Study A: An ethnographic study of the forty classrooms of the BTES Known Sample. Far West Laboratory for Educational Research and Development, San Francisco, CA.

162

Handout 1:   Excerpts from a Protocol

Narrative Overview

This entire narrative describes the Chapter I Writing Sample
procedure for about 22 first graders collected during their
regular class time.   Mrs. Abby, the teacher has her usual,
somewhat informal opening followed by the directions for the
sample.   As they work, Mrs. Abby begins to take dictation from
those who have finished and if they need to wait for her or have
completed the procedure, the children work with other materials
(mostly books) in other parts of the room.

Protocol Excerpt (Page 1)

	1.	There is the established opening, taking attendance

1. There is the established opening, taking attendance
2. while the children sit on the rug. One child
3. followed by another begins to look at the calendar
4. in the wall in front of them and slightly to the
5. right.

9:00
6. T.   Are you looking for what day it is?   OK, sit
7. down. (And she spends the next few moments going
8. through each page, month by month. By August she
9. tells them they will be second graders.

Frank   10. Someone expresses, "Second graders?!") I have (some
Melissa   11. writing) paper for you today...A special one with
Hector   12. your name at the top...a piece of paper for you to
Melona   13. write on. As soon as you get your paper, you can
Harry   14. write whatever you want to write.
Paul   15. Child: I'll make a picture first.
Ramona   16. T.   That's OK.
17. Child: (something about using crayons).
18. T.   We want to just use pencils today.
19. Ramona: How can we draw pictures?
20. T. (You'll have to do it with pencils.) Another
21. day we'll use crayons. (If you don't know how to
22. spell a word, like a name) say (a child's name),
23. write it how you think you'd write it. (A child
24. suggests 'V').
25. T. It has a 'V' just like (a child's name).
26. The teacher rather casually dismisses the children
27. to sit at tables in the 'rear' of the room. Three
28. girls sit down and spend time chatting at one of the
29. tables. Melona asks teacher for help. "Will you
30. help me (sound out words)?"

Ethnographic Summary

Page 1 (L 1-8) Oral language occurs as children respond to the
print environment and when the teacher treats their interest as
genuine. Several valuable concepts were introduced, reviewed, or

reinforced with this simple response to child-interest.

(L 8-25 to page 2 to L1) One of the most interesting aspects of this evaluation procedure is that most of the rules emerged from questions posed to the students, not specific pre-formulated directions from Mrs. Abby. The restrictions, no crayons, teacher can't help, are balanced by the overall informality and original requirement, "Write whatever you want to write."

18

THE COMPUTER-ASSISTED ANALYSIS OF QUALITATIVE DATA

Renata Tesch

During the past five years several scholars who are also competent computer programmers have developed software for the personal computer that is designed to relieve the naturalistic researcher of many of the tedious and time-consuming mechanical tasks that are part of the organizing process for qualitative data. The Ethnograph is one of the best known of these programs and it provides a good example of one basic approach that programmers have taken to facilitate text analysis. It is not a data base, i.e., storage-retrieval oriented, but analysis-process oriented. The software package will be introduced during this teaching activity. However, this is not a training session in the use of this program. Instead, the teaching activity acquaints researchers with the principles employed by this (and other) qualitative text analysis programs, and illustrates with computer screens how these principles are applied. The goal is to help researchers understand how the computer can be integrated in the conceptual analysis process.

MATERIALS

The Ethnograph sample disk
Sample data (your own)
Program screen transparencies, feature overviews (optional)

PROCEDURES

Introduction

Qualitative data in naturalistic evaluation consist of field notes or interview transcripts, and often a combination of both. If these data are highly structured (for instance, the interview proceeded along a formal schedule, producing only short responses), it is relatively easy to order them according to that structure. If they come in narrative form (open-ended answers to questionnaires and interview questions), the task is more difficult. The human mind is not equipped to deal with hundreds of pages of text at once. If the researcher is to discover patterns in the data, the data must be organized in such a way that s/he can look at smaller parts of the data and compare them with each other. These parts must be thematically related, i.e., they must pertain to the same topic. The task for the researcher, therefore, becomes to extract relevant text segments from the data and sort them according to their content. Eventually, everything in the data that thematically belongs together should be assembled in one place. Students should read chapter 9 in Patton (1980) before completing this exercise.

Conceptual Preparation for Organizing Data

In order to accomplish the task of organizing the data for analysis, three conceptual activities must be undertaken by the researcher: (1) the development of a categorizing system; (2) the determination of the units of analysis, and (3) the coding of the data (assigning units of analysis to categories).

I. Development of a Categorizing System

The development of a categorizing system for a naturalistic analysis is the process of determining what topics of relevance to the evaluation project are expected to be, or actually are contained in the data. There are two basic avenues for establishing such a system: (a) a categorizing system can be created from prior material, such as the theoretical framework adopted and/or the research questions that guide the evaluation (deductive method); or (b) a categorizing system can be constructed from the data themselves (inductive method). In most cases, the researcher will want to combine these methods, since that affords the greatest chance of capturing everything in the data that is pertinent to the evaluation.

A. Developing a Categorization System From the Research Questions or the Theoretical Framework

Have the students contribute their own research questions from a real or imagined evaluation project, or supply some examples. Ask them to abstract the major topics from these questions.

Example of a main research question:

How well does a recently implemented electronic network that connects adult students of a non-residential graduate program serve the needs of the institution's students and faculty?

Examples of specific questions:

To what degree was the electronic network seen by faculty and students as a desirable solution to unmet needs prior to the installation of the network?

What are the reasons for non-use by that portion of the faculty and students who have not become part of the network?

What do current users like and dislike about the system?

Examples of categories derived from these questions:

Attitudes toward electronic network
      students
      faculty
      administration

Non-use of the electronic network
      proportion of non-users
      reasons for non-use

Likes and dislikes about electronic network
      faculty
      students

B. **Developing A Categorizing System from the Data**

Have the students contribute their own research data from a real or imagined evaluation project, or supply your own examples. The data should be formatted in such a way that a wide margin is provided on either the right or left side of the text.

     Instruct the students to read the data carefully and note in the margin the topics that are talked about (in an interview) or described (in field notes). Make sure they distinguish between Topic and Content. The topic is what is talked or written about; the content is the substance of the message. For instance, the topic could be "the advantages of an electronic network." The content might be the "It is faster than mail, but does not require, as the telephone does, that the other person be available at the same moment." At this point, only Topics should be noted in the margins.

Example:

                          Researcher: How often do you log in on
                          the electronic network?

frequency of use   Respondent: Well, I know I am supposed
                          to log on every night to check my mail
                          but I find it a chore and often forget.

reason for use

> To be honest, I average about once a week. They're always after me to be more prompt.
>
> Researcher: What kinds of things do you communicate about on the network?
>
> Respondent: That's the problem. I don't have anything I want to communicate. I'm much more

attitude toward mail

> comfortable with the mail, and I don't really know why that isn't good enough. I will admit that my students <u>do</u> use the system a lot, and they want to negotiate

perception of student use

> their assessment contracts and ask questions about their dissertations and even submit their assessment examinations on the system. But I

reason for non-use

> type so slowly and painfully I just can't spend the time doing that.

Categories that emerged from this data segment

> attitudes toward mail
> frequency of use
> perception of student use
> reason for use
> reasons for non-use

II. Determination of the Unit of Analysis

The units of analysis are the portions of the text that contain the content to be categorized. For instance, in the above example the following would be a unit of analysis:

Researcher: How often do you log in on the electronic network?

Respondent: Well, I know I am supposed to log on every night to check my mail, but I find it a chore and often forget. To be honest, I guess I average about once a week.

This portion of the text is comprehensible by itself. It is just large enough to have meaning. The researcher's question might even be omitted, but its inclusion makes the meaning of the segments unmistakably clear. Analysis units can have any length, from a sentence to several paragraphs. The researcher must determine the boundaries, i.e., the beginning and end of the analysis unit for each relevant piece of the data.

Ask the students to mark the boundaries of the data text for which they previously determined the topic. One good way of marking such units is to run a square bracket from the line on which the unit begins to the one where it ends.

When this task is completed, ask the students to verify the viability of their units of analysis by extracting some of the segments and asking a fellow student to state the meaning of each segment. If there are more than one or two topics contained in the unit, it is too long. If no sense can be made of the text, the unit is too short.

III.   Coding of the Data

Coding or indexing the data is the process of assigning units of analysis to the categories of the organizing system. For this purpose, the names or labels that were given to the categories are abbreviated to form mnemonic codes. The Ethnograph permits ten characters; the abbreviations must remain within these limits.

Instruct the students to create meaningful abbreviations of the category labels they have developed. Once the students have turned their categories into a list of codes, provide them with the following instructions:

1.   Read your entire text to get a sense of the whole.

2.   Begin reading again. This time, decide for every sentence whether it is relevant for the purpose of the evaluation. If it is not relevant, ignore it.

3.   If the sentence is relevant, mark the line on which the sentence begins with the first horizontal line of a square bracket. Continue reading to determine the second boundary of the analysis unit, and finish the square bracket at the line where the unit ends.

4.   Determine the topic of the analysis unit and write the appropriate code in the margin at the beginning of the bracket.

5.   Re-read the text to determine whether all or parts of the unit are relevant to another category as well. If so, use another bracket and apply the appropriate code.

IV.   Use of the Computer

At this point in the process, the computer begins to be of help. Review the functions the software performs, as shown below. Once these are understood, the use of the software itself is accomplished by selecting one item from a menu of choices. The programs pick up text that has been prepared on word processors. The sample disk contains text that can be used for

practicing purposes.   Ask the students to "make up" analysis
units and codes for these sample data.

A. The Basic Functions Performed By Qualitative Analysis Software

The four most common groups of functions in analysis programs
are:

1. Main functions
    Attaching codes to segments of text
    Searching for the text segments according to the code and
    assembling them

2. Enhancement functions
    Ordering the retrieved segments alphabetically according to
    their codes
    Counting the frequency of the occurrence of codes in the
    data
    Searching for multiple codes (segments to which more than
    one code was attached)
    Searching selectively (through only a specified group of
    data documents)
    Searching for a particular sequence of codes (for segments
    that follow each other in a certain order).

3. Preparatory functions
    Importing files (picking up a document that has been
    created by a word processor)
    Numbering the lines of the data text
    Printing out paper copies of the data with line numbers
    attached

4. Housekeeping functions
    Retrieving files (data documents)
    Saving files
    Changing the directory (switching from one disk drive to
    another)
    Printing (entire documents, individual retrieved segments,
    or all segments retrieved in a search for one code or all
    codes).

(This list is available as a transparency from the author.)

B.   Introduction to The Ethnograph

      The Ethnograph requires that, under normal circumstances,
the coding is done first on a paper copy that is printed out by
the program after it has added numbers to each line of the data.
After that, the line numbers for the beginning and the end of an
analysis unit and the code are entered into a form provided on
the computer screen.   Each text segment (analysis unit) can be
simultaneously placed into several categories (several codes can

be attached). The Ethnograph permits several layers of overlapping, and in addition, smaller units within a larger segments can be coded separately (nesting).

It is easy to delete or change the coding again once it has been applied. The Ethnograph provides a separate function to accomplish modifications. After all data documents are coded, the researcher will want to instruct the computer to search for all codes through all documents and print out the results consecutively. This is the core of the computer process. The program can look for four or five code words occurring with the same segment.

V.   Demonstration

Use the Ethnograph sample disk to show the performance of the main functions only. (If you have an audience larger than your own computer's screen can accommodate, it is advisable to simultaneously show the screens overhead from a transparency. A set of transparencies of screen reproductions for the program is available from the author for $10.) Read carefully the instructions that come with the disks and familiarize yourself with the menu choices and terminologies of the programs. For the teaching activity proceed along the following steps:

A. Coding

Show the menu that appears when the program is loaded. It is called the PROCEDURE MENU. Point out the main functions: CODE and SEARCH. CODE works only on documents whose lines have been numbered (using the NUMBER function). The first action that the computer expects from the researcher is that s/he enter numbers and code names into a form. When C (for CODE) is selected from the menu, the user is first asked to provide the name of the file that is to be coded, and then to chose whether codes or sociodemographic (called "face-sheet") variables are to be attached to that data document. Sociodemographic variables are an enhancement function, not a main function. Your answer, therefore, is NO. Next, show the coding screen.

The cursor sits where the first entry in the form must be made (a line number for the beginning of an analysis unit), and jumps to the next entry spot whenever the researcher has entered a line number for the "start" and the "stop" of a segment, or a code name.

B. Searching/Assembling

When the researcher is ready to have the program search for the coded segments, s/he chooses S from the main menu (for SEARCH), and fills out two forms, one with the names of the files from which s/he wants the program to extract segments, and the other with the codes for which the program is to search. Show the NAMES OF FILES TO BE SEARCHED screen first. The researcher fills in the file names (up to 40 at a time) after the numbers.

Then show the CODE WORD for SEARCH screen. Here the researcher fills in the code words after the numbers (up to 80 at a time). Before the actual search begins, the researcher has the option to have the segments printed out according to the sequence in which the codes were entered into this form or in alphabetical order.

The computer will then print out one segment after the other, each divided from the next by broken lines. It includes for each segment the name of the file from which it was extracted, the name of the code for which the search was conducted, the names of additional codes that were also attached to the particular segment (if any), and a brief context description, if such information was provided by the researcher. The text of the analysis unit follows, with line numbers printed out to the right of each line.

DISCUSSION

The main notions to understand about computer-assisted analysis of qualitative data are:

1. The computer does not perform the actual analysis. It merely takes over the mechanical tasks that are part of organizing the data for later interpretation.

2. Several conceptual tasks must be performed by the evaluator before computer programs can be employed. They are: (a) the development of a categorizing system; (b) the determination of the units of analysis; and (c) the coding of the data (assigning units of analysis to categories).

3. Computer programs for qualitative analysis may be constructed in various different ways and use different terminology. However, all of them perform two main functions: the attachment of codes to segments of text, and the retrieval and assembly of segments that have been coded with the same code. All other functions are either preparatory to these tasks, or enhancements of the retrieval function, or they perform necessary electronic "housekeeping."

SOFTWARE INFORMATION

The Ethnograph program is for IBM personal computers and IBM compatibles, with MS-DOS. It requires 25K of RAM or less. The program and manual are copyrighted and can be ordered through the author. The cost is $150 per program. The sample disk (which comes with instructions provided by this author) costs $10. A set of transparencies with reproductions of the basic working screens of the program and with summaries of the program features is also available. The cost is $10 per set.

Other software programs for ethnographic analysis that are available for the IBM-PC include TAP (Text Analysis Package) and Qualpro. Hyperqual is a software package that is available for the MacIntosh computer. Information about these other software packages and sample disks are available from the author.

BACKGROUND READING

Patton, M.Q. (1980). <u>Qualitative evaluation methods</u>. Beverly Hills, CA: Sage.

19

UNDERSTANDING CONTENT ANALYSIS THROUGH THE SUNDAY COMICS

Hallie Preskill

The teaching of content analysis presents an instructor with an interesting challenge. Unlike studies reporting the findings of quantitative data collection and analysis, where the procedures and analyses are made explicit, qualitative evaluation studies employing content analysis data procedures are rarely described in detail. The decision rules and thought processes used in their analyses of interviews, field notes, and observations are often left out of articles and presentations. For the instructor trying to teach others about content analysis, this situation leaves one searching for meaningful learning activities.

In the past, I have brought in transcripts of interviews I have conducted and have asked students to code these data. This activity has been very useful in helping students develop a quick appreciation for the procedure. In spite of this activity's utility, I felt something else was needed to give the students more experience with real data.

The Comic Strip Activity

Recently I came across an article written in 1961 titled "A Content Analysis of Trends in Sunday Comics, 1900-1959" by Francis Barcus, published in an issue of <u>Journalism Quarterly</u>. In this article, the author describes a study he conducted that was a "sociocultural investigation into comic strips in the United States" that attempted to "trace trends and patterns of major themes, comic strip types, and use of characters since the beginning of the use of comic strips in the Sunday paper." The article describes in detail the coding procedures and categories that were established. The findings provide some interesting insights into the social and cultural changes of the American character as seen through the eyes of emerging cartoonists and illustrators during the 59 year period.

MATERIALS

1. Sunday comics from the local paper (one copy for each student)
2. Handout 1: Summary of Coding Categories
3. Handout 2: Comic Strip Types
4. Handout 3: Dominant Themes
5. Handout 4: Principal Characters

PROCEDURES

After reading this article, I thought it would be interesting to do a similar exercise, though on a much smaller scale. The activity was used in a graduate level class titled "Educational Program Evaluation." After completing a reading and mini-lecture on content analysis, the students participated in the following activity:

1. Students were asked to bring with them to the next class, the Sunday comics from one of the local newspapers. (They were asked to bring the comics from the same paper.)

2. Students read the Barcus article. The class discussed the analysis procedures, rules, and overall findings.

3. A summary sheet of the coding categories for (1) Comic Strip Types, (2) Dominant Themes, and (3) Principal Characters (Handout 1) was distributed.

4. A chart for coding the comic strips for each of the categories was distributed (Handouts 2-4).

5. With comic strips in hand, students were divided into groups of four (though larger or smaller groups can be established depending on the class size).

6. The students were given 30-40 minutes to read the comic strips and reach consensus in their group on how they should be coded and categorized on the handouts provided by the instructor. They were asked to keep a detailed log of their coding rules and the decisions they had to make during the coding process.

7. After the groups finished their analysis, a representative of each group shared its findings. Differences between groups were discussed, each emphasizing the decision rules used and issues that arose in the analysis process.

8. Students were referred back to the Barcus article to compare findings of one Sunday in 1988 to the findings of the

first half of the twentieth century. Of course, it was emphasized that more comic strips would need to be analyzed before any conclusive statements or generalizations could be made.

DISCUSSION

This activity worked extremely well in accomplishing the following:

1. Students became actively involved in coding real "data" and were better able to transfer their content analysis skills to coding interview data later on in the course.

2. The content of the exercise (comic strips) was humorous yet the topic of looking at American life through comic strips was also illuminating.

3. Working in groups allowed students to see the multiple perspectives that influence the analysis of data. In the conduct of qualitative evaluation this point is critical.

BACKGROUND READINGS

Barcus, F.E. (1961). A content analysis of trends in Sunday Comics, 1900-1959. Journalism Quarterly, 38(2), 171-180.

Holsti, Ole R. (1969). Content analysis for the social sciences and humanities. Reading, MA: Addison-Wesley Publishing Company.

Krippendorff, Klaus. (1980). Content analysis: An introduction to its methodology. Beverly Hills, CA: Sage Publications.

HANDOUT 1:   Summary of Coding Categories

A.   Comic Strip Types

Six Categories--Predominant nature.

1.   Serious--classical stories, historical topics, "social
     problems"
2.   Action and Adventure ("men of adventure")
3.   Humor--presumed intent is primarily light-hearted; "social
     satire" is involved
4.   Real Life--personal or interpersonal relationships,
     "soap opera"
5.   Fantasy--fairy tales, science fiction, non-human
     characters, non-earthly settings
6.   Other Types--not included in the above

B.   Dominant Themes

Based on characterization, activities of leading characteristics.

1.   Domestic situation (home, family, neighborhood)
2.   Crime, criminals, outlaws, police, detectives,
     corruption, etc.
3.   Association with historical events or activities, true or
     fictionalized
4.   Religion--stories from the Bible, churches, etc.
5.   Love and romance
6.   Supernatural, magic, occult, ghosts, etc.
7.   Nature, animals, forces of nature, etc.
8.   International settings and adventures
9.   Education and schools, teacher, etc.
10. Business and industry--occupational, dealing with
     executives, secretaries, etc.
11. Government and public affairs, politicians, the law,
     courts, legislation, etc.
12. Science and scientists--science fiction, technology
13. Entertainment world, mass media, sports, etc.
14. Armed forces and war, defense systems, combat settings
15. Literature and the fine arts, tales from classic
     literature, authors, artists, dance, etc.
16.   Other

C.   Principal Characters

Leading and continuous characters.
1.   Adults
2.   Teens, adolescents
3.   Infants and children
4.   Animal
5.   Other (e.g., robots)

HANDOUT 2:   Comic Strip Types

Serious	Action/Adventure	Humor	Real Life	Fantasy	Other

HANDOUT 3:   Dominant Themes

Domestic	Crime	Historical	Religion	Love/Romance	Supernatural

Nature	International	Education	Business	Government

Science	Entertainment	Armed Forces	Literature	Other

HANDOUT 4: Principal Characters

Adults	Teens	Infants/Children	Animals	Other

20

USING CASE RECORDS

Joseph P. Caliguri

The case record represents a detailed format for use in problem-solving for practitioners interested in a systematic approach to development of sound educational or organization practices. The case record also provides opportunities for practitioners to reflect theoretically on cases by seeking relevant literature to acquire further insights or support in regard to the case characteristics.

MATERIALS

Handout 1 provides pointers for using case records and definition of terms. Handout 2 provides a sample case record. A blank case record form can be constructed by interested readers by following the format provided in Handout 2.

PROCEDURE

The instructor can review the case record using transparencies or provide copies of the case record to students for independent study followed by a class session for further clarification.

Students are usually given a week to determine a problem situation in which the case record can be applied. The instructor, depending on class size, can hold one to one conferences with students or meet with groups of three to five students to reach agreement on implementation of the case record.

Time frames are then established for intermittent progress reports to the instructor and the class as well as target dates for case closure and submittance to the instructor.

An instructor may devise his/her own grading schema for the

case record work.   Some initial grading indicators are:

-Adherence to case record format and closure.

-Quality of effort and tasks in resolving a problem or modification of the case based on justifiable evidence related to unanticipated events or constraints.

-Demonstration by the student of the acquiring of knowledge, insights, and skills in problem solving, or identifying sound practices as indicated in progress reports and the final report.

HANDOUT 1:   Record-Keeping Guide--Definition of Terms

First, A Few Pointers

1.   Any situation or episode that requires your attention as a   staff person or administrator is appropriate for a case record.

2.   Try to complete the first side of the form before taking action.

3.   Be concise, but append additional paper if necessary.

4.   Give enough detail for other people involved to understand the situation and your thought processes.

5.   Your own growth and development as a professional will rest on your thoughtful (and frequent) completion of case records.

Front of Form

Case Title--your own invented name for the case.

Date--the day on which you became aware that there was a situation requiring your attention.

Trigger Event(s)--the occurrence(s) that made you aware that there was a situation requiring your attention.

Nature of Problem--the deviation from perfection; the imperfection you perceive in this situation.

Goal(s) of Action--what you will be trying to accomplish by your actions.

Possible Causes, Organization-Based--the one or two factors within your organization that seem likely to have caused the situation.

Possible Causes, Self-Based--the one or two aspects of your own behaviors, beliefs, values, or attitudes that may have caused the situation to arise.

Additional Information--details gathered before taking corrective action that seem to have a bearing on the situation.

Planned Solution--steps you plan to take to resolve the situation.

Target Date--the day by which you expect to have resolved the situation.

Back of Form

Key Events--the occurrences as you strive to implement your solution to the situation, and the date of each event.

Result--(Date: _____)--the actual outcome of your actions, and the day on which you checked on the result.

Further Reflections--any additional thoughts you have on the matter and readings in the literature bearing on the case record concepts and issues.

Another Thought or Two

We realize that writing case records--especially before taking action (as well as during and after acting)--is not at all easy. Your attempts to do so, however, and your thoughtfulness during this process, will be the sources of very important, new, professional knowledge for yourself.

What you get out of the process of case-record keeping is more important than what others gain from your thinking!

-You will find that you become aware of more factors to take into consideration.

-You will make better decisions about what actions to take.

-Your actions will be more efficient and effective.

-Your decisions will be more closely related to your longer-range plans and goals.

-You will become more proactive and less reactive.

-You will take troublesome situations less personally but more professionally.

HANDOUT 2:   Sample Case Record

Case Title: Test Results Feedback   Date: 9/11/85

Trigger Event(s).   During a casual conversation with a teacher, I became aware that the unit leaders in this school are not using the achievement test item analysis printout in planning unit instructional goals and objectives.

Nature of Problem.   A very valuable (and expensive) tool that could improve our instructional programs is being overlooked. Not using this tool contributes to unevenness in the school's instructional program.

Goal(s) of Actions.   To develop departmental goals and objectives that are congruent with results of the test item analysis.

Possible Causes, School-Based.   The testing process has, by default, been taken over by the guidance counselor. Results are reported only to parents and students regarding individual students.   The previous principal made no effort to use the test data to shape the instructional planning process.

Possible Causes, Self-Based.   I had assumed that unit leaders had been retrieving the item analysis and naively overlooked this matter.   Also, I didn't monitor the minutes of unit meetings closely enough; hence I wasted valuable time in installing this feedback loop.

Additional Information.   The central administration, in an effort to be cost-efficient, made a move to do away with this tool, but the information in this case record helped to blunt that attempt.

Planned Solution.   Work with unit leaders to discuss how to make the information gleaned from the item analysis a regular part of our instructional planning process.

     Shift from monthly to bi-weekly unit faculty meetings until the devised planning process is established.

     Check with teachers to determine whether test-related goals are being incorporated with regular classroom instruction.

Target Date: 10/31/85

Key Events

Date	Event
9/15/85	Met with unit leaders after school to review the item analysis printout from last spring's standardized test. Two of them did not know how to interpret the item-analysis results, so we spent 20 minutes reviewing what the item scores mean. Unit leaders were assigned the task of matching the test items with current grade-level goals and objectives before our meeting next week.
9/22	Second meeting with unit leaders. They all found some items that matched the current objectives well but many items that didn't. This lead to discussion of revisions of unit grade-level goals and objectives with involvement of the teachers. We also agreed to establish bi-weekly faculty unit meetings until curriculum revisions and teacher commitment are in place.
9/25	Sat in on the first curriculum related unit faculty meeting (while my Assistant Principal sat in on another). With few exceptions, teachers are enthusiastic about the tying of unit goals/objectives to test results, so discussions flowed smoothly. Most teachers are willing to recommend changes in grade-level objectives so as to shore up the areas in which students' item scores are at or below grade level.
9/26	Conferred with my A.P. about the unit meeting he'd attended. There was more faculty resistance there, possibly because I wasn't present in person. Teachers were objecting to "teaching to the test." We decided to switch units for the next bi-weekly meeting.
10/10	Sat in on social studies unit's second meeting. Teachers came prepared with recommendations for grade-level goals, but with some mutterings of dissatisfaction. I gave a "pep-talk" about raising our students' scores without sacrificing other subject-area objectives we had identified earlier. Some of the teachers expressed surprise about items that had attained low scores; these teachers seemed pleased to have gotten the feedback and enthusiastic about tying goals more closely to test results.

10/17   All units have revised their grade-level objectives, and teachers have been discussing various ways of orienting instruction to the new objectives without losing track of the major goals and objectives of the different classes.

10/19   Observed in one social studies class, one of the new objectives clearly part of the lesson-- possibly because I was present. Other spot-check observations planned for the coming weeks.

Result (Date: 11/3/85)

Reaction of the faculty has been very positive. The majority of teachers seem to enjoy this approach, since it clarifies the minimal expectations for each subject at each grade-level. Unit leaders have been surprised to discover the extent to which there is a hidden curriculum where content is being taught that really has no place in the school's general goals.

Further Reflections

As general system theory suggests, feedback is essential to keep the system on target. Without specific feedback, individual teachers (components) generate their own implicit goals, and the system disintegrates. The item-analysis printout from the standardized test offers one of many important sources of feedback. Eventually, I hope to provide class-by-class feedback of this sort.

III   NEEDS ASSESSMENT

21

COLLECTION TECHNIQUES FOR NEEDS ASSESSMENT

Julia Gamon

The purpose of the activity is for students to become familiar with collection techniques for needs assessment and be able to choose the best one for each situation.

Objectives

1. List steps in the Delphi technique and simulate its use.

2. Cite appropriate situations for a Q-sort and use it to identify competency needs.

3. Describe procedure for the Charrette technique and use it to identify resources and constraints.

4. Share news items regarding use of focus groups.

MATERIALS

1. Questionnaires (Handout 1) and envelopes for 1st round of Delphi. Second and third rounds will be done during a few minutes of subsequent class sessions.

2. Set of items for Q-sort (Handout 2).

3. Newsprint and markers for Charrette.

4. Newspaper, magazine, and journal articles that mention focus groups (need to watch for and collect these).

5. Handouts on Charrette (Handout 3) and focus groups (Handout 4).

PROCEDURES

1. Begin the Delphi technique

Interest Approach - Have a volunteer mailperson hand each student a sealed envelope with the first round of the Delphi (Handout 1). Tell them they have been selected as experts but not to open their mail yet. (Give them a few minutes at the end of class or at the break to open their mail and fill out the questionnaire.)

2. Introduction

Questionnaires are commonly used in evaluations, but there are other methods that may be effectively used to gather information and build ideas from individuals and from groups. Four possible methods are the Delphi, Q-sort, Charrette, and focus groups. Each of these has unique characteristics and strengths. All four are typically used for evaluation toward the beginning of a program. For example, in the CIPP (Context-Input-Process-Product) model these would be used at the context and input stages. The resulting data are usually in ordinal form. Knowing the procedures and characteristics of each technique will help in deciding which technique to use in a particular situation. Most of these procedures need one to two hours to do in an actual situation. The classroom versions will be very abbreviated.

3. Q-sort

A. Explanation. When used, procedure, types, and data analyses (see references)

B. Activity. Give each student Handout 2 containing ten competencies needed by evaluators and instruct student to tear on the lines and sort items into three piles (important, less important, least important) from the student's point of view. Give an example of how to sort, using one of the items.

C. Processing Activity. Ask students to share contents of their "important" piles, either with entire class or with their neighbors. Write on board topics and times each one is mentioned. Explain that this was an abbreviated version of a structured needs assessment Q-sort and results in ordinal data.

4. Charrette

A. Explanation. (Handout 3).

B. Activity. Divide the class into small groups and give each group a piece of newsprint and a marker. Ask each group to select a reporter. Choose an example, such as evaluation of the graduate student program, and ask groups to list on newsprint the resources and/or constraints related to an evaluation of the program. After each group has listed four or five items, instruct the reporter in each group to move to an adjacent group, taking with him/her the list of items on the newsprint and the marker. The reporter needs to explain to the new group the items on the newsprint and ask them to make additions and/or changes (may need more newsprint sheets).

C. Processing Activity. Ask reporters to share one item from their lists. Ask for feedback on the techniques, its strengths and uses.

5. Focus groups

A. Explanation. (See Handout 4).

B. Activity. Pass out articles and ask students to explain briefly how focus groups were mentioned in the article. Ask students who may have been involved in a focus group to share their experiences.

C. Processing Activity. Ask students to be alert for articles mentioning focus groups and to bring them to class. Summarize procedure and uses.

6. Finishing the Delphi

A. See references for explanation. Give class members a few minutes to open their mail and fill out first round of Delphi. Collect the questionnaires, and use their ideas for the second round of the Delphi at the next meeting of the class.

DISCUSSION

Techniques typically used for needs assessment are the Delphi, Q-sort, Charrette, and focus groups. Focus groups use homogeneous groups and taped nondirective interviews. Q-sorts use a predetermined set of piles with or without specific criteria for sorting. In the Charrette the ideas of one group are enlarged and refined by another. In the Delphi a series of questionnaires are mailed to experts. Knowing the unique features of each technique will help in selecting the best collection procedures for a particular situation. All of the activities related to these four techniques have been used over the last ten years in extension workshops and in courses on evaluation of agricultural programs and extension program planning at Iowa State University.

BACKGROUND READING

Gross, J.G. (1981). Delphi: A program planning technique.
     Journal of Extension, 19(3), 23-28.

Krueger, R.A. (1986).   Focus group interviewing: A helpful
     technique for agricultural educators. The Visitor, 73(1),
     University of Minnesota, St. Paul.

Moore, C.M. (1987). Group techniques for idea building. Beverly
     Hills: Sage Publications.

HANDOUT 1:   Example of a Delphi Questionnaire--First Round

To: Expert

From: Evaluator

We are examining the graduate student curriculum in an attempt to make it as relevant as possible to the needs of the students and of the profession.   You have been nominated by your peers as an expert in the field.   This study is important to the future direction of the curriculum and we need your opinion.   All forms will be treated confidentially.   No information will be released giving your name.

We are using the Delphi method.   This first round consists of two open-ended questions.   The next round will ask you to respond to results from the first round.

Thank you for your participation.

Question 1:   What are the strengths of the present graduate curriculum?

Question 2:   What changes would you like to see in curriculum, courses, or requirements?

HANDOUT 2:   Competencies Needed by Evaluators

Q-Sort Directions:

Fold paper on lines and tear into strips.   Place strips into
three piles "important," "less important," and "least important."

Oral Communication Skills

Knowledge of Evaluation Models

Writing Ability

Ethical, Moral Base

Familiarity with Object to be Evaluated

Statistical Analysis Skills

Understanding of Political Environment

Organizational and Management Skills

Knowledge of History of Evaluation

199

HANDOUT 3: Charrette

Explanation

The Charrette procedure is a group method of generating and prioritizing ideas. Each group leader collects ideas from a small group, then takes the list to a different group which adds to, refines, and prioritizes the ideas from the first group. The groups stay put; the leaders and lists move.

Time Needed

Approximately one hour, depending upon the number of topics to be discussed.

Uses

The Charrette may be used to draw up and rank order ideas such as needs, possible solutions, resources, constraints. It is ideal for large groups.

Procedures

1. Divide large group into small groups of six or seven members. Groups may sit in a circle, on both sides of a table, or in facing rows of chairs.

2. Ask each group to select a leader who will record the group's ideas. Give the leader a piece of newsprint and marker. (An easel, table, cardboard backing or other writing surface is needed.). Give out the discussion item. May want to provide an example of what is expected.

3. Allow time for groups to generate five or six responses (about ten minutes--give a warning two minutes before end of time). Call time and tell the leaders to take the responses from their groups and rotate to the next group. Groups may be numbered, or rotation may be clockwise.

4. In the new group, leader briefly reviews information from previous group, adds suggestions from new group, and asks group to prioritize items. Leader keeps list.

5. Group may then select new leader, receive new discussion topic and newsprint, and repeat procedure.

6. If desired, at end of session, each group leader can share top priority with large group. Or leaders can meet together afterward to prioritize.

Analysis.   Results in a separate set of ordinal data for each
small group.   Statistical analyses appropriate for ordinal data
are Spearman's Rho or Kendall's Tau.   An alternative is for group
leaders to meet together afterward, review individual priorities,
and reach consensus.

Strengths.   Large groups actively participate.   Ideas from one
group are built upon by another.   Interest level is high.

Weaknesses.   Because ideas lose their group and individual
identity, it may be difficult to find someone to take the
leadership for following through with the ideas that are
generated.

BACKGROUND READING

Gollattscheck, J.F. & Richburg, J.R. (1981). The Charrette as a
    group decision-making process for community-based
    institutions. Community Services Catalyst, 11(1), 22-25.

Rice, E. (1981). Access to vocational education: A planning
    system for local secondary and post-secondary program and
    facility accessibility: Step 3:   Generating strategies.
    Washington, D.C.:   Office of Vocational and Adult Education.

HANDOUT 4: Focus Groups

Explanation: Focus group interviews are group discussions
centered around a single theme.   Groups are homogeneous, and
there are usually at least three of them.   Discussions are tape-
recorded and carefully analyzed later.

Uses: Originally this was used as a market research tool to
evaluate potential customer response to new products.   Use has
spread to a variety of organizations interested in client
opinions about proposed or ongoing programs.   For example,
potential programs for new clientele can be revised before
expensive mistakes are made.   Intent is not to plan, advise,
vote, or reach a consensus but rather to thoughtfully consider
perceptions and viewpoints.

Procedures: A typical focus group will consist of a minimum of
three different groups, each with eight to ten people who share
some characteristics related to the question.   Over-recruiting is
necessary because of dropouts and some kind of incentive is
offered to participants.   The leader introduces the topic,
explains the need for the tape recorder, and then follows a
predetermined questioning route.   Plenty of time is allowed for
group members to offer insights, ideas, and clarification.
Procedure usually takes less than two hours.

     The leader needs to read suggested procedures carefully and
is advised to observe expert focus group interviewers.   It is
important to pay attention to wording and follow a natural
sequence of questions.

Analysis: After each session, the leader listens to the tape,
consults notes, and prepares a summary.   Summaries of three or
more groups are compared to note items of concern that surface in
more than one group.

Strengths: The breadth and quality of results obtained from
focus group interviews have been impressive.   Ineffective plans
are spotted in time to be revised or eliminated.   The interviews
can provide information in advance as to how participants will
respond to a program.

Limitations: Focus group interviews identify opinions but they
do not indicate the extent of opinions.   Ninety percent of
interviewees holding an opinion does not translate into 90
percent of total population with that same opinion.   Quantified
methods must be used to supplement focus group interviews if
measures of strength of views are needed.   Skills in selection of
participants, question development and sequence, and group
moderating are needed.

22

A QUICK LOOK AT THE NOMINAL GROUP TECHNIQUE

Oliver W. Cummings

Participants in this activity will:

-Learn the six steps in the Nominal Group Technique;

-Identify classes of problems that are amenable to use of NGT; and

-Review alternatives for analyzing and reporting NGT results.

Beaudin and Dowling (1985) reported that about 30 percent of trainers conducting studies of organizational or individual training needs used group discussion as a data collection technique. Further, group discussion frequently is offered as a key needs assessment method (e.g., Cummings, 1984; Cummings and Bramlett, 1984; Cureton, Newton, and Tesolowski, 1986; Newton and Lilyquist, 1979; Steadham, 1980). The group processes that might be used include brainstorming, focus groups, consensus groups, force-field analysis, Nominal Group Technique (NGT), or other currently popular group facilitation approaches.

One of the most popular group approaches is the NGT. Introduced by Delbecq, Van de Ven and Gustafson (1975), and more recently described by Moore (1987), the NGT has been touted as an approach for idea building in needs assessment (e.g., Harrison, Pietri, and Moore, 1983; Scott and Deadrick, 1982). The process is based on a structured approach and uses silent idea generation, structured reporting of ideas within the group, discussion to clarify reported ideas, and prioritizing ideas to develop a product in a short period of time. The product of the process is a rank-ordered listing of ideas produced in the group.

MATERIALS

The process involves capturing and posting ideas for consideration. The materials needed are listed below:

- seating--participants should be close to facilitator and facing each other (see figure 1)
- two flipcharts on easels
- two black markers, two red markers, and two green markers
- one roll of masking tape or push pins (to mount flipchart sheets on the wall)
- 200 3x5 index cards
- problem statement worksheets (enough for one per group member) (see figure 2)
- pencils and notetaking paper (for participants)
- name tents or tags

PROCEDURES

Using the process described here in a combination of lecture, discussion, and participation in a simulated NGT, evaluators can quickly learn this useful technique. The sample problem is appropriate to a hospital setting; however, the process is applicable to other settings. The instructor would simply have to pick a problem suitable to the audience.

When To Use NGT

It is important to match the technique to the problem with which the evaluator is faced. Use the NGT when:

1.   You need to generate many ideas about one question (issue, problem, etc.) in a short period of time.

2.   You need pooled intelligence to generate ideas related to an ill-defined problem.

3.   You want to assure equal opportunity for individual input to the group product and to override barriers of status and/or verbal aggressiveness of individual group members.

4.   You are not interested in team building within the group.

The key advantages of the technique are:

1.   It can be used within groups of varying backgrounds, culture, education, or work roles who share a common goal.

2.   It will guide the group to generate many ideas in a short amount of time.

3.   It enhances maximum and equal participation of each person.

4. It results in a tangible product at the end of the group meeting.

There are also limitations to the NGT process. Key considerations are:

1. NGT is used to <u>generate</u> ideas rather than to develop or design alternatives or to actively contrast and select "most appropriate" ideas.

2. Part of the success of the process is its novelty; it can be overused.

3. It is appropriate for dealing with only one question at a time.

Preparing for the NGT process

The NGT depends for its success on three essential elements:

1. Selection of the right participants.

2. Developing a precise, appropriate stimulus question.

3. Setting up and then following the structure of the process within the group.

<u>Selecting NGT Participants</u>. The participants for an NGT should be knowledgeable about the problem or issue under consideration. If differing points of view are to be considered, representatives of those points of view should be included. Various ranks or classes of people can be grouped together. The nature and scope of the question should dictate how homogeneous the participant group should be.

The size of the group should be from five to twelve participants. With fewer than five participants, the structure of the group is artificial. With more than 12 group members the conduct becomes difficult and too slow from the individual group member's perspective. With larger groups, the group should be split and two sessions run. If this is not possible, then an approach like Phillips 66 group (Phillips, 1948; Van Grundy, 1981, p. 113-114) or consensus group debriefing (Mellon, 1984) should be considered.

<u>Developing the NGT Question</u>. The question should be simply stated, but precise enough to elicit ideas at the appropriate level of detail. The question must be unidimensional; otherwise responses will be ambiguous. The evaluator should try out the proposed question to see if responses obtained are at the expected level.

<u>Materials and Logistical Needs</u>.   See the MATERIALS section of this chapter.

<u>Opening Statement</u>. The opening statement is used to set the tone for the meeting and is an important element in establishing the structure on which the success of the NGT depends. The statement should:

1.   Establish the facilitator's role as the person responsible for timekeeping, process management, and maintaining discipline.

2.   Confirm the participants' role and the importance of their unique perspectives to get their buy-in to the process.

3.   State explicitly the goal of the NGT session, the group's task, and how the results might be used.

4.   Train participants in the NGT process. Brief them in the steps and cover the rules for each step. The rules will be reinforced as each step is begun, as well.

<u>Step 1: Silent Idea Generation</u>. The objective of the first step is for individuals to silently and independently react to the problem statement and to generate possible alternatives. As leader, you pass out worksheets with the problem statement printed at the top and ask group members to respond to the statement using short (less than ten words) written phrases (see figure 2). By discouraging talking or moving around, you can promote an atmosphere for work and reinforce the structure of NGT. Step 1 provides time for members to respond to the problem with their own ideas, resulting in divergent responses. This step usually takes from six to 15 minutes.

<u>Step 2: Reporting of Ideas</u>. Allow each member of the group to share his or her ideas using the following process. First, ask someone to report one written thought. Record the idea, in the person's <u>exact</u> words on a flip chart. Then ask the next person for one idea and repeat the process. Take ideas serially around the table until all members have shared as many as they have to contribute. If anyone chooses to pass, simply go on to the next person. If the person who has passed thinks of another idea later, he or she should be encouraged to state it. (In other words, each time around, the facilitator should call on each person, even if they previously have passed.) When a reported idea stimulates a new idea for another participant, that person is encouraged to 'piggy back' and to report the idea when it is his/her regular turn. When a participant expresses an idea in a paragraph or two, rather than ten words or less, suggest tactfully that the participant think about how to express the idea succinctly and then report it on the next round.

As a leader, you must take care of two details during this step. First, each idea must be labeled with a letter of the alphabet (see exhibit 1). When the alphabet runs out, use double letters, then triple ones. This labeling makes the ranking of solutions easier in the last step. Second, discussion of ideas must be discouraged during this phase. The purpose of serial reporting of ideas is to equalize the opportunity to present ideas, particularly for less verbally aggressive participants. Discussion at this stage may cause certain ideas or people to receive more attention than others.

Step 3: Discussion for Clarification. Provide an opportunity for open discussion and clarification of all the generated ideas. Encourage group members to ask one another the meaning of words and phrases which appear on the posted lists. The discussion can and should convey the meaning, logic, or thought behind an idea. The discussion is not to be used to debate the issue or to argue the worth of an idea, but to clarify its meaning. Worth will be decided in the voting process of steps 4 through 6. Nonproductive discussion should be curtailed. Redundant items can be grouped during discussion (see exhibit 2).

Step 4: Ranking of Problem/Solution Importance (Preliminary Vote). The purpose of this phase is to "total up" the judgments of the group in order to determine the relative importance of the problems or solutions that have been identified. During this step, you distribute to each person five 3x5 cards and ask that each participant record the five items of highest priority from those listed on the flipchart (one selection per card). Have each person write one phrase and the identifying letter(s) on each card (see figure 3). Then ask the group members to identify the item of highest importance and rank it a 5, the next highest in importance a 4, and so on. About halfway through the voting process, remind participants that 5 = MOST IMPORTANT of the five highest priority items and 1 = LOWEST IMPORTANCE of the five. Collect the cards and tally points on a master sheet (see exhibit 3). It is important to note that ranking ideas in this non-threatening, private way makes possible the generation of a group judgment from each individual's judgments.

Step 5: Discussion of Preliminary Vote (Optional). A summary sheet (see exhibit 4) may be helpful in this discussion. During this discussion, participants may discover that their priority rankings were based on misinformation, misunderstanding, or unequal information. The subsequent clarification may produce a more definite consensus.

Step 6: Final Vote (Optional). For the final vote, use the same voting procedure as described in Step 4.

Analyzing the Vote and Reporting Results

When people select the "most important" problems or "best" solutions and then rank-order them, a two-stage voting process is taking place. First, from all the existing statements, the participants pick the most significant ones from their individual perspectives. Therefore, any item that draws a vote must be considered in the interpretation of results. Second, in the ranking, participants prioritize their most significant items. Thus, the intensity of the feeling about the votes should be considered in the interpretation. Table 1 provides a sample reporting format. Each element in this format contributes its unique information to the interpretation of the results.

Many ambiguities may arise in interpreting NGT results. In the example in table 1, for example, overall ranks based on a sum of the individual ranks, which is one accepted scoring method, yields somewhat different results than an overall ranking based on the frequency with which a category was ranked. As is true of many assessment techniques the results of the NGT are made meaningful through the exercise of informed judgment.

DISCUSSION

The NGT is one of several structured, small group approaches that can be used in the evaluation process. It has most often been used in needs assessment to generate categories of potential need and/or alternative solutions to perceived specific problems. The process is based on a set of rules and uses silent idea generation, structured reporting of ideas within the group, discussion to clarify reported ideas and prioritizing ideas to develop a product in a short period of time. The product of the process is a rank ordered listing of ideas produced in the group.

BACKGROUND READING

Beaudin, B.P., & Dowling, W.D. (1985). Data collection methods used to determine training needs in business and industry. Performance and Instructional Journal, 24, 28-30.

Cummings, O.W. (1984). Satisficing: A resource conservationist approach to needs assessment. Chicago P&I, 3, 1-8.

Cummings, O.W., & Bramlett, M.H. (1984). Needs assessment: A maximizing strategy that works for information development. A paper presented at the annual meeting of the Evaluation Network and the Evaluation Research Society, San Francisco, CA.

Cureton, J.H., Newton, A.F., & Tesolowski, D.G. (1986). Finding out what managers need. Training and Development Journal, 40, 106-107.

Delbecq, A.L., Van de Ven, H.A., & Gustafson, D.H. (1975).
    Group techniques for program planning: A guide to Nominal
    Group and Delphi processes. Glenview, IL: Scott-Foresman &
    Company.

Harrison, E.L., Pietri, P.H., & Moore, D.C. (1983). How to use
    Nominal Group Technique to assess training needs.
    Training/HRD, 20, 30-34.

Mellon, C.A. (1984). Group consensus evaluation: A procedure
    for gathering qualitative data. Journal of Instruction
    Development, 7, 18-22.

Moore, C.M. (1987). Group techniques for idea building. Newbury
    Park, CA: Sage Publications.

Newton, J.W., & Lilyquist, J.M. (1979). Selecting needs
    analysis methods. Training and Development Journal, 33, 52-
    56.

Phillips, D.J. (1948). Report on Discussion 66. Adult Education
    Journal, 7, 181-182.

Scott, D., & Deadrick, D. (1982). The Nominal Group Technique:
    Applications for training needs assessment. Training and
    Development Journal, 36, 26-33.

Steadham, S.V. (1980). Learning to select a needs assessment
    strategy. Training and Development Journal, 34, 56-61.

Van Gundy, A.B. (1981). Techniques of structured problem
    solving. New York: Nostrand Reinhold Company.

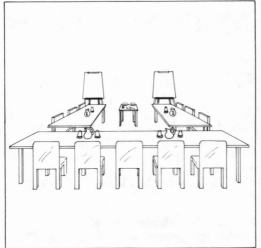

Figure 1. Room Layout

PARTICIPANT WORKSHEET

Problem statement: Specifically, what are the reasons for the lack of intradepartmental coordination at City Hospital?

* Any idea is important!
* Please respond silently and independently.
* Write down as many responses as possible.
* Make statements as short and specific as possible.
* Use specific action verbs such as to define, clarify, develop, complete, indicate, direct, research, etc.
* Try to avoid generalities such as to understand, to know, to be familiar with, etc.

Figure 2. Sample Phase 1 Worksheet

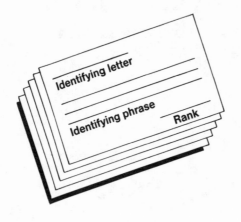

Figure 3. Format for Voting Cards

Identifying letter

Identifying phrase   Rank

Question: _ _ _ _ _ _ _ _ _ _ _ _ _ _ _ _ _ _ _
_ _

Total Vote	Rank of Total Vote	Frequency Category Selected	Rank of Frequency	Individual Rankings	Ideas Generated Within Categories
29	1	9	1	5,5,4,4,4,4,1,1,1	Category 1: — Idea 1: . . — Idea 2: . .
24	2	5	5.5	5,5,5,5,4	Category 2: — Idea 1: . . — Idea 2: . .
20	3	6	4	5,4,4,3,3,1	— Idea 1: . .
17	4	7	2.5	5,3,2,2,2,2,1	Category 4: — Idea 1: . . — Idea 2: . .
15	5	4	7	5,4,4,2	Category 5: — Idea 1: . . — Idea 2: . . — Idea 3: . .
14	6	7	2.5	3,3,3,2,1,1,1	— Idea 1: . .
13	7	5	5.5	4,3,3,2,1	— Idea 1: . .
7	8	3	8	3,2,2	— Idea 1: . .

Table 1
Sample NGT Reporting Format

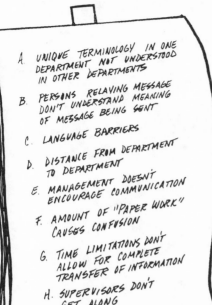

Exhibit 1. Sample of Posted Ideas

A. UNIQUE TERMINOLOGY IN ONE DEPARTMENT NOT UNDERSTOOD IN OTHER DEPARTMENTS

B. PERSONS RELAYING MESSAGE DON'T UNDERSTAND MEANING OF MESSAGE BEING SENT

C. LANGUAGE BARRIERS

D. DISTANCE FROM DEPARTMENT TO DEPARTMENT

E. MANAGEMENT DOESN'T ENCOURAGE COMMUNICATION

F. AMOUNT OF "PAPER WORK" CAUSES CONFUSION

G. TIME LIMITATIONS DON'T ALLOW FOR COMPLETE TRANSFER OF INFORMATION

H. SUPERVISORS DON'T GET ALONG

Exhibit 2. Grouped Ideas

A, B, R, QQ
B
C
D
E, H, TTT, U
F
G
H
I, M, X, K, L, M
J
K
L
M
N
O, BBB, V, UU
P, BB, CC, SS, SSS

Q
R
S
T
U
V
W, Y, EE
X
Y
Z, DD
AA
BB
CC
DD
EE
FF, AAA
GG
HH

Exhibit 3. Sample Voting Tally

A, B, R, QQ   5+4+4+2+2 / 6+2+1+1 = 21
B
C   9+3 = 6
D   2 = 4
E, H, TTT, U   4+3+4+2+2 = 15
F
G   2 = 2
H
I, AA, X, K, L, M   5+4+5+3+ 3=26
J   4 = 4
K
L
M
N
O, BBB, V, UU   3+5+5+5 = 18
P, BB, CC, SS, SSS

Q
R
S   2 = 2
T   5+4+3+3+3+ 2+1+1 = 22
U
V
W, Y, EE   5+4 = 9
X
Y
Z, DD   1+1+1+1 = 4
AA
BB
CC
DD
EE
FF, AAA   5 = 5
GG   1 = 1
HH   4+2+2 = 8

Exhibit 4. Preliminary Vote Results

CATEGORY	TOTAL VOTE
T	22
A, B, R, QQ	21
I, AA, X, K, L, M	26
O, BBB, V UU	18
E, H, TTT, U	15
W, Y, EE	9
HH	8
C	6
FF, AAA	5
Z, DD	4
J	4
D	2
G	2
S	1
GG	1

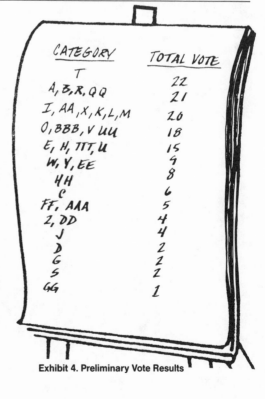

23

DEVELOPING FOCUS GROUP QUESTIONS FOR NEEDS ASSESSMENT

Donna M. Mertens

The concept of needs assessment is explained to students based on McKillip's (1987) **Need Analysis**. Need analysis is a tool for decision making that focuses on making judgments concerning the adequacy of services and the existence of solutions. The steps in need analysis include: (1) identification of users and uses, (2) description of the target population and service environment, (3) needs identification (describing the problems and solutions), (4) needs assessment (evaluating the needs), and (5) communication to decision makers.

One of the techniques that can be used for needs identification is the focus group interview. According to Krueger (1988), "The focus group interview is created to accomplish a specific purpose through a defined process. The process is to obtain information of a qualitative nature from a predetermined and limited number of people" (p. 26). A focus group study consists of conceptualizing the study, developing the questions, conducting the interviews, and analyzing and reporting the results of the data gathered. The activity described here provides students with a "conceptualized study," guidelines for developing questions, and an opportunity to apply those guidelines to a hypothetical study.

MATERIALS

I have developed a handout that describes the basic problem that emanates from the poor performance of deaf students in elementary and high school, and the university's desire to conduct outreach research that can enhance student performance. In order to begin such an outreach program, the university is proposing that a needs assessment be conducted to define the institutional contexts, identify the target population and assess their needs, diagnose problems underlying the needs, and identify ways to overcome barriers to conducting research in the schools.

PROCEDURES

1.   Students should already be aware of the process for planning an evaluation.   I used the model explained by Brinkerhoff, Brethower, Hluchyj, and Nowakowski (1983) to develop the first three steps of the evaluation plan for the hypothetical study.

2.   The conceptual background of needs assessment is explained in class and students are required to read McKillip's (1987) **Need Analysis**.

3.   The basic concepts of focus group interviews are explained. (See the opening discussion and Krueger, 1988.)

4.   The following characteristics of focus group questions are explained (see Krueger, 1988):

a.   Usually focused interviews include less than ten questions and often around five or six total.
b.   Focus group interviews use open-ended questions.   So, instead of asking, "Does your child play at the playground?," ask "Where does your child usually play?"
c.   Avoid asking dichotomous questions that can be answered yes or no.
d.   Avoid using "why" questions.   These questions can set off a defensive reaction by the respondent.   Modify the question, such as "What prompted you to want to participate in the program?"
e.   Carefully develop the questions.   Brainstorming sessions with colleagues or audience members is one way to generate questions.   Many questions can be generated this way and then priorities can be established to determine critical questions.
f.   Establish the context for questions so participants are ready to respond.   Provide enough information in each question so that the participants know where you are coming from.
g.   Questions should be arranged in a logical order, sometimes from general to specific.

5.   Provide the students with examples of focus group interview questions.   Sessions and Yanos (1987) conducted focus group interviews to determine desirable characteristics of a counseling agency.   They asked such questions as:

a.   What qualities would one look for in a counselor?
b.   What type of office setting would be preferable for the provision of counseling services?

c. If a person were seeking counseling, what days or hours
    would be most desirable?
d. What sort of services would be most desired-individual
    counseling, group counseling or family counseling?
e. What other factors should be considered in providing a
    counseling service to persons living in the eastern suburbs?

Krueger (1988) also presents many excellent examples (see
pp. 68-71). The following example is from a study by a
Cooperative State Extension Service that used focus group
interviews to develop a strategic plan:

> "I'd like each of you to take a few moments and fill out
> this list. (Pass out page). I've listed several categories
> of problems or issues that may affect you and others in your
> community. The categories include the following:
> work/business, family, leisure, community, and environment.
> Take a moment and jot down what you think to be the most
> important issues in each of these categories...Which of the
> issues that you mentioned on your list could be solved or
> lessened by education or information" (p. 70)?

6. Students are then given the attached handouts and asked
to brainstorm questions for the focus group interviews that are
described in the plan for the hypothetical study. If you have a
large class, this can be done in small groups of five or six
students. As you review the plan for the evaluation, be sure
that the students understand that the focus group techniques will
only be used to get answers to questions 3 and 4. As group
facilitator, the instructor can identify areas that have not been
addressed by their questions and can prompt students to think of
ways to use the "reflective" format for questions exemplified in
Krueger (1988, p. 70).

7. The students' plans are discussed in class, and their
ideas are synthesized. A draft of the questions can then be used
to discuss the next steps, such as preparing the introductory
comments. They can also be used as a basis for role playing a
focus group.

DISCUSSION

This activity provides a good opportunity for the students to
apply principles of developing focus group interview questions
within the context of needs assessment. In addition, it allows
them an opportunity to integrate their planning skills with the
concept of needs assessment.

BACKGROUND READING

Brinkerhoff, R.O., Brethower, D.M., Hluchyj, T., & Nowakowski, J.
    (1983). <u>Program evaluation</u>. Boston, MA: Kluwer-Nijhoff

216

Publishing.

Krueger, R.A.   (1988).   <u>Focus groups</u>.   Newbury Park, CA: Sage.

McKillip, J.   (1987).   <u>Needs analysis</u>.   Beverly Hills, CA: Sage.

Sessions, J.T. & Yanos, J.H.   (1987).   Desirable characteristics
   of a counseling agency.   Paper presented at the 1987 annual
   meeting of the American Evaluation Association, Boston, MA.

HANDOUT 1:   Research for Teachers of Deaf Students

Product 1:   Evaluation Preview

Object of the Evaluation.   The object of the evaluation consists of the needs of teachers of deaf students for research findings that will improve the students' learning and social development at the elementary and secondary levels.   School systems will include the greater metropolitan area and surrounding counties. Types of needs that could be identified include: the teaching process, teaching content, regular education students interacting with special education students, social and cognitive effects of mainstreaming, teachers' skill levels in teaching deaf students, self-concept, and memory processes.

Purpose.   The overall purposes for the needs assessment are to define institutional contexts, to identify the target population and assess their needs, to identify opportunities for addressing the needs, to diagnose problems underlying the needs, and to judge whether proposed objectives are sufficiently responsive to the assessed needs.

The specific purposes of the evaluation are:

1.   To build a network of teachers in the area who are interested in participating in research.
2.   To provide a basis for a realistic research agenda that will conform to the needs that the teachers have and to the faculty-researchers' expertise.
3.   To be responsive to the university's mission to serve the deaf community and to expand the amount of research done in deafness.

The results of the needs assessment will be used as justification for research proposals that will be written to outside funding agencies.

Audiences.   Principal investigators, administrators and teachers in the city and in surrounding counties will be important audiences.

Constraints.   The needs assessment will begin in October, data will be collected by May, and the final report and proposals will be finished by August.

Product 2: Evaluation Questions

1. What needs are suggested by the literature regarding the academic and social functioning of deaf students?

2. What needs are suggested by a social indicator analysis?
    a. What are the demographic characteristics of the students and teachers in the specified geographical area?
    b. What measurement data are already available regarding academic and social functioning of the students and teacher training in teaching deaf students?

3. What needs do teachers and administrators in the greater metropolitan area and surrounding counties express that could be addressed by research?
    a. Are the teachers and administrators in agreement?
    b. Are the needs different at the elementary and secondary levels?
    c. What training have teachers had in teaching deaf students?
    d. Would teachers be interested in participating in research that deals with:

        - cognitive learning processes?
        - facilitating social interaction between deaf and hearing students?
        - self-concept enhancement?
        - computer assisted instruction?
        - improved memory processes?

4. How can barriers to conducting research in the schools be minimized?
    a. How can the researchers conduct the research for the maximum benefit for teachers and students?
    b. At what level are teachers using research results in their teaching?
    c. What other research services are available in the schools?

Product 3: Data Collection Plan

Information Collection Procedure	Evaluation Question Answered	Schedule	Respondent (Sample)	Instrument Used
Interview with administra- tors	4c	Fall	All admini- strators	Resource Inventory Semi- structured interviews
	3,3a & b	Fall		
Social Indicator Analysis				
-Target Population Analysis	2a	Fall	All schools with deaf students	Frequency of admin., teachers, & students
-Risk Factor Analysis	2b	Fall Spring	All schools with deaf	Test scores; Teacher training
Focus Groups	3a - d 4a & b	Spring Spring	Volunteer teachers (50)	Semi- structured group interviews
Literature Review	1	Fall	ERIC & ECER	Theo- retical framework

IV PROPOSAL WRITING

24

PROPOSAL WRITING IN EARLY CHILDHOOD SPECIAL EDUCATION

Terry R. Berkeley

Students are required to respond to a Request for Proposals (RFP) to establish an innovative program in early childhood special education. Two aspects of the proposal focus on program evaluation: (1) a description of early intervention efficacy research; and (2) a program evaluation plan, including a program evaluation matrix of the program being proposed. The proposal submitted at the end of the semester is the final course requirement.

This particular requirement was developed because many students graduating from master's degree programs find themselves having dual responsibilities in teaching and program development and serving as administrators/coordinators of program efforts. Thus, it was felt that a course focusing on all components of a program (e.g., administration and management to working with advisory councils) would be helpful in meeting those employment demands, and this could be accomplished through the submission of a proposal under simulated conditions.

MATERIALS

Students are provided with the regulations accompanying Public Law 91-230, Amendments to the Education of the Handicapped Act of 1970, Section 623 of Part C, Handicapped Children's Early Education Program; an RFP packet (see Handout 1); and a copy of MOBIUS's Child Count Data in Special Education software. This software was published in 1985 by the Mobius Corporation, Alexandria, Virginia. It includes data on the number of handicapped children receiving special education and related services by age, by handicapping condition, by state, and on a national basis in programs whose legislative authority is either Public Law 94-142, the Education for All Handicapped Children Act of 1975 or Public Law 89-313 (1968) Title I, Section 103 (a) (5) State Operated Programs for Handicapped Children. The software is for use on IBM or IBM-clone personal computers using PC-DOS and MS-DOS. The data base requires 322,000 bytes. Recent contact with Mobius Corporation revealed the program is now in the public domain. In addition, proposals that have been successfully funded by the Handicapped Children's Early Education Program (under the direction of the Office of Special Education and Rehabilitative Services, U.S. Department of Education) are used as models. Each state has had several projects funded by this program, thus proposals are available from those organizations.

PROCEDURES

Students respond to the RFP in order to design an innovative program for young children from birth to eight years of age (any combination of ages derived from those ages is appropriate) and their families. A rationale for the program, a statement of need, staffing patterns (including job descriptions and performance appraisal methods), specification of program components, goals and objectives of the services delivery components of the program, the innovative aspect(s) of the program, the population of children and families to be served (including eligibility criteria), a statement of program philosophy and theories of development upon which the program is based, the program evaluation plan (including formative, summative and process designs), demonstration and dissemination activities, advisory board functions, prevention efforts, transition agreements with other agencies, including the schools, and transition plans and community liaison endeavors are all required in the proposal and are specified in the RFP. The students also must explain the geographic locale of the proposed project and detail urban, suburban and rural differences presented in those locales, and how the differences are reflected in the program.

Students work under simulated conditions. That is, the instructor of the course acts as the state director of early childhood special education services and students take on the role of prospective project directors working in a local agency requiring funds to begin a new program with a start-up budget of between $65,000 and $100,000 for the first project year. The RFP specifies the details of the technical assistance that is available from the state director of early childhood special education during the proposal preparation process.

DISCUSSION

In order for the simulation to run smoothly, the instructor must be willing to assist students in understanding the demographics associated with early childhood special education, how to use the

MOBIUS software program on special education child count data, and to read drafts of student proposals. This assures that students, who are usually unfamiliar with grants procedures, have the maximum opportunity to succeed with their work. Additionally, the instructor must be willing to meet with students to provide technical assistance to them as is the case when applicants are applying for funding from state or federal agencies. The result of this level of involvement has been quite positive in terms of the degree of innovation students have displayed, the quality of the writing of the proposals, and the ability of the students to demonstrate the utility of program evaluation in their efforts. In two instances, as well, students were successful in obtaining state and local support for new programs for young children with special needs and their families. In short, this is a labor intensive exercise for students and the instructor.

BACKGROUND READINGS

Berkeley, R., & Parkhurst, S. (1987). The utilization of process evaluation data: A conceptual itinerary based upon an examination of an early intervention program. Paper presented at the annual meeting of the American Evaluation Association, Boston, MA.

Bronfenbrenner, U. (1979). The ecology of human development. Cambridge, MA: Harvard University Press.

Fewell, R., & Vadasy, P. (1986). Families of handicapped children: Needs and supports across the lifespan. Austin, TX: Pro-Ed.

Linder, Toni. (1983). Early childhood special education: Program development and administration. Baltimore: Brookes.

Murphy, Jerome. (1980). Getting the facts. Santa Monica, CA: Goodyear.

Journals

Early Childhood: A Journal of the Division of Early Childhood.

Education Evaluation and Policy Analysis.

Evaluation Practice.

New Directions for Program Evaluation.

Topics in Early Childhood Special Education.

HANDOUT 1:   Request for Proposals

The State Director of Services for Young Handicapped Children and Families is announcing the availability of funds for demonstration projects to support innovative efforts that will provide comprehensive services to young handicapped children from birth to eight years of age (or any combination thereof) and their families. Funds to support these efforts were appropriated for the first time in June 1984. Priority areas for funding include: birth to three years of age, the at-risk (high risk) population, delivery systems in rural areas, and urban inner city services.   Thus, applicants must focus their attention on proposed efforts in at least one of these areas.

Proposals are due no later than 4:40 P.M., December 9, 1988. Proposals submitted after that time will not be accepted or considered under any circumstances.

Proposals submitted for consideration will adhere to regulations attached to this Request for Proposals in the following form:

1.   Technical Section. A separate document fully describing rationale, research, and theoretical underpinnings of the proposed effort, the local need for services to the group of children and families addressed in the proposal, description of the geographical area (demographics), description of the services presently being offered to the target population in the specific geographical area covered by the proposal, previous experience of the submitting agency, subsections detailing an administration and management plan, assessment activities, services to children, services to families, an advisory council, program evaluation plan, including formative, summative, and process, letters of support and other documentation considered to be important to support the proposed effort.

2.   Budget Section.   A separate document providing a detailed listing of the proposed expenses for the first year of the proposed efforts' operation, justification for expenses, and any additional supporting documentation to assist reviewers in understanding the nature of the budget.   There must also be a subsection of this document describing where continuation support will come from after state financial support terminates at the end of the second year of operation.

Proposals must be typed, double-spaced, and references, citations, etc. shall conform to the convention specified in the Publication Manual of the American Psychological Association, third edition.   Proposals must be submitted in duplicate to the State Director of Services to Young Handicapped Children and Families.   A cover letter must accompany the proposal specifying what the proposal is about, the amount of financial support being requested, the agency submitting the proposal and the primary contact person and that individual's home telephone number so that any questions arising during the review of the proposal can be resolved. The following schedule must be adhered to:

1.   September 30, 1988. Proposal outlines, partial bibliographies, and three minute pre-proposal presentations. The outline and bibliography must be typed and double-spaced.

2.   November 11, 1988. Proposal Program Evaluation Plan (draft) must be brought to a meeting of the applicants for discussion. This must include a draft of the evaluation matrix specifying: evaluation questions, sources of data, data collection methods, type of data analysis required, and when the data will be gathered. Also, applicants must submit a draft of their "transaction-antecedent-outcome" matrix that details the prospective process evaluation format.

3.   November 18, 1988. Proposal draft is due. This is not an optional requirement. The draft must be typewritten, double-spaced and include a complete reference list.

4.   December 9, 1988. Completed proposals must be submitted no later than 4:30 p.m. at the Office of the State Director.

The proposals to be submitted are in competition for grant awards of monies to support innovative endeavors in the area of early childhood special education. Proposed efforts are to be developmentally appropriate and the use of any child and family developmental theory or combination of theories must be appropriate to the age ranges of children to be served, as well as being appropriate for the families of those children. In addition, the developmental foundations must be explained in terms of program design, eligibility criteria, curricula base, and assessment procedures.

Assistance to applicants is available by telephone from the state director at 999-9999 during the day and at 888-8888 until 8:30 in the evenings. No calls will be accepted on weekends or holidays. Applicants are encouraged to see the state director by appointment on all issues related to an individual's proposal.

The state director reserves the right to award as many grants that meet the designated criteria of clarity, need, originality, innovativeness, and depth as are submitted. Also, there is no guarantee that any grants will be awarded if they are not successfully proposed. The maximum award will be at the level of $100,000 for the first year of support. The minimum award will be $65,000. Budgets should reflect a split between personnel and non-personnel items at 50 percent to 70 percent for the former and 30 percent to 50 percent for the latter. Personnel includes: salaries, fringes at 10 percent of salaries, and consultants. Non-personnel items include: equipment, materials, rent, telephone, postage, reproduction, computer time, food, staff development (no greater than $350 per staff member per annum), utilities, transportation, staff travel ($0.21 per mile), and insurance. Each applicant should provide a minimum of 20 percent matching dollars as a good faith contribution toward the continuation of the proposed effort after the termination of state financial support.

Eligible applicants include non-profit organizations engaged in human service efforts to handicapped and at-risk citizens, local school districts, colleges/universities, as well as public and private hospitals. Each applicant must adhere to the standards set forth in the Sections 502, 503 and 504 of the Rehabilitation Act of 1973 regarding issues of discrimination against the handicapped, removal of architectural barriers and civil rights of handicapped people. Each applicant must go beyond the parameters of Public Law 94-142, the Education for All Handicapped Children Act of 1975, Act 754, and the Public Law 91-230, Part C. This means that any child whose handicapping condition is not clearly identifiable as specified in any federal or state standards or regulations may be accepted into a program, e.g. the at-risk population. It is the intent of this competition to develop services at the highest level of quality that can be successfully replicated. Each applicant must submit a set of statements specifying their understanding and adherence to the provisions of the Rehabilitation Act of 1973. Also, a set of statements must be submitted by an applicant that assures that the civil rights of any individual are not abridged in any manner as a result of religion, ethnicity, sex, creed, race, sexual preference, or any other reason.

Applicants are encouraged to discuss their ideas about their proposal with individuals currently providing services to handicapped citizens and their families. The use of the materials and information provided by these "experts" must be acknowledged in the proposal. Individuals serving in these capacities can be obtained from the state director. Also, applicants are expected to conform to the tenets of normalization espoused by Wolf Wolfensberger and his adherents. Both the utilization of experts and the consideration of normalization will assist in assuring the highest quality of effort possible on behalf of individuals who happen to be developmentally disabled.

25

RESPONDING TO AN INFORMAL REQUEST TO EVALUATE:
WRITING A PROPOSAL

Elizabethann O'Sullivan

Agency personnel often approach evaluators to conduct a study.
If the agency is not required to solicit competitive bids, it may
not issue a request for proposal (RFP).   Still, the evaluator
needs to communicate what work will be done, when, and at what
cost.   The evaluator, based on his or her idea of what is
important, writes a proposal for agency review, comment, and
authorization.

     This exercise requires students to develop proposals in
response to informal agency requests. The instructor may use the
exercise to emphasize any of the following points:

1. what trade-offs occur between money or time, and what the
   research methodology is;
2. how to present a proposal, what its content and layout are;
3. what program features to emphasize, e.g.,
   effectiveness, efficiency;
4. how to apply methodological concepts appropriately
   and communicate them effectively.

MATERIALS

1. Comments on proposal writing (Handout 1)

2. Sample RFPs and proposals (optional)

3. Case Study (Handout 2)

PROCEDURES

1. Background Information Needed

The case study involves a research question to which most students can respond. Students with course work in research methods should be able to select a reasonable methodology with little difficulty. The initial questions raised by the exercise should concern the logistics of presenting a proposal: what to include? how to include it? how much detail to include?

Published details on how to prepare a proposal are sparse. Sample RFPs, responses to RFPs, material on proposal writing such as Weidman's (1977) article, cited in the readings, work well to fill in the gap. Appropriate examples may be gathered from local agency contacts. Alternatively, instructors may contact the author for exemplary proposals. Handout 1 summarizes briefly the general content of proposals, but reviewing actual examples should improve the students' proposals.

The exercise works best after the class has covered material on different evaluation approaches and how they vary by client needs (similar to Handout 1 or Rossi and Freeman's chapter 2).

2. Initiating the Exercise

Handout 1 and any exemplary materials should be discussed briefly in class. Comment on both the content of a proposal and its format. Encourage students to incorporate their own ideas of what would make a clear and attractive proposal.

Assign the case study and first four questions (see Handout 2) as homework. Ask students to make copies of their answers to share with their teammates. The questions ask each student to develop his or her ideas of what should be included; during the in-class portion of the exercise the individual ideas will be integrated into draft proposals. Combining individual and team efforts increases the efficiency of the exercise. More important, it demonstrates the value of individual contributions and the need for group interaction to develop a sound proposal.

3. Organizing to Draft the Proposal

Assign teams to answers questions 5 and 6. The availability of copies of the individual answers to question 2 should speed up the drafting of the methodological section and improve its presentation.

4. Outlining the Proposal

The class as a whole or the individual teams should agree on an outline for the proposal. The goal of outlining is to come up with a strategy that leads to a logical, well-organized proposal. A proposal writer has a wide degree of latitude in deciding on an outline. A lengthy discussion is unnecessary since several alternatives will work equally well.

The discussion of the content should identify elements that are critical to a proposal (methodology--data collection strategy, sample design and size, types of measures; budget; schedule). Avoid letting students read too much into the case study. It is based on an actual case, and the level of detail approximates what was known by the evaluator. Assuming conditions far beyond those indicated can lead to a proposal that is inappropriate for an agency's resources, interests or its constituent relationships. Extensive debate on content may be postponed until the proposal is drafted.

5. Drafting the proposal

Give the teams a time limit to work through question 5. Leave five to ten minutes at the end for each group to organize an oral presentation (question 6) of its proposal. Instruct the groups to budget their time so that all elements of the proposal are covered. Let them know that some elements of the proposal may be less well developed and more tentative.

6. Oral Presentation of the Proposal

Point out to the class that good listening and questioning skills are as important in one's professional development as good presentation skills. Furthermore, preparing with a "dry run" before one's peers is common.

Ask one team to act as presenters and to present its proposal orally. The others are to take on the role of agency personnel, and raise questions and comments. The goal of the listeners is to make sure that the evaluation team has the best possible proposal. Through their questions they prepare the evaluators to improve their presentation and to answer questions effectively.

The initial questioning should center on the methodology: Is it feasible given the time and budget constraints? Will it answer the agency's questions? Have limitations that will affect interpretation of the findings been discussed? Have alternative methodologies been considered? Should alternative methodologies be included in the proposal?

Questions on the budget and activities should ask: Are they adequate to carry out the planned study? Do they seem reasonable? Does the probable information from the study justify its cost?

　　　To conclude the exercise the class should decide what changes to make in the proposal, how to improve the oral presentation, and what the written proposal should look like.

7.　Possible Approaches

The actual proposal focused on the first year to avoid assuming the evaluation needs of a program that had not started. The first year study documented program operations with data collected on client characteristics and services offered. The staff and evaluators determined what data to collect. After the program's first quarter a report was written from the initial data collection. Based on staff reaction, the data collection and reporting were further modified.

　　　The proposal noted problems in assessing program effectiveness. First, start-up problems may lessen a program's initial effectiveness. Second, evidence of community benefits should be interpreted cautiously; for example, an improvement in one community might be offset by deterioration in a neighboring community. The proposal suggested that the evaluators would study effectiveness by differentiating between "successful" and "unsuccessful" clients. The proposal also called for efficiency measures to determine service costs and to link costs with client outcomes.

DISCUSSION

This exercise balances the practical issues of evaluation against the methodological concerns. Focusing discussion of the oral presentation on methodological issues will be most worthwhile. Writing a proposal is a valuable and necessary skill, but it also requires students to recognize the trade offs in conducting applied research and to communicate ideas clearly.

　　　Teams of four or five students work best. Random assignment of team members usually yields interesting discussions and presentations. Alternatively, teams may be formed to maximize class diversity. The hardest part of the exercise is getting the "listeners" to question effectively. Having each team work on the same case study lessens this reluctance.

BACKGROUND READING

Rossi, P. H., & Freeman, H.E. (1985) Evaluation: A systematic approach. Beverly Hills: Sage Publications.

Weidman, D.R. (1977). Writing a better RFP: Ten hints for obtaining more successful evaluation studies. Public Administration Review, (November/December), 714-717.

233

HANDOUT 1:   Comments on Proposal Writing

Evaluators write a proposal to communicate and record their plans for conducting a program evaluation.   Normally, a proposal delineates the roles and responsibilities of both the evaluators and agency and details time schedules and budget needs.   The specific content of the proposal, including the order and detail of its content, depend on the needs and interests of the agency. The following are commonly found:

o   Problem statement
o   Objectives of evaluation
o   Methodology
    . Data collection strategy
    . Sample design and size
    . Types of measures
o   Evaluation products
o   Budget
o   Schedule.

Remember that the proposal may be reviewed by a variety of personnel with different levels of interest in the project. Thus, the format should be concise, attractive, and easy to follow.   An article (Weidman, 1977)* on how to write a request for proposal (RFP) has suggestions on how to avoid evaluations that do not meet agency expectations or that get bogged down on irrelevant or controversial issues.   Included among the suggestions are the following:

-Important constraints, such as limitations or expectations for
    methods of data collection or analysis, should be explicit.
-Quantitative analysis should be limited to available (or
    obtainable) and reliable data.
-Opinions should be measured only if the program was intended to
    change opinions.
-Observations based on data analysis and the evaluators' judgment
    should be clearly differentiated.
-At least one measure of program accomplishment should be
    included.
-The number of questions the evaluation is meant to answer should
    be limited.
-Frequent informal progress reports are preferable to formal
    written reports.

----
*Weidman, D.R.   (1977).   Writing a better RFP: Ten hints for
    obtaining more successful evaluation studies.   Public
    Administration Review,   (November/December), 714-717.

HANDOUT 2:   Case Study: A Youth Services Project

The Wood County Commissioners have funded a two year demonstration project, Forest Youth Services (FYS), to provide comprehensive services to juvenile offenders in the Forest Community. FYS will coordinate services to meet clients' academic, social, and emotional needs. FYS is funded for two years; at the end of the second year the commissioners want it evaluated.

Kevin Hall directs FYS. He is a trained social worker who has worked at Juvenile Court. He plans to hire a secretary and a social worker and to contract with individuals or groups for all other services.

Hall calls you his second week on the job. He wants to plan for the evaluation now before the program begins. He knows that your expertise is in applied research and evaluation not in children's services.   (He has spoken to local experts in children's services and feels that they are more interested in program development than in evaluation.)

You meet with Hall. You learn that he has $4,000 budgeted for evaluation in the first year; additional money budgeted for training and computer consultation may also fund evaluation activities. His immediate interest is to develop a data base. He has ordered a computer; however, he has virtually no computer experience.

The specific details of the program are vague. He has not yet solicited referrals, and services will be tailored around individual client needs.   He estimates an active client population of roughly 40 youths and their families.

He gives you the report that led to the development of FYS. The report documents the lack of services available to youths, inadequate use of services by troubled adolescents, and poor integration of services offered to youths and their families.

He has prepared some documents for your review. They are summarized below.

FYS--Overview

FYS recognizes that the needs of individual clients are unique, wide ranging and vary over time. Therefore, the system must be flexible. The service needs of a client, an individual, or family will be defined through an interagency process on an individual client basis. Services may include skills development, structured recreational activities, and academic tutoring. Services should be delivered in the community and involve the family as much as possible.

Goals and Objectives.

Goal. The aim of the project is to reduce the incidence of juvenile crime within the target population through a coordinated system of prevention and intervention programs.

Objectives. The program's objectives are as follows:

.to deliver services in one central community based location

.to reduce the number of repeat offenses from youths in the target population

.to facilitate linkages and referrals identified in individual service plans

.to identify and document service gaps in the community.

Evaluation Questions

Has the incidence of juvenile crime within the target population been reduced? If so, to what extent can the change be attributed to the program?

What was the full cost of the results obtained?

Were certain parts of the program more or less effective than others?

What kinds of students benefitted most or least from the program?

Service Flowchart

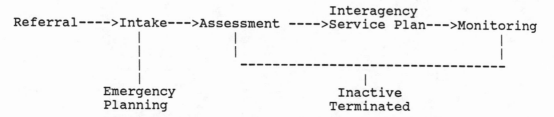

Hall tells you that he wants to contract with you to do the evaluation and related work. He wants you to write a proposal that he can discuss with his board of directors. You tell Hall that you can prepare a draft proposal for his review within the week.

1. Outline the components of your proposal

    a. What will be its major categories?
    b. How will they be ordered?

2. Write a rough draft of the sections of your proposal that cover the research plan, e.g., the measures, data collection strategy, sample, and so forth.

3. List the activities required to conduct the study.

4. List the items that should be included in the budget.

Work with your classmates to:

5. Develop a rough draft of your written proposal, including a time schedule, budget, and list of "deliverables," e.g., reports.

6. Hall calls you and asks you to make a presentation of your proposal to the board, prepare a "dry run" of your presentation.

V PERSONNEL
EVALUATION

26

A HANDS-ON EXPERIENCE IN CLINICAL SUPERVISION

Joseph P. Caliguri

Included in the quest to pursue better ways to evaluate the
classroom performance of teachers is the clinical supervision
model.   Its basic strategy is to use classroom observation
techniques to provide teachers with objective feedback on their
instructional performance.   This guide presents information about
hands-on experience in a required clinical supervision course for
education administration degree students.

A "nuts-and-bolts," knowledge-based text familiarizes
graduate students with a seven-step planning process through
which the supervisor and the teacher collaborate on deciding what
will be observed and evaluated.   The seven steps are listed on
Handout 1.   A text array of observational techniques are then
reviewed to select one to fit with the teacher's concerns.
Classroom observation techniques that are explained in the text
include: selective verbatim, at task, verbal flow, movement
patterns, anecdotal records, and video and audio recording.
After the classroom observation session is scheduled, a nine-step
feedback conference is arranged in which the supervisor presents
the analysis of data from the selected observational technique
(see Handout 1).

Arrangements for the hands-on experience are scheduled early
in the course by the graduate students with volunteer colleagues
in their own schools or organization.   Direct involvement allows
students to gain initial seasoning in collaborative planning, use
of classroom observational techniques, and feedback of data based
results.

A review of clinical supervision reports over time indicates
consistently high valuing by students for promoting collaborative
roles and generating of trust in supervisor/teacher

relationships. Several of the observational techniques can be used in any organization that has a teaching function. The clinical supervision approach can facilitate decisions for professional growth or can be used as a contribution to a systematic teacher evaluation system devised for managerial decisions.

MATERIALS

Handout 1 outlines the planning and feedback conference steps. Included are questions and answers concerning clinical supervision.

PROCEDURES

1. Read the text chapters on clinical supervision process and clinical supervision techniques.

2. Study an actual clinical supervision project provided by the instructor.

3. Conduct a class session to review text and project material (see Concept section).

4. Include in the review session the following guidelines for recruiting volunteer teachers for the clinical supervision hands-on project:

a. Students should contact teachers they have access to and explain clearly the purposes of the course assignment. Secure agreement with at least two volunteer teachers.

b. Set up a time frame at the convenience of the volunteers to initiate the planning conference and to allay any fear that they will be personally identified in the project report for the course assignment or that the results will be submitted to their superiors.

c. Conduct the observations.

d. The feedback conference should be conducted as soon as possible after the planning conference and observation schedules have been completed.

e. Type the report and submit it to the instructor.

f. At the appropriate time, the instructor can conduct class sessions to critique the progress of hands-on projects. In small classes, the instructor can schedule one to one conferences with students to critique the progress of the hands-on experience.

g. The hands-on clinical supervision projects as a class
    assignment can be tailored by the instructor to meet the
    needs of particular class participants. The course time
    frames and number of projects for this assignment can vary
    depending on class size and characteristics and the way the
    instructor desires to use the material. Students can be
    encouraged to continue improving their competencies on their
    own after the course is completed.

BACKGROUND READING

Acheson, Keith A., & Gall, Meredith Damien. (1987). Techniques in
    the clinical supervision of teachers. New York: Longman,
    Inc.

Tanner, Daniel, & Tanner, Laurel. (1987). Supervision in
    education. New York: Macmillan Publishing Co.

HANDOUT 1: Clinical Supervision

Purpose

When you begin working with a teacher using the cycle presented in this program, the first phase is a <u>planning conference</u>. Because you need to know various observation techniques for this step, you became familiar with the observational techniques first. In the planning conference, both you and the teacher contribute information and ideas to figure out what you ought to look at in the observation, how you can record what happens, when you should observe, and what the two of you will do with the results.

Constraints

It is important to be realistic about the number of contacts that you can have with a particular teacher. If your schedule limits you to two sessions per month, for example, your planning cannot include a cycle in which your observation and discussions would be needed for three consecutive days. The kinds and intervals of participation that are feasible should be understood by both the supervisor and the teacher before making plans.

Getting Started

How do you find out what to look at? One of the ways is to use the techniques explained in this lesson. "Translate abstract concepts into observable behaviors." That's particularly useful when the teacher has discovered a problem or identified a concern on his/her own. In your early contacts with a teacher, however, you may want to limit your attention to concrete behaviors. After a few observations, both you and the teacher will be able to explore together even complex abstractions and devise observational methods for collecting pertinent information.

Elements of the Planning Conference

The supervisor will conduct a conference in which the teacher will:

A.   Describe the lesson to be observed.

B.   Describe what he/she will be doing during the lesson.

C.   Describe expected student behaviors.

D.   Predict problems, rough spots, weak points, concerns, etc.

E.   Agree upon the observer's role (what will be observed and what data will be collected).

F. Ask the teacher to state the lesson objectives, strategies, and techniques.*

G. Arrange the classroom observation time.

Getting the teacher to describe the lesson objectives (student outcomes), the options among two or more teaching strategies, and plans for using specific techniques that make up a strategy will help him/her be clear on what he/she intends to do and will also give ideas on what you can plan to observe. Once the teacher states what the students are to learn from the lesson, he/she has the basis for deciding what instructional approaches will aid that learning.

Read the following typescript of a conference held prior to a poetry lesson:

T: My objectives for today are to get the students to develop criteria for evaluating poetry.

S: How will you achieve that?

T: They will analyze these five poems in small groups.

S: How will you form the groups?

T: I have evaluated the students each time we've worked on poetry and I have formed the groups based on their previous success--more or less homogeneously, I guess.

S: What kind of guidelines or directions will you provide?

T: I decided not to use discussion guides. The students will have a definite task that should provide enough direction. The task is that they must develop a list of criteria for evaluating poems.

----
* A strategy in this course is an overall approach to an instructional session. A technique is a specific behavior or instructional session. A technique is a specific behavior or skill that the teacher performs while implementing the strategy. In football, a pass play or a running play is a strategy; blocking, running, tackling, and throwing are skills or techniques.

The supervisor has in mind a number of questions which he/she will continue to pursue with the teacher in order that both fully understand the proposed strategy and activity.

1.   Why did he/she select a small group approach?

2.   What instructions will be given orally?

3.   Will the less competent groups complete the task?

4.   How will the groups differ in their handling of the problem?

The Feedback Conference

Importance.   The feedback conference is a part of the cycle that requires the fullest use of the supervisor's understanding of himself/herself, of communications skills, and of professional expertise.   For many, it is a sticky situation.   Consider the realities of the supervisor's job...

Constraints.   Most supervisors have teaching schedules and other responsibilities in addition to the supervision assignment and, as a result, have less time than they'd like to spend with each teacher.   Even if one wanted to be the ultimate authority figure, telling every teacher what's wrong and how to fix it, he/she couldn't find enough time to maintain that role.   And teachers recognize easily that the supervisor who says, "I wouldn't do it that way," may not have to walk into the classroom and demonstrate that his/her way works.   So the risks, the exposure, and the mistakes are the teacher's, while the supervisor watches and waits for the opportunity to tell him/her what he/she did wrong.

Objectives.   As you face these realities, there are two factors to consider: your limited time and the most constructive use of it to encourage the development of the teacher's skills.   Part of the task of the supervisor is to help the teacher to become self-analytical and self-directed instead of being dependent upon another's evaluation of his/her daily instruction.   If self-direction and self-analysis can be agreed upon as goals early in the interaction between teacher and supervisor, this will help to clarify the role of each.   The supervisor uses objective information, elicits views and feelings from the teacher, asks clarifying questions, and maintains an attitude that communicates that the teacher is an intelligent professional capable of analysis and decision making.   The teacher then is freed to analyze, interpret, and make decisions.

Elements of the Feedback Conference

The supervisor will:

-Provide the teacher with persuasive data
-Elicit feelings, inferences, and opinions.
-Ask clarifying questions
-Listen more and talk less
-Acknowledge, paraphrase, and expand the teacher's statements
-Avoid giving direct advice
-Provide specific praise for performance and growth
-Provide opportunities for practice and comparison
-Elicit alternative techniques and explanations.

Format. The format for the feedback conference emerges naturally from the normal sequence of planning, observing, and communicating. The supervisor shares the data collected, the teacher analyzes it, and both work to interpret the conclusions of the analysis in order to construct subsequent goals and procedures.

Opening the session is quite easy when the teacher knows exactly what the supervisor has been doing in the classroom. The poetry teacher in the previous example is likely to come in and ask, "How did the kids in those two groups work today?"

You answer, "Here's the chart that shows what each contributed," or "Let's listen to the tape and see." Notice how neatly the supervisor has avoided the analysis and evaluation that he/she wants the teacher to perform. Even though the supervisor has had time to review and analyze the data, he/she is not drawing inferences and stating conclusions. If he/she said, "Let's listen to the audiotape and see whether you might want to work with a few students more intensively," he/she would be controlling his/her listening--minimizing the teacher's analytical ability.

Technique. The teacher must be provided with objective observational data. Providing the teacher with these data is a technique that demands not only the data's presentation ("Here's the chart...") but also the obligation to return continually to the data for clarification, explanation, and additional points for discussion. In our ideal world, no supervisor would leave objective data in a notebook while conducting a subjective, non-data based conference.

A characteristic of a conference in which objective data are being used is that the teacher and the supervisor will be talking about the data rather than talking about each other. This is not to say that the supervisor will never offer an opinion, but it does mean that he/she will not start by stating a conclusion or drawing an inference. There will be times, while a supervisor is presenting data, that a teacher will ask for an opinion or a conclusion.

Overview of Clinical Supervision

Q: What is clinical supervision?

A: A systematic and carefully planned program of supervising a teacher, to assist the teacher to grow professionally. Typically, the clinical supervision process incorporates several cycles of pre-observation conference, observation, analysis of observational data, feedback conference, and evaluation of the cycle.

Q: How many cycles are considered necessary?

A: The answer depends on the teacher's needs. While the issue has not been carefully researched, experience suggests that a minimum of five cycles is required to effect major improvement.

Q: Which teachers can profit from clinical supervision?

A: All teachers can profit from clinical supervision periodically in their careers. New teachers and teachers experiencing special problems in the classroom need it most of all.

Q: Who can provide clinical supervision?

A: It is best provided by someone who has had training and experience in the skills of planning, observing, analyzing, conferring, and evaluating. That individual might be an administrator, a supervisor, or an experienced teacher with special responsibilities and training.

Q: Should all teachers in a school receive clinical supervision?

A: As indicated above, all teachers can profit from the intensive assistance of clinical supervision. Even very experienced and competent teachers from time to time in their careers should have the benefits of clinical supervision. However, a great deal of time is required for clinical supervision to be effective, it seems reasonable to focus clinical efforts on teachers who request it or on those whom the principal feels are especially in need of it.

A: Will the observations made as part of the clinical supervision process be used also to rate or evaluate the teacher involved?

Q: It seems desirable, in the opinion of most experts, to
    separate supervision and evaluation. Ordinarily, therefore,
    supervisory visits should not have an evaluative focus.
    However, the answer to this question is best determined by
    administrators and teachers consulting together under the
    guidance of district policy and developing an explicit
    agreement about the issue.

Q: What written records will be made of the clinical
    supervision?

A: Supervisors will probably keep two types of written records.
    First many supervisors will keep a "clinical supervision
    log," which briefly notes the following: name of the
    teacher observed, class or period observed, date of
    observation, date and time when feedback conference was
    held, and a brief summary of the conference. This log is
    intended solely as a record for the supervisor.

    Second, in addition to holding a feedback conference, the
    supervisor will probably give the teacher a written report,
    which includes the following: date and time of observation,
    class or period observed, chronological summary of important
    teaching and learning transactions, teaching strengths
    noted, and issues requiring discussion.

27

TENSIONS AND ACCOMMODATIONS AMONG ADMINISTRATORS
AND TEACHERS ABOUT STAFF APPRAISAL

Joseph P. Caliguri

This case focuses on the tensions of school staff and the accommodations of administrators in validating what actually exists in passing judgment on evaluation of staff. It is used to examine the concepts of staff self-esteem and leniency of administrators in the evaluator role as a first step. As a second step, it is used to explore alternative ways of improving staff performance. As a problem case in terms of the solution fitting the problem, fundamental characteristics of evaluation provide potential for the case to be utilized in other organizational settings.

MATERIALS

The case study is included in Handout 1. The case study activities consisted of site observations, informal interviews of 10 percent of the staff centering on perceptions of staff evaluation and suggestions for improvement.

PROCEDURES

This case was written for use in various basic management courses at both the undergraduate and graduate levels. It has been introduced in general and in educational administration courses to exemplify the complex interactions between practicing staffs and administrators in relationship to staff evaluation. The case has been reviewed and approved by management officials to insure that the facts are indicative of administration concerns in these particular school systems.

The case is also used by the author as a first step in encouraging examination of innovative approaches to staff appraisal espoused by authoritative writers and researchers in the field of educational evaluation. Some instructors prefer to discuss the case first, and then link in conceptual themes. Others prefer the reverse presentation techniques, and still others prefer to role play some of the case content first and then focus on concepts, problems, and issues.

Class discussions are conducted that are organized around the following three areas:

Part A. Section 1

Is the appraisal system unsuitable for improving staff performance?

Issue.   The appraisal system generates more negative than positive effects on evaluators and evaluatees.

-Philosophy and goals of staff handbook
-Staff evaluation procedures
-Concept of self-esteem
-Concept of administrator leniency or accommodation.

Part B. Section 2

Authoritative writers and researchers in the field of educational evaluation are advocating alternative approaches to this traditional staff evaluation system. Among the approaches advocated as more defensible are:

-Use of item sampling of standardized achievement tests involving different pupils completing different segments of a test; that is, each pupil taking less than the total test in order to yield an overall estimate of group progress.

-Use of criterion reference tests or selection of tests items from tests by local school staffs.

-Use of affective measure instruments related to student attributes, interests, and valuing behavior as a part of instructional analysis plans of teachers.

-The disclosure free concept suggested by Edwin Bridges in which teachers can use various means of evaluating their performance bereft of public record: results of staff activities; tangible products of their activities, and methods of performance; development by teachers of documentary techniques such as activity logs containing selected subjective and objective information bearing on their classroom performance, and narrative reports on the quantity and quality of extra-curricular staff tasks related to job performance.

The case study focused on teachers and administrators. What questions and/or perceptions may other actors such as central office personnel staff, support system staff, students, and parents have about evaluation procedures and process?

Part C. Section 3

Is this case study generalizable to other school districts to a large extent?

-Philosophy and goals of staff handbooks
-Staff evaluation procedures
-Concepts of self-esteem
-Concept of administrator leniency of accommodation
-Other issues and concerns.

Is the case study generalizable to other organizational settings, i.e., business, industry, governmental, social service agencies?

-Similarities in settings and personalities
-Differences in settings and personalities
-Other factors.

BACKGROUND READING

Beecher, Russell S. (1979). Staff evaluation: The essential administrative task. Phi Delta Kappan, 60(7), 515-517.

Bridges, Edwin H. (1974). Faculty evaluation--A critique and a proposal. Administrator's Notebook, 22(6), Midwest Administration Center, University of Chicago.

HANDOUT # 1:   Case Study for
Tensions and Accommodations Among Administrators
and Teachers About Staff Appraisal

Evaluation refers to judgment of merit about things, people, and
programs.   More noticeable is the point that the strength of
evaluation is its potential to threaten in order to penetrate and
its promise of decisions leading to improvement of performance.
Unless it does threaten and promise, it is a waste of resources
or becomes a pretence.   In one urban school district, a revised
staff evaluation system shaped by an evaluation task force of
school-community representatives is in its first year of
implementation.   To gather information in its implementation, a
case study in one secondary school was conducted.   Supplementary
sources of information are also included, and the case is limited
to the administrators and staff.

Questions and Related Issues

Is the appraisal system unsuitable for improving staff
performance?

The formal evaluation procedures generate more negative than
positive effects on evaluators and evaluatees.

How can the appraisal system be improved or strengthened?

Little attention is given to developing supplementary evaluation
activities and techniques as a means of coping with the
limitations of the formal system.

From Intentions to Outcomes

On-site observations during the visitations generally showed a
traditional teaching style of presenting text material or
explaining a topic, encouraging student responses, and making
assignments of seat work and/or homework.   Classroom management
controls were highly evident in terms of consistency and action,
especially by experienced teachers.   Also evident was a thread of
sedative or tranquilizer teaching styles--student seat-work
focusing on duplicated material and a passive teacher role for
most of the school day.   The major activities of the school
principal and his/her assistants related to administrative
routines and school management controls.   An instructional
motivator visited teachers who requested assistance or teachers
who were advised by the principal that the instructional
motivator would be available for assistance.

What the Interviews Said About Staff Evaluation

Data Places: The most apparent cues selected from reading and
rereading the interview material shows some substantiation about

evaluation as threatening to one's self-worth and job security. For instance, many teachers are ambivalent about the administrator's expertise in subject matter areas as echoed in this statement:

> The principal can't judge me because he lacks expertise in my subject matter field. Unless he can spot real difficulties he should use instructional supervisors or curriculum specialists to judge my expertise, especially if I am rated as needing improvement and job target plans are needed.

On the other hand, there was more agreement by teachers that the administrator as evaluator can make judgments in areas such as basic classroom procedures and student behaviors. Ambivalence about the administrator's role in evaluation was further pronounced by this comment:

> This policy and procedure of having two classroom observations and a final conference becomes mostly a showcasing action by teachers unless the administrator visits classrooms almost daily. All the principal really sees is how well teachers prepare and not how well they really teach. Spontaneous visits to the classroom can help to keep us on our toes.

More distinctive points relating to role conflict for administrators were noted in these expressions:

> Principals can get into conflict with teachers who refuse to sign the evaluation form because principals do not get across their expectations for classroom teaching to staffs. And, principals need to be competent also in handling disagreements with teachers who are displaying poor performance or plain incompetency, or who are dissatisfied about their role.

In concluding this phase about teacher's views, one experienced teacher asked to sum up her impressions made these points:

> My first impression is that the evaluation system is a vast improvement from the one previously used by the district. Two visits and a follow-up conference are preferable to the previous practice of one visit. However, there are areas of the evaluation form which do cause concern.

> It would be difficult to determine the clarity of objectives on one or two visits. I question an administrator's ability to suggest an appropriate job target when necessary for the variety of subject areas in the secondary schools. Asking a teacher who is having difficulty to assist in the process might be like asking a drowning man to save himself.

As with any evaluation tool, fairness and impartiality cannot be guaranteed.*

Two visits may not isolate those teachers who have chronic classroom problems such as lack of knowledge, poor teaching or classroom management skills. How does this new evaluation system make it any easier to eliminate people who are ill suited to the profession? Will the tenured person with persistently poor performance continue to be offered a contract until retirement?

Overall, the staff commentary partially exemplifies some of the resisting views and the apparent vulnerabilities administrators face in regard to questions about their evaluation competencies. Turning to the administrator, intermittent conferences involved with examining his ongoing ratings, discussion of staff commentary, and co-observation of one teacher exhibiting poor classroom management practices. In a summary discussion of his work, he exclaimed:

I had 45 staff evaluations to do with the assistance of an assistant principal, and I also had to follow the timetable prescribed by the district procedures. It's very time consuming--so much so that even though I rated two teachers as unsatisfactory, I did not make a recommendation for termination proceedings according to the schedule.

I can use more assistance from instructional supervisors or a curriculum-instruction specialist added to my staff. You're right about suggesting that I add more specific reasons about the checkmarks I make on the rating form, otherwise teachers think I am doing a fast job on them.

Complementary Commentary. To add to the commentary from one school, additional sources of information are included at this point. In one of the district's reports on meetings of administrators and instructional supervisors, one administrator said:

---

*After reading this excerpt in the case, one elementary teacher coming up for tenure showed the author her superior ratings and defined fairness as the ability of administrators to desist from rating teachers strictly on personal likes or dislikes.

In my opinion, the new evaluation forms and directives are very cumbersome and time consuming. I spent over 50 hours evaluating eight teachers. The detail is necessary where improvement is required. Perhaps it is superfluous where performance is excellent.

In another report from a graduate student interviewing five secondary administrators in a nearby school district, uncomfortableness about job targets was attested by these remarks:

Job targets approach tends to exclude comprehensive assessment of important areas of teaching, like personality problems of teachers.

There seems to be a natural tendency on the part of administrators and teachers to avoid weak areas when writing job targets.

In connection to this local focus, a recent national survey of public secondary school principals reported these statements in reference to staff evaluation:

Regarding instructional matters, principals do not formally evaluate teachers very frequently, nor do most principals observe teaching in classrooms often.

On the other hand, it appears impractical for principals to control instructional matters or to uncover incompetence or inadequate teaching given the influence of teacher organization agreements and complicated grievance procedures.

Does the Solution Fit the Problem?

If we assume analytically that the formal evaluation system is a solution that does not fit the problem of improving staff performance, the question of what can be done to strengthen the appraisal system and the issue emerges of reducing self-esteem tensions of staff and managerial leniency or accommodations. During the experience of this case study very few perceptions and suggestions related to addressing this question and its accompanying issue. An exception was a summary presentation of the case study to another secondary school staff in the district in which two small groups of teachers sequentially simulated a teachers' lounge feedback to the presentation. Among the most provocative comments were:

Administrators can only do in depth evaluation of staff if they are limited to eight or nine staff appraisals during the year.

Linked to this statement, one staff member stated that:

> Public education has to develop quality control measures or standardized-teaching-learning practices if we are to develop evaluative criteria upon which staff appraisals are based.

Another experienced staff person exclaimed that:

> Job descriptions with measurable performance standards should be devised which can be the target for staff evaluation rather than the present costly and ineffective system.

Clarification of Concepts

Self-Esteem and the Teacher. When self-esteem is challenged by negative information about performance, staff tend to strongly discount it even if it is perceived as valid because it constitutes a loss of face and a possible threat to job security. Under these conditions, it is unlikely that improved performance will occur. Many of the defensive oriented comments made by teachers seem to reflect on this threat combined with conditions they perceive in relation to school resources, and student and parent support problem.

The School Administrator and Leniency Aspects of Managing Staff Evaluations

A major goal of the staff evaluation system is the improvement of staff performance. Outcomes of staff evaluation tend to be soft or less than rigorous creating a leniency aspect or an overstating of staff qualifications and contributions. A rating of satisfactory for 43 of 45 teachers may have added some validity to the concept of leniency. This particular administrator chose to occupy a major portion of his time with school control activities. Little attention was given to developing on-going contacts and activities with the staff in regard to curricular-instructional matters of the school. Also, by limiting ratings which can be appealed or questioned by the staff, an administrator can exchange positive evaluations for staff loyalty, support, and compliance commonly called a trade-off.

VI ISSUES IN EVALUATION: REPORTING, UTILIZATION, AND ETHICS

28

INFORMATION PORTRAYAL AND USE

Gabriel Della-Piana

This exercise in "portrayal" of evaluation information is based on a particular conceptualization of use (Weiss, 1982), a perspective on information portrayal (Della-Piana, 1981), and a perspective on data collection (Della-Piana and Della-Piana, 1984). Data must be gathered in a way that serves the purposes of portrayal, which is to foster understanding of the form and workings of the object of evaluation. The strategy for portrayal involves presenting data in the form of juxtapositions of data sets that not only illuminate structure and process of what is evaluated but also creates dissonance that involves users in making their own interpretations and judgments.

MATERIALS

1. Illustrative data set juxtapositions
2. An illustrative portrayal

PROCEDURES

1. Clarify the Conceptualization of Information Use

Evaluators do not agree on what constitutes "use" of information, nor on how appropriate use might best be fostered (Patton, 1988; Shadish and Reichardt, 1987; Weiss, 1988). There does seem to be agreement that it is a rare circumstance in which information from an evaluation "switches a decision from A to B by the power of its evidence and analysis" (Shadish and Reichardt, 1987; Weiss, 1982). It is also generally agreed that in practice, evaluation informs rather than dictates a decision. It contributes to an understanding of issues, causes of problems, and the dynamics of interventions to be "taken into account" in making a decision. See also: Cousins and Leithwood (1986), Cronbach and Associates (1980), Lindblom (1987), Lindblom and

Cohen (1979).

Describe this conceptualization of information use. Have students discuss the following two "theses" from Cronbach and Associates (1980, p. 11):

The evaluator is an educator; his success is to be judged by what others learn.
Those who shape policy should reach decisions with their eyes open; it is the evaluator's task to illuminate the situation, not to dictate the decision.

Note to the Instructor. There should be two outcomes to this discussion or debate on the theses. First, students should get a conception of how information is used in making decisions. Second, students should see the need for presenting information in ways that contribute to "understanding" by a broad range of participants in the decision making.

2. Clarify the Perspective on How Information Travels to Decision Makers and How It Is Used. The findings and ideas from an evaluation may "travel" to decision makers in a number of ways. It is useful to think of this travel in terms of how it is mediated, the path it takes, and how it is used.

Smith (1982) has edited a book that discusses a variety of forms of mediation including graphic displays, oral briefings, adversary hearings, television presentation, committee hearings, and briefing panels. Weiss (1988) describes a variety of channels or paths through which information travels effectively to decision makers. Two of the channels are: staff of the policymakers (research and public relations specialists or administrative aides) and special interest groups (professional associations, unions, consumer groups, etc.) that "get to" the policymakers. As contrasted with traditional "reports" that do not get read or used, these channels get attention because of their credibility, pressure, and accessibility. Weiss (1988) also contends that policymakers use information in four ways: as warnings that things are going wrong, as guidance for improving policies or programs, as reconceptualizations or new ways of thinking about an issue, and as mobilization for support through providing a way to build a convincing case with a coalition of relevant people.

Conduct a discussion of the following situation referring to the concepts of information travel and use sketched out above.

Rachel Carson's Silent Spring focused attention on matters of environmental pollution and destruction. This caused much public "awareness and concern." In this climate it was easy for scientists to get policy makers to listen to them. How would you have proceeded differently at that time in reporting on your research or evaluation in the following two contexts: (1) the policy-shaping community <u>agrees</u> on values relevant to the recommendations but <u>disagrees</u> on the facts; (2) the policy shaping-community <u>disagrees</u> on values and <u>agrees</u> on facts.

<u>Note to the Instructor</u>. In context 1, "specialists" who know about and are able to communicate the "facts" are essential. In context 2, "representation" from the diverse value orientations is essential (Cronbach and Associates, 1980, ch. 4). Focus discussion on how information might travel (mediation and path) and get used (warnings, etc.) in the two different contexts.

3. <u>Clarify Data-Gathering Strategies:</u> <u>Analyzing Instructional Sequences</u>. The portrayal of information to decision makers in a way that helps them see "how things work" requires <u>gathering data</u> that has a good chance of illuminating how things work in the program to be evaluated. Have students carry out the following exercise to get experience in gathering some data in a form that might illuminate the "workings" of an instructional sequence.

<u>Develop a Framework for Analysis</u>. There are many possible frameworks for the analysis of instruction. One possibility is presented in Handout 1. That framework was developed for analyzing computer-based instruction, but it may be generalized to instruction mediated in other ways. For suggestions on building frameworks in the form of a matrix for data-gathering and display, see Miles and Huberman (1984).

<u>Try Out an Instructional Sequence on Yourself and One Other Person</u>. Select some instructional material for a tryout. The author regularly uses an unpublished instructional unit in the area of "counseling" he has designed for this task (available on request from author) <u>or</u> allows students to select a short instructional unit in a paper-and-pencil or computer-based format. Have students try out the instructional material on themselves prior to trying it out on another student.

Use the following procedures for the tryout:

1. I am "trying out" this instructional material on a skill needed in counseling (or whatever material was chosen for the tryout). Your responses will help me to see how the instruction works and how to get information from someone as they go through a unit of instruction like this.

2. "Think out loud" as you go through the material, so I can get some idea as to what the directions and instruction mean to you.

3. I will make notes (or tape) your comments to get some sense as to how the material works and what might be changed.

4. When you have difficulty (if something is unclear), let me know, and I will rewrite the material "on the spot" so I have a record of what you looked at while responding.

5. I might ask you questions occasionally, to find out what you were doing and thinking as you worked out your responses in a section of the instruction [Note to evaluator: do this especially after long pauses with no thinking aloud or where a student changes a response and does not think aloud or where you simply are not sure what was discriminative for (or what cued) a particular response].

Analyze the Data from Your Tryout: Descriptive Level. Have students use the framework in Handout 1 to conduct a descriptive analysis of the data they gathered in the tryout of the instructional unit. Have them summarize the data under the nine data sources.

Note to Instructor. In conducting the analysis students will find that some kinds of data were not gathered. Where possible, have them get that data, too. For example, an "ideal-based" data source in Handout 1, item 7, is "valued courseware-related accomplishments as judged by an appropriate policy-shaping community." Students might talk with subject matter experts in the area of the instruction that was used to see if the accomplishment in the instructional material is highly valued and if there are other "models of appropriate performance" for this kind of accomplishment.

4. Clarify the Design of Portrayal Strategies

There are three phases to the experience of trying out portrayal strategies. After discussing the three phases as outlined below, have students try out the design of portrayal strategies by taking their own data through the three phase portrayal process.

Grasping the Portrayal Perspective. The perspective for portrayal that is the focus of this exercise is what we have called "juxtaposition of discontinuities." The intent is to portray data from two or more sources, giving contradictory or jarring or dissonant information. The result hoped for is to involve the information users in making their own interpretations and judgments for their own purposes (see Della-Piana and Della-Piana, 1982, 1984).

Any two or three of the nine data sources presented in Handout 1 may be juxtaposed to "involve" users in interpreting the results. For illustrations of the possibilities, see Della-Piana and Della-Piana (1982, p. 14).

Selecting the Data Sets To Be Juxtaposed. Since the data were presumably gathered to illuminate "how the program (or strategy) to be evaluated actually works," then they should provide the possibilities for illuminating structure and process.

Some of Patton's (1986) "principles" for reporting findings are relevant here: Have users speculate as to results and present data juxtaposed with these speculations. Strive for simplicity, balance (multiple interpretations of both so-called positive and negative results), clarity, and representation of the range of structures and processes that are in the design for data collection.

Here is one illustration of the kinds of juxtapositions that are possible with data sets from Handout 1:

> An author's objective for a drill and practice program is "to increase accuracy and rate of performance in arithmetic fundamentals through massive practice and immediate feedback." The author's instructional strategy includes 60 percent of the time on any frame devoted to feedback such as fireworks flashing across the monitor and correct answer confirmation. Student performance includes loss of interest, missing feedback, and punching in responses without much conscious attention, for 20 percent of the students.

Designing the Portrayal. For an illustrative design see Handout 2. Also, remember that the portrayal form (mediation) does not necessarily commit you to a particular path to get the report to the decision makers for an intended use.

DISCUSSION

The possibilities of portrayal formats within the perspectives of the unit are endless. What students should be learning or experiencing is how to conceptualize portrayal intent within the perspective outlined above, and how to compose portrayal formats that meet that intent. The problem with examples, although they are included for instructional value, is that they are often taken as the only way the perspectives may be applied. Thus, it is important to have students analyze their own work from the vantage point of criteria derived from the perspectives and frameworks of the unit. The author has tried out various portions of the above unit in program evaluation and product evaluation courses in which students were enrolled from nursing, physics, education, psychology, sociology, and educational administration.

BACKGROUND READINGS

Cousins, J.B., & Leithwood, K.A. (1986). Current empirical research on evaluation utilization. Review of Educational

Research. 56(3), 331-364.

Cronbach, L.J., & Associates. (1980). Toward reform of program evaluation. San Francisco: Jossey-Bass.

Della-Piana, G. (1981). Literary and film criticism. In N. L. Smith (ed.), Metaphors for evaluation. Beverly Hills: Sage, pp. 211-246.

Della-Piana, G., & Della-Piana, C. (1982). Making courseware transparent: Beyond initial screening. Research on Evaluation Paper & Report Series, No. 76. Portland, OR: Northwest Regional Educational Laboratory.

Della-Piana, G., & Della Piana, C. (1984). Computer software information for educators. Educational Technology, 19,(10), 19-25.

Lindblom, C.E. (1987). Who needs what social research for policymaking? In W.R. Shadish Jr. & C.S. Reichardt (eds.), Evaluation Studies Review Annual, 12, 163-184.

Lindblom, C.E., & Cohen, D.K. (1979). Usable knowledge. New Haven, CT: Yale University Press.

Miles, M.B., & Huberman, A.H. (1984). Qualitative data analysis. Beverly Hills: Sage.

Patton, M. (1988). The evaluator's responsibility for utilization. Evaluation Practice, 9(2), 5-24.

Patton, M. (1986). Utilization focused evaluation. Beverly Hills: Sage.

Shadish, W.R. Jr., & Reichardt, C.S. (eds.). (1987). Evaluation Studies Review Annual, 12. Beverly Hills: Sage.

Smith, N.L. (ed.) Communication strategies in evaluation. Beverly Hills: Sage.

Weiss, C. (1982). Measuring the use of evaluation. In E.R. House et al. (eds.). Evaluation studies review annual, 7, Beverly Hills: Sage, pp.129-145.

Weiss, C. (1988). Evaluation decisions: Is anybody there? Does anybody care? Evaluation Practice, 9(1), 5-19.

HANDOUT 1: Nine Data Sources and Illustrative Kinds of Data for Evaluating Software
(from Della-Piana and Della-Piana, 1984)

Data Sources

Kind of Data

Author-Based

1. Objectives specified in courseware, manual, or other supportive material.

2. Objectives inferred from analysis of instructional strategy.

3. Objectives inferred from analysis of final mastery test.

(a) Collection of objectives stated within the courseware (on the computer monitor) or in other supportive material. The objectives may be reorganized according to some system for formal specification of objectives.

(b) Evaluator-inferred objectives as determined by going through the "course" as a student and noting what the instructional strategies appear to teach.

(c) Evaluator-inferred objectives as determined by evaluator analysis of final mastery test or submastery tests.

Student-Based

4. Instructional path of student in relation to computer interaction and supportive material.

5. Student performance on submastery and final mastery tests as function of aptitude.

6. Student interaction with teachers, aides, peers, or "noncourse" sources of information.

(d) Hard-copy printout of student responses while going through computer-aided instruction.

(e) Workbook (or other comparable response sheet) responses associated with the courseware package.

(f) Structured interviews with students after completion of instructional segments on critical points within the instruction.

(g) Observation of students during instruction re: interaction with computers, supportive materials, peers, or others, and follow-up interviews of key persons.

(h) Student performance on submastery and mastery tests.

Ideal-Based

7. Valued courseware-related accomplishments as judged by appropriate policy-shaping community.
8. Generalization of power of valued accomplishments.
9. Economy or worth of instruction as a ratio of valued accomplishments to costs of instruction.

(i) Judgments of value of alternative models of accomplishments as determined by a committee using some sort of informed consensus process.

(j) Estimates of generalization power of valued accomplishments based on empirical tryout data or informed hunches. (Does mastery generalize to other valued accomplishments?)

(k) Estimation of the worth of instruction based on actual/estimated costs and judged value of the accomplishments.

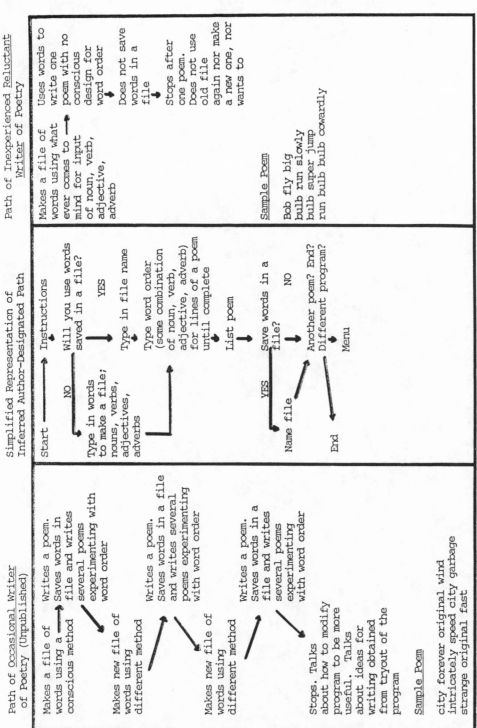

Path of Occasional Writer of Poetry (Unpublished)

Writes a poem. Saves words in file and writes several poems experimenting with word order

Makes a file of words using a conscious method

Writes a poem. Saves words in a file and writes several poems experimenting with word order

Makes new file of words using different method

Writes a poem. Saves words in a file and writes several poems experimenting with word order

Makes new file of words using different method

Stops. Talks about how to modify program to be more useful. Talks about ideas for writing obtained from tryout of the program

Sample Poem

city forever original wind
intricately speed city garbage
strange original fast

Simplified Representation of Inferred Author-Designated Path

Start → Instructions

Will you use words saved in a file?

NO → Type in words to make a file; nouns, verbs, adjectives, adverbs

YES → Type in file name

Type word order (some combination of noun, verb, adjective, adverb) for lines of a poem until complete

List poem

Save words in a file?

YES → Name file

NO

Another poem? End? Different program?

Menu

End

Path of Inexperienced Reluctant Writer of Poetry

Uses words to write one poem with no conscious design for word order

Makes a file of words using what ever comes to mind for input of noun, verb, adjective, adverb

Does not save words in a file

Stops after one poem. Does not use old file again nor make a new one, nor wants to

Sample Poem

Bob fly big
bulb run slowly
bulb super jump
run bulb bulb cowardly

HANDOUT 2: Flowchart of Simplified, Inferred, Author-Designed Path Through MECC "Poetry" and Two Student Paths (Della-Piana and Della Piana, 1982)

29

ETHICS AND EVALUATION: PROBLEMS, ISSUES, AND USEFULNESS

Valerie J. Janesick

The study of evaluation requires some consideration of the ethical dimensions inherent in evaluating. Consequently, prospective evaluators would be well served by the serious treatment of ethics as either a separate course in its own right or as a component of an evaluation course. Two relationships in particular put the evaluator into a role that may include ethical dilemmas: (1) the relationship between evaluator and client or funder; and (2) the relationship between the evaluator and participants under evaluation. In some cases, the ethical complexities are compounded when both relationships overlap or coincide. For example, the client may also be one of the participants under evaluation in the project.

In addition, an overriding ethical question overshadows almost all evaluation projects. That question is: In whose best interest is the report written? Many scholars feel that the question ought to be seriously considered before, during, and at the close of any evaluation. The best-interest question may put the evaluator in an awkward position since the evaluator is being paid to write a report that may have controversial, negative, or damaging information in it. Should the evaluator disclose this information? If so, who is in jeopardy by disclosing the information? Might the evaluator feel compelled to write the report in a style that sidesteps the controversial and damaging information, in order to meet the deadline? If the evaluator is dependent on money from outside contracts, is there a danger that the final report will inevitably contain an overwhelming amount of positive information? These ethical questions are among the many that are bound to materialize within the context of most evaluations.

MATERIALS

Handout 1: Overview of Approaches to Ethics
Handout 2: A Comparison of Kohlberg and Gilligan
Handout 3: Dilemmas Evaluators Face

PROCEDURES

1. Establish the framework for understanding the common approaches to ethical questions: rational, emotive, situation, and stage developmental (see Handout 1).

2. Since the stage developmental approach is a recent and useful tool for studying ethical dilemmas, introduce students to Kohlberg's theory and stages and the recent criticisms of Kohlberg's theory (Gilligan, 1982).

3. Introduce two or three moral dilemmas. It is often a good technique to begin working on dilemmas from a classic example such as any of the Kohlberg dilemmas. Then, after trust and communication are established, proceed to your own examples. One example I like to use is one from personal experience working as an evaluator (see Handout 2). Two other examples are also included in Handout 2.

4. Design a mechanism for presenting the dilemma, discussing it and coming to a solution of some sorts. Then try to classify all responses according to Kohlberg's scale.

For example, in Case 1, the student/evaluator is faced with the ethical dilemma of what to do in terms of reporting findings. On the one hand, the participant has declared on tape a specific behavior that might cause negative repurcussions. On the other hand, the evaluator feels these data are extremely relevant to some portion of the final report. Yet, the participant makes the false claim that these words were never spoken. What should the evaluator do and why? Some possible responses students may generate include:

1. The evaluator should allow the participant to delete those comments after all, the participant entered into this social contract and would not willingly want to jeopardize his job. The greatest good in this case is protection for the participant.

Kohlberg Scale Stage 5: Social Contract. Since the greatest good is relative to the person who is at the least advantage.

2. A good evaluator would see that his/her participant must be protected. If not, he/she may not get another evaluation job.

Kohlberg Scale Stage 2: Instrumental Relativism. Since the evaluator is worried about the next evaluation job, not the particulars of the immediate case.

3. The evaluator should just let the participant do the editing of the material. After all, a good person would do this so that no embarassment will come of it.

Kohlberg Scale Stage 3: Good boy - Nice girl. Since morality is viewed as what a good person would do.

In this application, students have the opportunity to place responses on the Kohlberg scale (see Handout 3). If the students want to use the Gilligan scale as well, you will have both perspectives accounted for and allow for more diverse interpretations of the same behaviors.

DISCUSSION

The value of discussing ethical problems and dilemmas is the rich sharing of opinions at all levels of the Kohlberg scale. This enables students to learn from one another as well as to practice problem-solving techniques individually and collectively. Students usually are enthusiastic about discussing moral issues and questions. They begin to see how the role of an evaluator includes dealing with moral dilemmas, and questions of values and ethics in a discrete way.

BACKGROUND READINGS

Gilligan, C. (1982). In a different voice. Cambridge, MA: Harvard University Press.

Hyde, A.A. (1987). Theory used in ethnographic educational evaluations: Negotiating values. Anthropology and Education Quarterly, 18(3).

Kohlberg L. (1976). Moral stages and moralization: The cognitive developmental approach. In T. Lickona (ed.), Moral development and behavior: Theory, research, and social issues. New York: Holt, Rinehart, and Winston, pp. 31-53.

The Encyclopedia of Philosophy.

HANDOUT #1: Overview of Approaches to Ethics

1. Ethical Objectivism

In this approach, there are objective criteria about what is right or wrong. The assumption is made that people agree on this.

Sometimes called: The rational approach to ethics, or the idealist approach.

Chief proponents: Plato, Kant, St. Thomas Acquinas, John Locke, et al.

2. Ethical Subjectivism

In this approach, what is right or wrong is intuitively known. People will follow their emotional, gut reaction.

Sometimes called: The emotive approach to ethics, or the naturalist position.

Chief proponent: Bertrand Russell.

3. Ethical Relativism

In this approach, ethical principles are always in conflict and ethical disagreements follow cultural lines. The s i t u a t i o n defines the ethics. There is no objective right or wrong.

Sometimes called: Situational Ethics.

Chief proponent: Westermarck.

4. Stage Developmental Ethical Approach

In this approach, moral development follows a certain specified stage progression. The six stages of Laurence Kohlberg's moral development scale include (1) punishment-obedience, (2) reciprocity, (3) conformity, (4) law and order, (5) social contract, and (6) universal, ethical principles. The assumption is made that higher stages are better. Moral dilemmas are used to decide the reasons for solutions to the problem. By this one can assess the appropriate level on the scale.

Sometimes called: Cognitive Developmental Approach.

Chief proponents: Kohlberg, Gilligan.

Kohlberg

Preconventional level		Conventional level		Postconventional level		
Stage 1	Stage 2	Stage 3	Stage 4	Stage 5	Stage 6	Stage 7
Punishment & obedience	Instrumental relativism	Good boy, nice girl	Authority & law & order	Social contract	Principled ethical morality	Integration of self & others
In which punishment is exacted to fit the crime	In which you scratch my back & I'll scratch yours	In which a good boy (or girl) would do this or that	In which I obey even an unjust law at any cost	In which the greatest good for the greatest number is sought	In which equity and the value of life are primary	In which the holistic connection fostering life are protected

Gilligan

Stage 1	First Transition	Stage 2	Second Transition	Stage 3
Self-survival	Care for others	Self-sacrifice	Reconsideration of relationship	Integration of self & others through interdependence
In which one gives all to self, disregarding the other	In which the stage 1 activity is looked upon as selfish	In which care for others to exclusion of self occurs	In which the disequilibrium caused by self-sacrifice is examined in the light of the concept of goodness	In which care is the self-chosen principle concern for relationship and condemnation of hurt

---

* Please note that terms describing the Gilligan stages are a synopsis composed by Francine Siedlecki.

HANDOUT #3: Dilemmas Evaluators Face

Each year students and colleagues who take part in evaluations
have been kind enough to share with me true stories that fall in
the category of ethical dilemmas.   I am indebted to all who
prompted my creation of these examples. They know who they are.

Case 1

Imagine you are evaluating a federally funded project on teacher
effectiveness at the community college level. You interview a
number of teacher-participants in the project on tape, and, in
the course of one of the interviews, a teacher discloses that he
smokes marijuana with his students. He states that this gives
him "credibility and effectiveness" with his students, most of
whom are older than he is. He also states that he feels "he can
tell his students anything and can count on their cooperation in
learning any of his course content in psychology." After you
begin writing your report you include a short paragraph on
"factors that influence the success of the students." You list
as common activities social gatherings that may sometimes include
smoking dope.   You show this to the participant who says, "I
never said that." Remember, you have his words on tape.

Questions:

(a)   What would you do in this case?
(b)   What would you change, if anything, in this situation?
(c)   What ethical concerns are to be addressed?
(d)   What is the most sensible solution for all persons involved
      here--the evaluator, the practitioner, and the funder?

Case 2

You are an evaluator of a small federally funded music and arts
summer camp program for handicapped high school students.   You
are in charge of evaluating communication between students and
staff, the content of the music courses in piano, voice,
composition and performance and career opportunities.   The
program will serve 25 students with a staff of seven instructors
for five weeks. Funding for the program is about $65,000. All
students will evaluate their instructors, and the director will
evaluate the instructors. You have the opportunity to see all
the evaluations and see that in every instance, students are
dissatisfied with the poor quality of instruction and lack of
teacher preparation and performance opportunities.   All
instructors are personal friends of the director who hired you.
It is clear that the content of the classes is far below standard
from the data provided in the written evaluations and from the
interview data you collected.

Questions:

(a)   How would you handle this?
(b)   What would you recommend for improvement?
(c)   What is the role of the evaluator in this case?
(d)   What ethical issues are raised in this case?

Case 3

You have just contracted to evaluate a program that receives
federal funds in a large urban school district. You have pages
of testimony, documents, taped interviews, and questionnaire data
that testify to the success of this gifted and talented K-8
program.   In the course of the evaluation, almost in its last
month of six months of work, the director of the gifted and
talented district-wide program, and the person who hired you,
requests a meeting with you. At this time, the director tells
you that the report you write will be used as part of an argument
to cut the program and eliminate it from the district in order to
pave the way for the closing of that particular school.

Questions:

(a)   How would you handle this?
(b)   What recommendations would you make for improvement?
(c)   What is your role as evaluator in this case?
(d)   What ethical issues are raised in this case?

VII   POLICY ANALYSIS

30

POLICY/GOAL PERCENTAGING

Stuart S. Nagel

This software is designed to process a set of (1) alternatives to be evaluated, (2) criteria for judging the alternatives, and (3) relations between alternatives and criteria in order to choose a best alternative, combination, allocation, or predictive decision rule. The program can be applied to such areas as law, government, business, personal, or other decision making.

For example, in the field of law, the program can be applied to such practice problems as (1) whether to go to trial or settle out of court in civil and criminal cases, (2) how to allocate time or other resources across a set of cases, (3) which of various laws should be adopted for achieving a set of goals, (4) what decision should be reached in resolving a legal dispute, and (5) what level of activity should be engaged in for a given matter in which doing too much or too little may be undesirable.

MATERIALS

To use the software, one needs to obtain the floppy disks and the basic documentation from Decision Aids Inc., 1720 Parkhaven Drive, Champaign, IL 61820, (217) 359-8541.

PROCEDURES

The best way to use the software is to have a course that involves many controversial substantive or methodological problems, e.g., medical school admissions, evaluating cities, optimum level of busing, counseling for the poor, and evaluating energy sources. Think of each problem in terms of one or more alternatives for resolving the problem, one or more criteria for judging the alternatives, and relations between the alternatives and the criteria. That kind of thinking lends itself well to a spreadsheet or matrix presentation with the alternatives on the rows, the criteria on the columns, and the relations in the cells. The software can then generate a summation column at the far right showing an overall evaluation for each alternative or combination. The software can also indicate what it would take to bring a second or other-place alternative up to first place.

DISCUSSION

To stimulate involvement where there are five students per microcomputer, the students can be grouped in terms of their ideological or substantive interests. For example, with 25 students, the five sets might cover relatively strong liberals, mild liberals, neutrals, mild conservatives, and relatively strong conservatives. To facilitate interaction across such groups students should be encouraged to suggest new alternatives, criteria and compromises perhaps better than the expectations of either side. An illustrative problem might be how to provide legal services for the poor. The class might create a new data file to examine alternative policies such as salaried government lawyers versus unpaid volunteers. The goal might be inexpensiveness, accessibility, political feasibility, and competency.

BACKGROUND READINGS

Nagel, S. (1985). Using microcomputers and policy/goal percentaging for teaching policy analysis and public policy. In P. Bergerson and B. Nedwek (eds.), Teaching public administration. St. Louis, MO: Programs in Public Policy Analysis and Administration.

Nagel, S. (1986). Evaluation analysis with microcomputers. Greenwich, CT: JAI Press.

Computer: Any IBM compatible computer

Operating System: The standard disk operating system.

Sectors: The program uses standard 5 1/4 inch diskettes.

Bytes: The program requires 192-256K of memory.

Copyright: The program is copyrighted.

Fee: For $45, one can obtain a program disk, two data file disks, three self-teaching tutorials, one data file manual, and a binder of summarizing articles.

VIII THE EVALUATOR'S TOOLS: STATISTICS, MEASUREMENT, AND COMPUTERS

31

STATISTICAL SOFTWARE EXPERT SYSTEM

George A. Marcoulides

ZEERA is a computer program designed to interact with users and help them understand and perform statistical analyses. ZEERA uses the tools of artificial intelligence to function as an expert system in the area of statistics. The objectives of this software are twofold: (1) to assist users of statistical techniques in choosing correct procedures, and (2) to enhance learning and increase material retention through computer-provided feedback. In its present form, ZEERA is limited to statistical hypothesis testing.

ZEERA consists of two functional areas: the work area and the help area. The work area of the system lies inside a main border where all input and operations are performed. Because of the different types of statistical problems that can be encountered, the expert system's decisions are gauged by user responses to sets of questions. It is extremely important, therefore, that the interaction between the user and the system be clear and error-free. For this purpose, a second border area is provided that acts as the help area. When an inappropriate response is given by the user, the help area provides hints and samples of acceptable responses to guide the user.

MATERIALS

Materials consist of one diskette and one back-up diskette. Documentation is included on the diskette.

PROCEDURES

ZEERA proceeds by introducing itself to the user and asking the user to specify a problem for consideration and analysis. ZEERA then scans the user's answer input and continues producing questions that reflect its responses to the input. When ZEERA finally determines the appropriate statistical procedure for the problem at hand it prompts the user for the necessary data. ZEERA has both complete and partial file handling capabilities. If the user has the raw data available, ZEERA will perform a complete analysis. If, on the other hand, the user has already computed some of the intermediate values, ZEERA can also accept these values.

Consider the following problem assigned to a student taking a course in elementary statistics:

The scenario: a researcher is doing an experiment to determine if students do better on manual dexterity tasks when rock music is playing in the background rather than classical music. The researcher feels that rock music will stimulate students to work faster. To test this hypothesis, 11 students were given two minutes to trace 15 mazes while listening to music. The first group of five students listened to classical music while the remaining six students listened--in a different room, of course--to rock music. The researcher now wants to proceed with the analysis. What type of analysis should the researcher perform, and what are the results?

With the help of ZEERA the student is guided in selecting and computing an independent t-test.

DISCUSSION

This program was developed over two years and tested in different situations. This version of the program was tested out on a number of students registered in elementary statistics courses at a large state university. The program was the focus of an experimental study in which two groups of subjects were compared (Marcoulides, 1988). Results indicated that those students who used ZEERA in their studies were able to retain more information and perform better on examinations. The benefits of using ZEERA include: (1) it can increase the accuracy of selecting appropriate statistical procedures, and (2) it can increase the retention of material being studied.

BACKGROUND READING

Marcoulides, G.A. (1988). Improving learner performance with intelligent computer based programs. Journal of Computer-Based Instruction, (accepted for publication).

Marcoulides, G.A. (1988). An intelligent computer based learning program. Collegiate Microcomputer, 6(2), 123-126.

Computer: Any IBM compatible computer.

Operating System: MSDOS.

Sectors: Two.

Bytes: 128K minimum.

Copyright: Marcoulides, G.A.

Fee: $13 to cover diskette and postage.

32

CHARTING STUDENT PROGRESS

Geofferey Masters, George Morgan, and
Mark Wilson

The aim of this software and accompanying documentation is to introduce educators and educational researchers to the potential benefits of using Item Response Theory (IRT) to construct local variables rather than rely on standardized measures. In the booklet, "Charting Student Progress," we discuss the construction of:

1. an elementary-school fractions chart;
2. a high school reading chart; and
3. an attitude chart concerning the quality of school life.

Using these examples, we describe the steps taken to develop the items that represent the variable, how to check that the psychometric model and the data are in concordance, and how to interpret the IRT estimates for both groups and individuals. These examples are drawn from our common backgrounds in education, but the technique is applicable wherever sums of dichotomous items (e.g., test scores) are used to mediate between latent variables and empirical responses. We intend that the learner will have a conceptual rather than statistical understanding of the technique. The accompanying software does the book-keeping, analysis and reporting in graphical format, and provides examples of the major components of the technique, such as calibration of items, checking model-data misfit, interpreting the variable, and diagnosing individual misfit. A test construction and administration package is also supplied which can be used to generate computerized tests, to administer them to students, and to organize the student responses for the analysis.

MATERIALS

1.   Booklet: Charting Student Progress
2.   Software (on floppy disks) and User's Guide called "CHARTS"

PROCEDURES

Learners attend a half-day workshop that follows the booklet
"Charting Student Progress" and several examples using a
microcomputer.   The materials are designed to be self-
explanatory, however, with sample data that allow the reader to
work through each of the examples him/herself.

DISCUSSION

The best way for someone to learn how to use the program is to
apply it to a real problem.   With this in mind we encourage
workshop attendees to bring along a data set that can be analyzed
on a consultive basis after the workshop (i.e., in the
afternoon).   Typical data sets would be composed of curriculum-
based achievement tests that had been locally developed, results
(item-level) from standardized achievement tests where local
calibration and validation are needed, and locally developed
checklists and attitude scales.

     The IRT methods introduced by the above materials extend
also to polytomous response data such as Likert scales and
partial credit rating schemes. A computer analysis package
(PC-CREDIT) and accompanying materials for this important area
are available from Mark Wilson.

BACKGROUND READING

Wright, B.D., & Stone, M. (1979). Best test design. Chicago:
     MESA.

SOFTWARE INFORMATION

     1.   CHARTS presently runs on the Apple IIe/c (running under
PRODOS); an IBM-PC version (running under MS-DOS) is under
preparation (the analysis package is now available, the test-
administration package will not be ready until later.)

     2.   It is distributed on two single-sided floppy disks, one
for example data and outputs and one for the actual program.

3.   Copyright is held by the Australian Council for Educational Research (ACER).   The materials are distributed as part of the workshop but may also be purchased independently from ACER when published.   The address for information about publication data is: Australian Council for Education Research, Radford House, Frederick St., Hawthorn, Victoria 3122 AUSTRALIA.

4.   Workshop fee varies;   ACER has not yet established a price for the software and printed materials.   Contact Mark Wilson for pre-publication information.

33

ACTIVITIES FOR TEACHING REGRESSION TO THE MEAN

Jack McKillip

Regression artifacts plague applied research and are difficult
for students to understand. Three class activities are described
that aid presentation of a classical, errors-in-measurement
explanation of regression to the mean: (1) a clairvoyance test
(Hunter and Horwitz, 1977); (2) dice-rolling exercise
(D.T. Campbell); and (3) computer-generated data simulation and
analysis. Student readings are recommended, and test questions
are suggested.

This chapter is based on a presentation at the 1987 annual
meeting of the American Evaluation Association in Boston. Most
of the material is taken from others, especially Don Campbell. I
have adapted it for my teaching and urge others to do the same.

MATERIALS

For clairvoyance test--nothing; for dice rolling--one die for
each student and a recording sheet (given as table 1); for
computer simulation--access to SPSSX (control language given in
table 2).

PROCEDURES

1. Clairvoyant Methodology Aptitude Test (Hunter and Horwitz, 1977)

Students are told to number a piece of paper from 1 to 10. They
are given a ten-item true-and-false test about research methods--
The Clairvoyant Methodological Aptitude Test (CMAT). Instead of
reading the questions, I transmit the questions psychically,
sending them one by one. The student's task is to respond true
or false, correctly. (Humorous aides: have a stooge ask for a

question to be repeated; send a two-part question.)

After the final question is sent, students are told to correct their own papers. The correct answers are posted (e.g., TTFTFFFTTF), and the class distribution is charted and displayed. (At this time such ideas as expected value for an individual's test score--i.e., five correct--can be introduced.) Next, those students "most in need" of remediation (e.g., scores of 4 or lower) are told to go to the back of the room to meditate as their treatment. After a short time they are brought back and retested. Their posttests are scored and the distribution of their scores is displayed--and they are congratulated for the marked improvement.

The expected value of posttest scores is discussed and I introduce the classical notion that:

$$\text{Observed Score} = \text{True Score} + \text{Error Score}.$$

I explain regression to the mean in this case as due to the observed scores being 100 percent error--regressing all the way back to the expected value of the population.

2. Dice-Rolling Exercise (Don Campbell)

A die and a worksheet (table 1) are distributed to each student. The worksheet has spaces for construction of a pretest and a posttest for two groups (A and B) with ten observations (subjects) in each group. Test scores are made up of equal parts of true score and error. Error components are determined by independent rolls of the die.

The class proceeds one group at a time, first working on Group A pretest. True scores are given. (Campbell uses two dice, one for the true score and one for the error component.) Students construct Observed Scores by rolling the die to generate the error term (e.g., Error 1) and adding this number to the True Score. It is important that students put all numbers on the sheet. Once pretests are completed, posttest scores are constructed. Students then average the True Score, Error 1, and Observed Score columns--averaging is quite easy since there are ten observations. Students should now have a feel for a number of assumptions and implications of the classical test theory explanation of regression to the mean.

-The expected value and variance for Error 1 and Error 2 are the same but the actual values are uncorrelated.

-Both true scores and error scores contribute to (and are correlated with) observed scores.

-Selecting an observation because it has a high (low) observed score will, on average, select an observation with a high (low) error score.

Next I use the bottom panel of table 1. Students match observations on Pretest Observed Scores. They compute the mean Posttest Observed Score for each of these categories. For example, posttest scores are averaged for the observations that had 4 on the pretest. Inspection of the second column of the bottom panel of table 1 will show a pattern of compression, or regression to the mean. Students observe that this compression is an artifact of their dice rolls and not due to a constriction in the variance or changes in true score. In fact, the same pattern will result if matching is done on Posttest Observed Scores and mean Observed Pretest Scores are computed instead.

Finally, students complete the middle panel of table 1, constructing Group B scores. True scores for Group B are two higher than those from Group A. The point I want to illustrate is that even though there was no treatment effect (i.e., neither Group A nor Group B changed true scores from pretest to post-test), matching on observed scores from different populations can create the impression that there was one. For example, the lowest subjects (observed pretest scores <= 5) in Group A might receive remediation. A control group is constructed by matching on observed pretest scores from Group B. (Obviously, no matches can be made for pretests scores of 2 or 3 from Group A). Students figure pretest and posttest scores for the treated (Group A) and control group (Group B). The pattern will show that, although the treatment appeared to help (Group A scores improved from pretest to posttest), the control group improved even more. Inspection of the change in error scores from pretest to posttest within group will explain this pattern. Variations on this exercise are possible: (1) make the Group B low scorers the treated group and watch how wonderful the treatment is; and (2) treat the most meritorious (high pretest observed score) and show either a bias for or against treatment depending on the choice of treated group. These variations make good homework assignments.

3. Computer Data Simulation

The third activity builds on the second and follows the presentation of Campbell and Erlebacher (1970). Simulated data are created according to a classical test theory model similar to the Dice-Rolling Exercise using a random number function. The SPSSX control language to generate data similar to that of the Dice-Rolling Exercise is presented in table 2. Use of SPSSX, or any of the other computer packages, allows me or my students to test various aspects of my Regression to the Mean presentation with a much larger sample size than is convenient to work with by hand. Some of the aspects of the regression phenomenon that I examine are: (1) the classical test theory assumptions of uncorrelated error and the correlation between observed scores and error: (2) the effects of variation in reliability on the amount of regression from pretest to posttest--table 2 generates pretests (or covariates) of five levels of reliability; (3) ability of ANCOVA or regression analysis to adjust for pre-existing differences between groups--the MANOVA statement in table 2; and (4) the effect of varying the reliability of measurement, and changes in the reliability of measurement from pretest to posttest, on the accuracy of ANOVA, ANCOVA, and repeated measures ANOVA. When doing this exercise, I usually give each student a copy of the printout and go through it in class.

The relationship between the weights given to the True and Error components in the COMPUTE statements of table 2 on the one hand and the reliability of the computed scores is given by this formula:

$$r_{xx} = \frac{(\text{Weight True})^2}{(\text{Weight True})^2 + (\text{Weight Error})^2}$$

Note that even with the covariate that has 90 percent reliability (PRE90) ANCOVA (ANALYSIS + POST50 WITH PRE90) still indicates Group A and B differ at posttest over and above differences existing at pretest (F (1,198) = 5.00, p < .02). Given the data-generating steps, we know this conclusion is false.

DISCUSSION

Regression artifacts are common in both applied (e.g., Reichart, 1985; Seaver, 1973) and basic research settings (e.g., Conolley and Knight, 1976; McKillip, 1978). One example I use:

A superintendent wants to evaluate a newly adopted pre-algebra text to be used with the eighth grade. Of course, she wants a rigorous evaluation, concerned especially with the appropriateness of the text for some of the less mathematically inclined students. She compares the students' nationally normed math scores for seventh grade with their scores for eighth grade (i.e., after having used the text for a year). She is happy to find an average gain of 1.3 grade equivalent units. Furthermore, she is especially pleased to find that lowest fifth of the class (on the seventh grade test) gained 1.7 units. The only problem presenting itself is that the highest fifth of the class (again from the 7th grade test) gained only .9 units. She concludes, much to her surprise, that the text is especially good for the slower students but something more challenging may need to be done for the best math students.

What the superintendent discovered, at least in part, was regression to the mean. The approach of examining extreme subgroups of a population (the top and bottom fifths) guaranteed the results she found. [Note: One variation of the Dice-Rolling Activity is to have students add two points to the posttests of all observations (to allow for maturation). Groups of two or three students can then re-enact the experience of the school superintendent evaluating the pre-algebra text that I described.]

In addition to these class activities, I have students read Furby's (1973) presentation and give them the reference to Campbell and Erlebacher (1970). Furby's article is particularly important because she attacks the myth that regression is due to unreliability in measurement--believed partially because of the simple test theory model I use (i.e, $O = T + E$). With this model, reliability and validity are confounded. Furby demonstrates that regression will occur with "reliable" measures when they are used as proxies for a concept other than that for which they were designed, e.g., sex of kindergartners as a measure of reading readiness. Regression to the mean is caused by the use of less than perfectly valid measures.

For test items, I construct scenarios like the story of the superintendent and the new pre-algebra text or this one from Tversky and Kahneman (1974):

In a discussion of flight training, experienced instructors noted that praise for an exceptionally smooth landing is typically followed by a poorer landing on the next try, while harsh criticism after rough landing is usually followed by an improvement on the next try. The instructors concluded that verbal rewards are detrimental to learning, while verbal punishments are beneficial, contrary to accepted psychological doctrine.

The student should be able to recognize and explain the operation of regression to the mean, including the direction of biases that might occur.

A more challenging approach to testing (Reichart, 1985) has students read Seaver's (1973) JPSP article and find a regression artifact. Mark (1986, p. 60) gives a regression explanation for another study cited by Cook and Campbell (1979, p. 129)--the selection cohort design used to evaluate Sesame Street. Students who can identify regression-to-the-mean interpretations for these studies surely understand the topic.

BACKGROUND READING

Campbell, D.T., & Erlebacher, A.E. (1970). How regression artifacts in quasi-experimental evaluations can mistakenly make compensatory education look harmful. In J. Hellmuth (ed.), <u>Compensatory education: A national debate</u>, Vol. 3: Disadvantaged child). New York: Brunner/Mazel. Reprinted in E.L. Struening and M. Guttentag (eds.), <u>Handbook of Evaluation Research</u>, Vol. 1, 1975. Sage: Newbury Park, pp. 597-617.

Conolley, E.S., & Knight, G.P. (1976). Anderson's personality trait words: Has their likableness changed? <u>Personality and Social Psychology Bulletin</u>, <u>2</u>, 300-307.

Furby, L. (1973). Interpreting regression toward the mean in developmental research. <u>Developmental Psychology</u>, <u>8</u>, 172-179.

Hunter, W.J., & Horwitz, S. (1977). Regression: That's mean. <u>CEDR Quarterly</u>, <u>10</u>, 18-19.

Mark, M.M. (1986). Validity typologies and the logic and practice of quasi-experimentation. <u>New Directions in Program Evaluation</u>, <u>31</u>, 47-66.

McKillip, J. (1978). Comment on "Anderson's personality trait words: Has their meaning changed?" <u>Personality and Social Psychology Bulletin</u>, <u>4</u>, 289-291.

Reichart, C.S. (1985). Reinterpreting Seaver's (1973) study of teacher expectations as a regression artifact. <u>Journal of Educational Psychology</u>, <u>77</u>, 231-236.

Seaver, W.B. (1973). Effects of naturally induced teacher expectancies. <u>Journal of Personality and Social Psychology</u>, <u>28</u>, 333-342.

Tversky A., & Kahneman, D. (1975). Judgment under uncertainty: Heuristics and biases. <u>Science</u>, <u>185</u>, 1124-1131.

Table 1
Dice-Rolling Exercise Work Sheet

Observation #:	Pretest			Posttest		
Group A	: True : Score	: Error 1 :	:Observed: : Score :	True : Score:	Error 2 :	:Observed : Score
1	: 1	:	:	: 1	:	:
2	: 2	:	:	: 2	:	:
3	: 3	:	:	: 3	:	:
4	: 4	:	:	: 4	:	:
5	: 5	:	:	: 5	:	:
6	: 6	:	:	: 6	:	:
7	: 2	:	:	: 2	:	:
8	: 3	:	:	: 3	:	:
9	: 4	:	:	: 4	:	:
10	: 5	:	:	: 5	:	:
Average	: 3.5	:	:	: 3.5 :		:
Group B	: True : Score	: Error 1 :	:Observed: : Score :	True : Score:	Error 2 :	:Observed : Score
1	: 3	:	:	: 3	:	:
2	: 4	:	:	: 4	:	:
3	: 5	:	:	: 5	:	:
4	: 6	:	:	: 6	:	:
5	: 7	:	:	: 7	:	:
6	: 8	:	:	: 8	:	:
7	: 4	:	:	: 4	:	:
8	: 5	:	:	: 5	:	:
9	: 6	:	:	: 6	:	:
10	: 7	:	:	: 7	:	:
Average	: 5.5	:	:	: 5.5 :		:

Mean Pretest Observed Score :	Mean Posttest Observed Score :	Mean Error 1	: Mean : Error 2
2	:	:	:
3	:	:	:
4	:	:	:
5	:	:	:
6	:	:	:
7	:	:	:
8	:	:	:
9	:	:	:
10	:	:	:
11	:	:	:
12	:	:	:

Table 2
SPSSX Listing to Generate Regression to Mean Example

```
--------------------------------------------------------------------
UNNUMBERED
TITLE 'REGRESSION TO THE MEAN DEMONSTRATION DATA SET'
DATA LIST FILE=INLINE RECORDS=1
     /1 GROUP 1
VALUE LABELS GROUP 1'A' 2'B'          ....[1]
SET SEED =1432756                     ....[2]
DO IF (GROUP EQ 1)                    ....[3]
COMPUTE TRUE=TRUNC(UNIFORM(6))+1
COMPUTE ERROR1=TRUNC(UNIFORM(6))+1
COMPUTE ERROR2=TRUNC(UNIFORM(6))+1
ELSE
COMPUTE TRUE=TRUNC(UNIFORM(6))+3
COMPUTE ERROR1=TRUNC(UNIFORM(6))+1
COMPUTER ERROR2=TRUNC(UNIFORM(6))+1
END IF
COMPUTE POST50=TRUE+ERROR2
COMPUTE PRE10= .5*TRUE + 1.5*ERROR1            ....[4]
COMPUTE PRE30= .8*TRUE + 1.2*ERROR1
COMPUTE PRE50=TRUE+ERROR1
COMPUTE PRETO=1.2*TRUE + .8*ERROR1
COMPUTE PRE90=1.5*TRUE + .5*ERROR1
VARIABLE LABELS
     POST50 'POSTTEST OR CRITERION WITH RELIABILITY=.5'
     PRE10 'PRETEST OR COVARIATE WITH RELIABILITY=.10'
     PRE30 'PRETEST OR COVARIATE WITH RELIABILITY=.31'
     PRE50 'PRETEST OR COVARIATE WITH RELIABILITY=.5'
     PRE70 'PRETEST OR COVARIATE WITH RELIABILITY=.69'
     PRE90 'PRETEST OR COVARIATE WITH RELIABILITY=.90'
BEGIN DATA
*data (200 records. 100 with 1 in column 1 and 100 with 2 in
column 1)
END DATA
--------------------
```

Note: "...." notes for this table only. Table 2 is continued on
the next page.

[1] Groups A and B are similar in construction to the groups
     in the Dice-Rolling Exercise.
[2] Use of same seed guarantees the same random numbers.
[3] Generates dice roll-like inputs, ranging from 1 to 6 for two
     groups differing on true score by 2.
[4] Generates covariates of low (10, 30) medium (50) and high
     (70, 90) reliability.

Table 2 Continued
SPSSX Listing to Generate Regression to Mean Example

```
MANOVA POST50 BY GROUP (1,2) WITH PRE10,PRE30,PRE50,PRE70,PRE90,
TRUE/
     ANALYSIS= POST50/              .......[5]
     PRINT=OMEANS/
     DESIGN=GROUP/
     ANALYSIS= POST50 WITH PRE10/       ........[6]
     PRINT=PMEANS/                       ........[7]
     DESIGN=GROUP/
     ANALYSIS= POST50 WITH PRE30/
     PRINT=PMEANS/
     DESIGN=GROUP/
     ANALYSIS= POST50 WITH PRE50/
     PRINT=PMEANS/
     DESIGN=GROUP/
     ANALYSIS= POST50 WITH PRE70/
     PRINT=PMEANS/
     DESIGN=GROUP/
     ANALYSIS= POST50 WITH PRE90/
     PRINT=PMEANS/
     DESIGN=GROUP/
     ANALYSIS= POST50 WITH TRUE/        .......[8]
     PRINT=PMEANS/
     DESIGN=GROUP/
FINISH
```

Note: "...." notes for this table only. Table 2 continued from
previous page.

[5] Produces ANOVA on post-test scores only.
[6] Produces ANCOVA on post-test scores with covariates of
     increasing reliability.
[7] Produces adjusted means for ANCOVA.
[8] Uses perfect covariate, i.e., a perfect measure of pre-
     existing group differences.

34

USING MICROCOMPUTER DATABASE MANAGEMENT SOFTWARE TO SOLVE EVALUATION DATA MANAGEMENT PROBLEMS

John J. Bowers

Much of data "analysis" is actually data management, because it more typically involves entering, organizing, and retrieving data rather than mathematical computation. Thus, microcomputer database management system (DBMS) software may be more appropriate for many evaluation projects than statistical analysis software. Data management includes such tasks as designing data files by determining their structure and content; adding, changing, and deleting data; organizing the data into files whose data fields can be joined together; and retrieving the data in specified ways for decision making and reports.

This activity introduces the basic elements of a relational database, the model used by most microcomputer DBMS software. It provides an example of one type of database, an item bank containing data on test items. It concludes with an exercise that allows students to design their own databases.

This activity assumes that the students have some knowledge about what a database is, and possibly some skills in setting up databases. The purpose of this activity is to take them one step further into the logic of relational databases and how they can help in the management process.

MATERIALS

Tables 1 to 3 at the end of this chapter should be used as handouts. Table 4 should be reserved until after students have completed the exercises.

PROCEDURES

1.   Introduce the Basic Concept of a Database

Refer to table 1. Review the definition of a database. Perhaps students could present examples of databases they have used in the past. Probably some will have experience creating a complex database for storing data on test or questionnaire items. An item bank used in developing multiple forms of a test is one kind of database and will be used here as an example.

In the test development process, items are repeated from one test form to another, and historical data must be maintained on the usage and performance of each item. Items must be selected from the item bank/database based on various criteria, such as content classification, difficulty, and discrimination. The item bank/database is used to maintain and organize an item population that is constantly changing as item data are changed, new items added, and old items deleted.

2.   Introduce the Concept of a Relational Database

Refer to table 1 again to review and discuss the additional features that characterize a relational database. Explain that microcomputer DBMS software are usually based on the relational database model, in which data are organized into a series of flat, two-dimensional table files. There can be any number of files, each with its own record structure and its own data. Data from these files can be joined on the basis of a single data field common to the joined files. A relational DBMS typically includes a high level query language that can join data from different files or use data in one file to organize data in another. The query language can be used interactively to enter queries from a keyboard or as a programming language.

Table 2 is an example of the various data files that might make up an item bank/database. The "type" and "width" of each field are typical descriptors for data fields in most microcomputer DBMS. Explain that data from these files may be linked to provide answers to any number of possible queries. For example, "What is the difficulty and discrimination of all items in content Area III in their last use?" would require linking the POOL and HIST files on their common field, IBNO, the item bank number. The query, "List item reviewer comments for all items in Area III that have a difficulty between 50 and 90 in their last use," would involve linking three files--POOL, HIST, and COMMENTS--on their common field, IBNO. This linking is possible through the database query language and would be invisible to the user. Only the resulting data, listed in the desired order, would appear on the computer screen or printer.

Once students grasp the basic concept of joining data from
two files on the basis of common fields, they will quickly see
that a database can consist of any number of flat table files and
that data can be retrieved by joining records from two or more
files based on shared, common fields. Before leaving table 2,
note that other files containing data about key terms or words in
each test item, and data about each test form could also be added
to the database to provide more information and answer even more
complex queries. It may be useful to explore with the students
what fields these files might contain.

Introduce next the two elements of database design: (1)
__Content__, the variables and values for each item contained in the
database; and (2) __Structure__, the organization of that content
into files, records, and fields. Briefly, content is determined
by the process the database must serve, the extent to which the
DBMS must provide preprogrammed reports or respond to
spontaneous, unplanned decision needs, and the types of queries
that need to be answered. Structure is determined by a process
called __normalization__, which produces the most efficient
organization of the variables into files and fields. For an
extensive discussion of database design and an example of how the
structure in table 2 was developed, see Bowers (1985).

One important result of normalization is that each file will
have one or more key fields that uniquely identify each record in
that file. For example, in table 2 the POOL file has a single
key field, IBNO, the item bank number. Other items might have
the same content classification or author, but no two items have
the same item bank number. Therefore, the IBNO field ensures
that each record in the file is unique. The HIST file has a
compound key, the fields FORM and NUM, representing the test form
code and the sequence number of the item on the test form,
respectively. There will be many items on the same test form and
many that have the same sequence number on different test forms,
but each item record in this file will have a unique combination
of test form number and sequence number, making these the key
fields.

Conclude with the two exercises in table 3. Some suggested
answers are available in table 4, but many others are possible.
For further suggestions and discussion, see Bowers (1986).

BACKGROUND READING

Bowers, J. (1985). Designing an item bank: Practical guidance
    from a database management approach. Paper presented at the
    Annual Meeting of the American Educational Research
    Association.

Bowers, J. (1986). A microcomputer-based system to manage
    health professions test development and item banking

activities.   Paper presented at the Annual Meeting of the
American Educational Research Association.

Codd,   E.F.   (1982).   Relational   database: A   practical
foundation for productivity.   Communications of the ACM,
February.

Date, C.J.   (1976).   An introduction to database systems.
Reading, MA: Addison-Wesley.

Kalman, David.   (1984).   What is a database management system?
Data Based Advisor.

Martin, James.   (1976).   Principles of database management.
Englewood Cliffs, NJ: Prentice-Hall.

Table 1
Characteristics of a Relational Database

A database should meet three basic conditions:

1. It should not unnecessarily repeat data or require its repeated entry. For example, it should not be necessary to reenter common data about a test item in a bank (e.g., its classification) every time the item is used.
2. The database must be able to serve multiple users who have different purposes for using it. This implies that the data are independent of the programs that use the data. Thus, the same program can use more than one database and the same database can be used by more than one program.
3. There must be a common, controlled approach to adding, changing, deleting, and retrieving data within the database. Every database should have a data dictionary that describes the structure and organization of the files and the structure and content of the variables (fields) in each file.

To these conditions, a relational database adds the following:

1. Data are organized into a series of flat two-dimensional table files called <u>relations</u>. For example, an item bank constructed on the relational model would contain a minimum of two files, one a master file with one record per item containing relatively constant data about the item, and the other a usage file with each record containing data about one use of an item. There can be any number of independent files, each with its own record types and its own data.
2. Each file contains only one record type. For example, master data and usage data records would not be mixed in one file.
3. The logical structure (i.e., how data are displayed--in list or table form) is separate from the physical location of the data on a disk. The data can be listed in an order that is logical and useful to the user, entirely independent of the location of the data on the disk.
4. The data in each relation (table) are independent of data in other files. For example, data could be added about a new item to the master file even though the item had never been used and had no usage record.
5. The DBMS has a high level query language that can join data from independent files on the basis of data fields common to the joined files. Thus, it can use data in one file to organize data in another file. For example, the question "What is the average difficulty of items in content category A written by item writer X?" would involve relating data from the master file, the usage file, and an item writer file.

Table 2
Example of a Database Structure for an Item Bank

File name: POOL
Content: Each record stores relatively constant data about an item.

Field	Type	Width	Description of variable
IBNO*	Character	4	Item bank number; unique identifier for each item.
CONT1	Character	3	First level of the item's classification in the test content outline, e.g., I, II, III.
CONT2	Character	1	Second level content classification, e.g., A, B, C.
MKEY	Character	1	Position of correct response in master version of the item: A, B, C, or D.
FMT	Character	2	Item format code, e.g., multiple choice, true-false.
LINES	Numeric	2	Item length; number of typed lines it occupies.
STATUS	Character	2	Item status, e.g., active, inactive, needs revision
GRAF	Character	3	Type and length of graphic, if any.
WCODE	Character	3	Item writer code. Each has a unique code number.
DATEIN	Date	8	Date item was originally entered into item bank.
COMMENT	Logical	1	Coded true (T) if a comment exists in the COMMENTS file for this item. Else, coded false (F).

File name: HIST
Content: Each record stores data on one use of a test item on a test form.

Field	Type	Width	Description of variable
ID*	Character	4	Item bank number; unique identifier for each item.
FORM*	Character	4	Test form number; unique identifier for this form.
NUM	Character	3	Item's sequence on this test form.
FKEY	Character	1	Position of correct response in this use of item.
FUNC	Character	2	Item's function on this form: e.g., equator, pretest.

DIFF	Numeric	3	Item's difficulty in this use, i.e., percent of examinees answering correctly.
DISC	Numeric	4	Item's point biserial discrimination in this use.

File name: COMMENTS
Content: Each record stores a comment from an item reviewer about one item.

Field	Type	Width	Description of variable
IBNO*	Character	4	Item bank number; unique identifier for each item.
DATE*	Date	8	Date the comment was entered.
TEXT	Character	60	The text of the comment.

File name: WRITERS
Content: Each record stores data about an item writer.

Field	Type	Width	Description of variable
WCODE*	Character	3	Item writer code. Each has a unique code number.
LAST	Character	15	Item writer's last name.
FIRST	Character	10	Item writer's first name.
ADD1	Character	25	Item writer's address, line 1.
ADD2	Character	25	Item writer's address, line 2.
CITY	Character	15	Item writer's address, city.
STATE	Character	2	Item writer's address, state.
ZIP	Character	9	Item writer's address, zip code.
ASSIGN	Numeric	2	Number of items writer has been assigned to write.
AREA	Character	3	Content area of writer's assignment.

*Indicates a key field, i.e., a field that makes each record unique. Data from the POOL, HIST, and COMMENTS files can be joined based on their common field, IBNO. Data from the POOL and WRITERS files can be joined based on their common field, WCODE.

Note: Bowers (1986) has suggested other files that could be useful in an item bank database: a KEYWORDS file storing one or more important words or terms from each item; and a FORMDATA file storing summary data about each test form, the number tested, mean, standard deviation, and reliability.

Table 3
Exercises in Designing Relational Database File Structures

For each of the two examples below, do the following:

1. Specify two or more files appropriate for the database and some of the fields that would be in each file. For each file, specify the key field or fields that would make each record in that file unique.

2. Specify how the files could be linked on common, shared fields.

3. Suggest some questions that might be asked and how data from two or more of the files could be joined to answer them.

Example 1: A Social Service Agency

Imagine that you work in a social service agency or department in a large city that must keep track of the persons it serves through various public and private agencies and the nature of these services. These agencies can include prisons, hospitals, nursing homes, drug programs, halfway houses, and so on. The problem is that individuals may be served by a widely varying number of agencies. An elderly man may be in one institution, a nursing home, permanently. However, a young woman who has a drug problem may be in a foster home, a hospital, a drug treatment house, and a juvenile detention center over a period of several months. Develop a file structure for use by a relational DBMS that can help keep track of these persons, the services they receive, their present location or institution, how many institutions they go through, and so on.

Example 2: School Testing Office

Imagine that you work in a school district testing or research and evaluation office that must find a way to retrieve student performance data easily. The office must respond quickly to queries from administrators, the school board, and the public regarding patterns of student performance on local and national tests and may need to retrieve data based on many criteria. Data on nationally standardized tests may be received on individual computer tapes but it is difficult to pull data across years and tests from separate tapes. Develop a file structure for use by a relational database that could help to maintain, organize, and retrieve data on individual students and groups of students, their performance on various tests, and the characteristics of the tests.

Table 4
Suggested Answers for the Exercises

Example 1: A Social Service Agency

1. Person file. One record for each person. Possible fields: name, Social Security number, sex, race, date of birth.
2. Contact or service file. One record for each contact or service provided to a person by the agency. Possible fields: the person's Social Security number, the date the person entered a certain institution, the code number for that institution, the services provided, the expected length of stay or date of discharge.
3. Institution file. One record for each institution used by the agency. Possible fields: institution's name, its unique code number, its location, and characteristics such as capacity, staff, and services.

By linking all three files on their common fields (Social Security number and institution code number), it would be possible to answer the question "How many white males over the age of 65 are presently in nursing homes that have a capacity greater than 50 persons?"

Example 2: School Testing Office

1. Student file. One record for each student. Possible fields: student's name, a unique student identification number, sex, race, address, parents' names, date of first attendance, and grade placement at entry. This file could also be used for other administrative purposes.
2. Scores file. One record for each test form taken by a student. Possible fields: the student's unique identification number, a unique test form code, the date of administration, the student's total score and subscores, and percentile rank. The key fields would be the student's identification number and the test form code number (assuming that no student takes the same test form twice).
3. Test information file. One record for each test form administered, whether it was developed locally or nationally. Possible fields: a unique test form code, the test name and publisher, content, national norms, and local norms.

By linking all three files on their common fields (student identification number and the unique test form code), it would be possible to answer the question, "What was the mean score, each year, on test X, broken down by race and sex, for the ninth graders who have attended school in this district since the fifth grade?" It could also generate a report showing a given student's performance with respect to national norms.

Index

312